CREATIVE Fly Tying and Fly Fishing

CREATIVE Fly Tying and Fly Fishing

Rex Gerlach

foreword by A. I. "Pal" Alexander

STOEGER Publishing Company

To all beginning fly fishermen, with the hope that this book will truly enhance their enjoyment of the sport of fly fishing.

ISBN: 0-88317-047-7

Published by Stoeger Publishing Company
55 Ruta Court
South Hackensack, New Jersey 07606

First Stoeger quality paperback edition, January 1978

This Stoeger Sportsman's Library Edition is published
by arrangement with Winchester Press
Distributed to the book trade by Follett Publishing
Company, 1010 West Washington Boulevard,
Chicago, Illinois 60607 and to the sporting goods
trade by Stoeger Industries, 55 Ruta Court,
South Hackensack, New Jersey 07606

In Canada, distributed to the book trade and to the
sporting goods trade by Stoeger Trading Company,
900 Ontario Street East, Montreal, Quebec H2L 1P4

Printed in the United States of America

CONTENTS

Foreword

FLY FISHING and its subordinate art, fly tying, have a long and fascinating history. The amount of literature they have spawned is enormous, and rightly so; neither one has ever been easy.

In the early beginnings of fly-fishing history the angler was obliged not only to fashion his own flies but to make his own hooks, line, and rod as well. It took a lot of determination and perseverance to become a fly fisherman!

As the technology of making lines and rods improved, the fly fisherman's burden was eased considerably and more of his attention was focused on the fly and its presentation. In many ways, though, the fly making became more complicated. Professional tiers made their handicraft akin to black magic by combining exotic feathers and materials into creations that could not be readily duplicated by less than an expert tier. The result was full-dressed Atlantic salmon flies that rivaled museum art and trout flies such as the Royal Coachman, the Parmachene Belle, and the Silver Doctor, which brightened the hat bands and fly books but boasted of no real-life counterparts. This is not to say that these fanciful creations did not catch fish—they did, and they still do, particularly on lightly fished waters and with unsophisticated fish.

It was on English chalkstreams that the fly fisherman's art was formally joined with science under the guidance of such illustrious fly fishers as Alfred Ronalds, Frederick M. Halford, and G.E.M. Skues. The latter two differed bitterly on presentation, the dry fly versus the wet fly, but nevertheless, scientific method was their keynote and they made exhaustive studies to correlate their fraudulent imitations with the natural flies.

In America, before the turn of the century, fly fishing was in the Dark Ages compared to England. The wet flies for bass and trout were mainly gaudy attractors with few exceptions. The T. H. Chubb Rod Co., of Post Mills, Vermont, in their catalog of 1896, and perhaps earlier, offered a wide variety of terrestrial imitations for both trout and bass. They also had floating flies, buoyed up by cork bodies, but, for the most part, dry-fly fishing was relatively unknown.

In 1890, Theodore Gordon requested and received a number of dry flies from Frederick M. Halford, in England. From these flies, Gordon gleaned the mechanics of dry-fly construction, but, astutely, he realized they imitated nothing on the Neversink, Willowemoc, or Beaverkill, his favored fishing grounds. Consequently, Gordon created his own patterns which matched the naturals and, along with his disciples, adopted the philosophy that the most successful flies were those that imitated nature.

English fly patterns in the United States and Canada, particularly for trout and Atlantic salmon, have persisted to some degree even up to the present time, but as fishing has attracted legions of followers and the fish have become wary, selective, and scarce, more and more fly patterns and methods have been developed specifically to catch them. On our hard-pressed waters, haphazard fly selection and methods produce meager results.

American fly-fishing development is still very much in its infancy, although it has seen the birth of the streamer fly, the heavy-hackled and hair-wing dry flies for rough water, deer-hair bass bugs, and flat-bodied nymphs, to name but a few innovations. In recent years, on Canadian waters, we have even seen the lordly Atlantic salmon succumb to very simple—but deadly effective—hair-wing wet flies.

In the future, fly fishing is going to be more difficult, more demanding, and more challenging than ever before. Our inland waters are dwindling, and easy access coupled with the increase of newcomers to the sport will favor the angler who has done his homework and done it well. The reader of *Creative Fly Tying and Fly Fishing* will find that Rex Gerlach has presented a comprehensive review and analysis of the best of our current fly-fishing and fly-tying methods and techniques. Not only will it prove to be informative to both the veteran and tyro angler alike, but, more importantly, I think, he has admirably succeeded in his avowed purpose of providing the stimulus for thoughtful inquiry and experimentation, the two keys to future successful fly fishing.

—A. I. "PAL" ALEXANDER

Acknowledgments

THE AUTHOR expresses his sincere thanks and appreciation to the following individuals and firms for their invaluable contributions to the research efforts for this book.

Abercrombie & Fitch Co., A. I. "Pal" Alexander, P. G. "Perk" Angwin, Dan Bailey, Joseph D. Bates, Jr., Berkley and Company, George M. Bodmer, Paul W. "Bill" Butler, Duncan Campbell, Lou Corona, Cortland Line Co., H. A. Darbee, Bob Elliot, Stan Engle, Art Flick, James H. Gilford, Lt. Col. Lee Gomes, USAF (ret.), George F. Grant, Larry Green, Grits Gresham, Edward Haaga, Jesse Harden, Warren Hartung, Herter's Inc., Milt Huber, Jack Hutchinson, Ray Johnson, Milt Kahl, Stuart Kaplan, William Keane, Jim Kilburn, Lefty Kreh, Paul Kukonen, Bud Lilly, William C. Lynch, Tom McNally, Tom Nixon, The Orvis Company, Parks Fly Shop, William W. "Billy" Pate, Percy Tackle Co., Phillips Fly and Tackle Co., Wally Powell, John Propp, Milt Rosco, Fenton S. Roskelley, Scientific Anglers, Inc., Warren Schoth, A. E. Sherar, Don Shiner, Richard Simons, Mark Sosin, Robert D. Stearns, Thomas H. Stouffer, Doug Swisher, Bob Terrell, Terry Tyed Flies, Irwin M. Thompson, Ted Trueblood, John Veniard, E. Veniard, Ltd., A. A. "Tony" Whitney and Simion V. Yaruta.

Special thanks are due Jim Gilford for the color photograph of a mayfly and to Robert D. Stearns for the photograph of a fly-caught permit (Fig. 3).

The author's sincerest appreciation goes to Edward Patrick Murphy, who produced the finished line art and renderings; to Milt Kahl, Paul Kukonen, Pal Alexander, and Ken Anderson, for sketches later converted into line artwork; and to Donna Lowe, for her assistance in proofreading the completed manuscript. And to my wife, Joan, for her aid in proofreading the galley and page proofs.

—R. G.

CREATIVE Fly Tying and Fly Fishing

Chapter 1

The Creative Approach

Virtually anyone can tie an artificial fly that will occasionally catch fish. And virtually anyone can attack a piece of water so persistently that he will chance into occasional fish by virtue of sheer perseverance. But the satisfactions of fly fishing are subtle and complicated, from the anglers first venture through a lifetime of rewarding and productive fishing experiences. Fly fishing is like an *affair d'amour* rather than a major contact sport—it is a truly recreative act in which the longer and more delicate the courtship, the more intimate and intriguing the relationship becomes.

Fly fishing and fly tying are quite separate activities, yet an indissoluble marriage takes place between the two when, to paraphrase the late innovative flyfisher James E. Leisenring, one dresses and presents an artificial fly to a fish in a way the fish can appreciate. This intensely sought union of skills and attitudes within the fly fisherman is what I mean by "creative" fly tying and fishing.

Artificial flies and methods of fishing them are creative when they either successfully depart from traditional forms or enhance in new ways one's ability to catch fish with proved techniques. How well an angler succeeds in accomplishing either of those goals during his fly-fishing career pretty much depends upon his willingness to adapt to the constant changes that constitute the very essence of the sport.

From a practical point of view, the most important aspect of fly fishing is how the fly appears to the fish. Most experienced fly fishermen can recall numerous apparently near-perfect simulations of aquatic and terrestrial creatures that have flown from tying vise to tippet on the wings of eager anticipation, only to be proved dismal failures at attracting fish. Most may also recall during this moment of remorseful reflection an even larger number of artificials that seem to bear little resemblance to living fish foods yet consistently prompt fish to fall all over one another in the race to take them in. Such is the great paradox confronting the fly-tying fisherman.

How an artificial fly looks to a fish, once it rests upon or sinks beneath the surface film, depends largely on the materials from which it is dressed, the style in which it is tied, the craftsmanship of the fly dresser and the manner in which it is ultimately drifted on or manipulated through the water. The angler has considerable imaginative control over most of these factors, provided of course he elects to use it, as we shall observe in the following chapters.

Fly fishing is essentially a form of subtle communication between angler and fish—a deceitful proposal from the fisherman that either triggers an instant of supreme delight for the fish, arouses its instinctive wariness, or meets with total indifference, depending upon the *quality* of the message. If the angler succeeds in imparting fish-enticing behavior in his artificial, and if the fish responds with a rise or a strike, then an act of creative fly fishing has taken place. And, as far as this creative aspect is concerned, it makes little difference if the fish is hooked, played or landed, provided the angler's fly-tying and presentation efforts are rewarded.

All of the other elements contributing to the pleasures of fly fishing—the beauty and mood of the lake, stream or saltwater setting, the mettle of the fish, the artful landing, the tender flesh or possibly releasing the fish unharmed—tend to be subordinate to that electrifying instant when the angler's skills cause the fish to take. And that's what this book is all about—ways and means to combine fly-tying and fishing skills so as to create the magical illusion that causes a fish to take in a fly.

The Magic Formula

There was once a wise old physician who, when asked by his young assistant which of all the modern medicines provided the most dramatic cures, replied: "Young man, it's commonly referred to by a four-lettered word—*work!*"

Truly creative angling with flies is also the result of work. It is the work of observation and experimentation, study and evaluation—the kind of work that frees a flyfisher's intellect from the errors of ignorance, prejudice, inexperience or bad advice. Creative fly fishing is a lifelong exercise in applied environmental science, demanding more than a passing acquaintance with the sciences of biology, entomology, limnology, zoology, ichthyology, taxonomy, morphology and ecology, not to speak of a reasonable proficiency in the arts of casting, fly tying, wading and boating—all combined into a gentle and pleas-

urable regimen of refreshing mental and physical activity.

The fish are the professors in this college of angling. They assess but two grades for our performance: "A" when we catch 'em, "F" when we don't.

Truly creative fly tying and fishing begin with the systematic study and observation of game fish, the environments they inhabit, the creatures upon which they prey and the angling methods known to consistently impart fish-enticing behavior to artificial flies. The learning process is similar to that involved in developing competence in any art—one first studies the art from its historical origins to the present time, then learns fundamental skills that allow basic performance, then refines this performance through practice, and ultimately achieves a sufficient level of skill and insight to permit creative efforts.

Although a beginning fly fisherman usually strives for perfection from the outset, he learns very quickly that he has embraced a most unforgiving preoccupation that surrenders grudgingly at best to the pedestrian performer. As a result, most well-intentioned neophytes soon begin to seek proved techniques and artificials that will give them an edge on the fish—methods and flies developed by the sport's creative innovators, sensitive and observant anglers the likes of Charles Cotton, Alfred Ronalds, Theodore Gordon, George M. L. La Branche, Edward R. Hewitt, James E. Leisenring, Art Flick, George F. Grant, Lee Wulff, Pete Hidy, Tom Nixon, Vincent C. Marinaro, Joe Brooks, Ted Trueblood, Doug Swisher, Carl Richards, Sid W. Gordon, Roderick Haig-Brown and a host of others, many of whom will never share their wisdom via the printed word. It is by acquainting himself with their methods and theories that the learning flyfisher gains the insight to wrestle his individual angling problems with objectivity, imagination and confidence.

We will begin with a discussion of tackle—for tackle is always the beginning angler's first concern. But the beginner should remember that neither tackle nor technique is the true first subject: first is the fish itself and its natural behavior. A tremendous variety of aquatic and terrestrial creatures serve as foods for game fish. The most important of those organisms will be considered individually in Chapters 9 through 13. They include aquatic insects and their nymphal, larval and pupal forms; crustaceans such as shrimp and crayfish; annelids (worms) such as waterworms and leeches; mollusks such as snails and clams; forage and game fishes; rodents; snakes; frogs; eels; small birds; bats; and a host of other creatures. Just a few are shown in Fig. 1. Each of the living organisms that constitute a major or minor part of the fish's diet has configuration, colors, buoyancy, transparency or opacity, and behavioral characteristics that identify it to the fish as food. The angler's fly-tying and fishing methods are merely attempts to simulate those characteristics of certain of the basic fish foods. That's the goal, and tackle is only a means to achieve it.

Fig. 1.

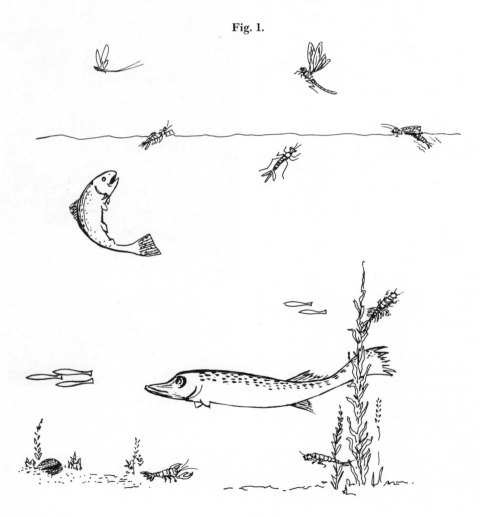

Chapter 2

Tackle for Fly Fishing

I T IS an all too common failing to con-
fuse the relative importance of fishing
tackle and fishing skill. Modern tackle
plays an essential but often subordinate
role to both casting technique and presentation in the luring of many important
game fish to the fly Except when angling
for the heaviest and most physically active
game species, the rod serves as little more
than a lever and transmitter through which
the angler imparts calculated messages to
the fly via the line and leader.

Naturally, when very long casts are necessary, the rod's relative importance increases. And in the case of very powerful
fishes, the rod can be of paramount importance, affecting one's ability to hook, play
and land the quarry.

Much the same is true concerning reels.
They are basically simple contrivances on
which to hold line in order to prevent it
from becoming twisted or tangled. Here
again, however, there are exceptions, such
as reels designed to aid in playing and
braking very heavy or fast-moving fish like
salmon, sailfish, tarpon, steelhead, bonefish
and other battling species.

Fly lines and leaders very often are the
most important tackle items, aside from
the flies themselves. They are the direct
means of communication through which
the angler's messages are conveyed to the
fly for observation by the fish.

Certainly, the vital question when se-

Fig. 2. Under normal trout and panfishing conditions, extremely long, powerful rods are seldom required. When fishing "fine," the angler
should select a rod that will allow him to control the line at both close and longer distances.
The rod should be light but not too short, or
line control will be difficult.

lecting rods, reels, lines and leaders is whether they perform the tasks and withstand the particular stresses imposed upon them by the angler and the game-fish species. In selecting equipment, one must make every effort to *match the tackle* to the characteristics of the water and the fish.

Fly Rods

Whether a species of fish requires the use of ultralight, medium or powerful basic tackle, an angler with limited casting experience will probably enjoy fishing more and fish more productively if his fly rod has an action that is somewhat tolerant of casting imperfections. For the most part, fly rods with relatively full-length flexing actions are probably best for both beginners and advanced casters. Such a rod may be quite stiff or gently "limp."

Fly rods that are excessively "tippy," or overly soft in the butt section, are sometimes effective in deft hands but require very precise timing on the part of the caster to realize their full potential. Excitement and anticipation tend to impair the timing of even the most accomplished casters. Any fly rod that forces a fellow to concentrate more on his casting than on the actual fishing of the fly cannot be considered the best choice for a general-purpose rod. That's the opinion of one who owns some twenty fly rods, yet regularly fishes with only five. The fifteen or so mostly unused rods were accumulated dur-

Fig. 3. When long casts or heavy, fast-moving sportfish are the quarry, the fly rod's role in playing the fish becomes increasingly important. Angler Mike Schamroth needed a powerful rod as well as great skill to land this 11-pound, 5-ounce permit—a very nice trophy.

ing the early part of my angling career when enthusiasm vastly exceeded judgment. Certain fly rods like the Orvis Battenkill series; the Scientific Anglers, Inc., System rods; the Fenwick rods and other superb casting instruments crafted by such distinguished manufacturers as the Winston Rod Co., H. L. Leonard, the Payne Rod Co., Hardy Bros., the Phillipson Rod Co., the Garcia Corp. and Pezon et Michel are accepted by the fly-fishing fraternity as exemplars of casting pleasure and efficiency.

From a practical point of view, if one plans to do a lot of bass, pike, muskie, salmon, steelhead or saltwater fly fishing, then he should consider the inherent advantages of a rod capable of handling 9-, 10- or 11-weight lines. The heavy lines simplify the casting of large, wind-resistant hair- and cork-bodied bugs, outsized streamers and bucktails. And the longer rods used with heavier lines provide greater leverage for long-distance casting and the playing of weighty fish.

All but the largest and hardest-mouthed game fish can be hooked and controlled on light-to-medium-weight casting instruments. But pike and muskies especially have hard mouth parts and such powerful jaws that a very powerful rod is usually necessary to break the jaw tension and set the hook. Much the same is true in the case of certain saltwater species with hard mouth parts. So anglers seeking pike, bass and muskies in weedy or stump-choked areas of lakes and sloughs, and anglers seeking outsized saltwater fish, like tarpon and billfish, must consider a rod's ability to set the hook and to apply enough pressure on a fish to regain lost line and backing.

On the other hand, limestone-stream specialists want to be able to make supremely delicate presentations of the fly on gossamer-fine tippet material. Often, therefore, very light double-tapered fly

lines (AFTMA line weights 3 to 6) are appropriate, and such lines call for correspondingly lighter-action rods, although not necessarily shorter ones. At the risk of being charged with heresy by the short-rod buffs, I consider it only fair to point out that very short rods significantly limit an angler's ability to control the line once it lies upon the water and, in some cases, to impart certain important manipulations like mending the cast, which will be described at length in a later chapter.

Fly Lines

Not only does the fly line serve as the connecting link between rod and leader during the presentation of the fly and the ensuing fight with the fish, but it also controls to a high degree the depth at which the fly runs and the limits of casting distance. The line also provides the weight required to flex the rod during the cast.

There are six types of commercially available fly lines, designated by their relative abilities to float or sink: (1) floating, (2) sinking-tip, (3) intermediate sinking/floating, (4) slow-sinking, (5) fast-sinking and (6) extra-fast sinking. Their uses are shown in Fig. 4. Some anglers modify these lines to increase their sinking rates by splicing in short sections of plastic-coated, lead-cored trolling line. Other anglers occasionally modify the factory tapers with spliced-in sections of fly line in order to alter their casting characteristics. Each type of fly line is available in several tapers that adapt it to a range of casting and fishing situations.

Tapers are described as: (1) level, (2) double taper, (3) weight-forward taper, (4) bug taper, (5) saltwater taper, (6) shooting taper or shooting head and (7) lead head. These are shown in Fig. 5. Lead-head lines are usually level shooting heads dinged up by anglers out of 20- to 35-foot lengths of lead-core trolling line. As mentioned earlier, some flyrodders splice sections of the same lead-core line into conventional weight-forward and shooting-head fly lines. These bastardized lines, too, are also sometimes referred to as lead heads.

Level fly lines are uniform in diameter from end to end. They are available in floating, intermediate and sinking types over a wide range of AFTMA line weights (Fig. 6.) Long ago, level fly lines played a useful role in fly casting on American and European waters. That was in the days when fly rods were noted for their buggy-whip actions. Even the most gentle mod-

Fishing types	Line taper	Sinking fly-line types							Floating fly-line types		
		I	II	III	ST	WH	LH	SH	Regular	BT	SWT
Dry flies	DT,WF								x		
Wet flies	DT,WF	x	x	x	x			x	x		
Nymphs, shallow	DT,WF	x			x				x		
Nymphs, deep	DT,WF		x	x		x	x	x			
Streamers, shallow	DT,WF	x			x				x		
Streamers, deep	DT,WF		x	x		x	x	x			
Saltwater, surface	WF									x	x
Saltwater, shallow	WF	x			x	x					x
Bugs	WF									x	x

KEY:

DT — Double-tapered
WF — Weight-forward
I — AFTMA-designated for "slow-sinking" line
II — AFTMA designated for "fast-sinking" line
III — AFTMA designated for "extra-fast-sinking" line
ST — Sinking tip (front 6 to 8 feet)

WH — Wet-head (front 30 feet sinks)
LH — Lead-head (an all lead-core line, or one into which sections of lead-core line have been spliced)
SH — Shooting taper or shooting head
BT — Bug-taper
SWT — Saltwater taper

Fig. 4. Fly lines for freshwater and saltwater fly fishing.

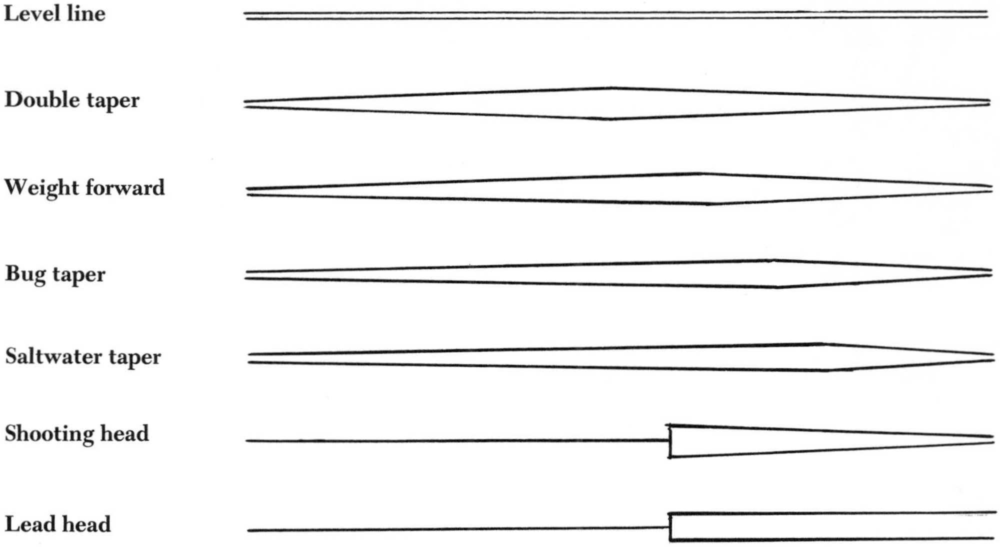

Level line

Double taper

Weight forward

Bug taper

Saltwater taper

Shooting head

Lead head

Fig. 5. Fly-line tapers.

ern rods are relatively stiff compared with the limber wands of a century ago. Modern rods, being stiffer, demand lines with pro-

Weight code	Specified weight (grains)	Allowable tolerances (grains)
4	120	114-126
5	140	134-146
6	160	152-168
7	185	177-193
8	210	202-218
9	240	230-250
10	280	270-290
11	330	318-342

Fig. 6. AFTMA fly-line weights. Weights are based on first 30 feet of line, exclusive of any taper or tip. (There are 437½ grains in one ounce.) Line weights 1, 2, 3, and 12 have been omitted from this table because they have limited applications to normal fly-fishing situations.

gressive weight distribution in order to realize their full casting potential. There are, however, two functions which level fly lines can serve well. One is to troll flies on or beneath the surface. The other is to act as floating "shooting line" backing a shooting head. Floating shooting line allows a moderately expert angler to make casts approaching 100 feet and, at the same time, mend those casts once the line is on the water. More about this in the next chapter.

Double-tapered fly lines are larger at the center than at the tip ends. Each end of a double-tapered line consists of a foot or two of small-diameter level line, usually trimmed off or at least reduced in length before attaching the leader butt. Advantages of the design present themselves in angling situations requiring maximum accuracy, line control and delicacy. At distances in excess of 70 feet, double-tapered lines are difficult and tiring to cast.

Weight-forward fly lines are tapered heavier at one end than at the other. The casting weight is concentrated in the front

30 or so feet of the line. The remainder is small-diameter running line. Advantages of the weight-forward design are striking when casting farther than 60 feet. For one thing, it allows a *proficient* caster to extend his range to distances approaching the entire 90 feet of the line. With the casting weight concentrated in the front 30 feet, it is relatively easy to drive long casts directly into the wind, even with large, wind-resistant flies. But the weight-forward line does have a few drawbacks, the most noticeable being that the heavy forward taper does not allow an angler to cast as delicately as with double-tapered lines.

Be that as it may, a weight-forward fly line is often the best choice for fishing in the wind, casting to cruising game fish in still waters and fishing on rivers where wading is severely limited yet long casts are required. Possibly the greatest benefit occurs when it is essential to make the long casts that allow one to impart a very long effective retrieve of a nymph or streamer over deeper lake shelves and tidal flats and channels.

Bug-taper and *saltwater taper* lines are essentially variations on the weight-forward design. In these lines the weight is even more dramatically concentrated toward the tip ends than in conventional weight-forward lines. This increases casting distance with a minimum of backcasts. It also aids in presenting highly wind-resistant artificials under breezy or windy conditions.

Shooting-taper fly lines, also known as shooting heads, are roughly 30-foot-long single-tapered fly lines—large at the butt end, small at the tip. Their role in creative fly fishing is to present the fly at distances approaching 130 feet. Shooting heads also allow the flyfisher to achieve extremely long drifts of the fly in an attitude broadside to the current.

Shooting heads are commercially available in floating, intermediate and sinking models. Consistently productive fishing with these lines requires no small amount of skill in long distance casting.

The shooting taper is rigged for fishing by its spliced, butt-end loop to about 100 feet of 15- to 30-pound test moderately limp monofilament, or to an equivalent length of floating, braided, level shooting-line of fine diameter (usually .029 inches). Although the flat monofilament used in tournament-casting distance events facilitates incredibly long casts with a shooting head, it does encounter considerable resistance from water—enough to virtually require the use of a stripping basket when it's used for fishing. Because many experienced anglers prefer to hold the recovered shooting line in long loops between their lips, the limp, round monofilament materials like Maxima and Kroic, which are supple yet not too limp, are recommended when a stripping basket is not employed. Finally, the remainder of the reel drum beneath the "head" and the shooting line is filled with 100 to 300 yards of 20-pound-test braided Dacron backing line. The casting technique involves the "double haul" described in Chapter 3.

Depending upon the depth, speed and direction of the current, the cast is directed up and across, straight across or down and across the current. Additional line is very often played out before the fly begins its across-stream swing if a longer and deeper than normal run of the fly is desired.

As the recovery is made, the shooting line is gathered into long loops which are either held in the caster's lips or allowed to fall in coils in a stripping basket strapped to his waist.

One popular type of stripping basket is made from canvas stitched to a wire frame. Another good one is made out of fiberglass (Fig. 7). Slots or loops along the rear side of the basket accommodate the angler's wad-

Fig. 7. This excellent stripping basket is made out of fiberglass. It is strapped to the upper waist with the wading belt.

Fig. 8. Strip the monofilament or braided shooting line into the basket in long pulls. Some anglers hold the rod under the upper casting arm and employ both hands for the maneuver.

ing belt. The basket is strapped outside the waders to the upper waist.

In using a stripping basket, some anglers find it most convenient to hold the fly rod under the upper casting arm and strip in shooting line with both hands during the recovery (Fig. 8). A container other than the commercial type can be rigged to function as an emergency stripping basket. Some anglers have been known to slice a couple of belt slots in a cardboard box. Rubber or plastic dishpans also serve as makeshift stripping baskets.

Fig. 9. The tangle-free line gathers in the stripping basket.

Lead head denotes any one of several possible modifications of conventional fly lines aimed at enhancing their ability to sink. It can also describe a shooting head constructed by the angler from a weighed section of lead-cored, plastic-coated trolling line (Gladding Mark V is the best I've tried to date).

One type of lead-head line consists of a shooting-taper sinking fly line, to the tip of which is spliced a 1-to-2-foot section of 18-pound-test leaded line. In another type, two or three shorter pieces of leaded line are spliced in at intervals in the conventional shooting head. Still another consists of a short section of leaded line spliced into the tip of a floating weight-forward line to form a sort of super "sink tip."

Lead heads made entirely of leaded trolling line usually run from 15 to 25 feet long. They are spliced or nail-knotted directly to monofilament shooting line. Such lines are most popular with West Coast flyrodders seeking Chinook salmon and winter-run steelheads in the deeper stretches of rivers. The outsized Chinooks, especially, tend to hug the bottom of a river during their upstream spawning runs, and lead heads are great aids in getting flies down to where they are.

It takes some practice to learn how to cast a lead head safely. It can be downright dangerous if cast with the same methods used to develop velocity in a conventional shooting head, because the lead head offers very little wind resistance. It develops tremendous speed with a minimum casting effort, dropping to a dangerously low level during a normal "high" back cast.

The safest way to cast a lead head (if there really is a safe method) is to allow *all* of the head portion to flow through the tip guide on the first back cast (Fig. 10). The forward cast is then made with a single gentle haul on the shooting line. Unless you want to court disaster, do not false cast with a lead-head line. Once you've fished out your cast, lift it into a high back cast, allowing the head to carry four or five feet past the rod tip and to drop nearly to the surface behind you. Then, with a single haul on the shooting line, send out the forward cast on a high arc aimed well above the intended target. Be prepared to duck!

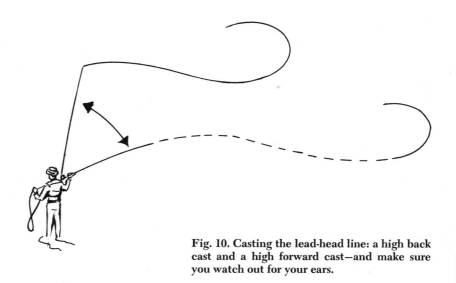

Fig. 10. Casting the lead-head line: a high back cast and a high forward cast—and make sure you watch out for your ears.

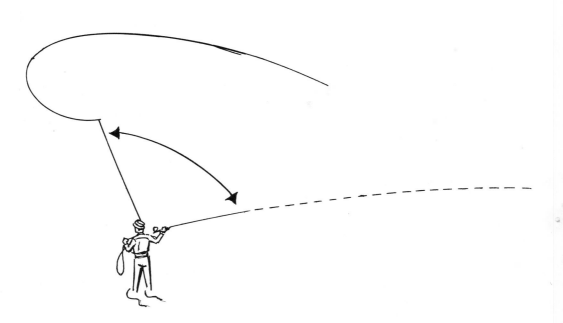

Chapter 3

Fly Casting

FLY-CASTING TECHNIQUE has undergone some dramatic changes during the past century and a quarter. Essentially, the methods of modern-day fly casting are the natural outgrowths of certain revolutionary developments in rod- and line-making technology. The trend in rod design has gradually drifted away from long, heavy rods with relatively slow actions toward lighter, stiffer, quicker, more powerful casting instruments capable of imparting tremendous velocity to fly lines.

The development of modern fly rods really began in 1862 when Samuel Phillippe of Easton, Pennsylvania, glued together into rod sections split, planed strips of Calcutta bamboo cane. A number of other fine craftsmen soon began to produce the split-cane fly rods, including Hiram Leonard of Bangor, Maine.

Early-day split-cane rods basically followed the designs of the solid-wood rods preceding them. Prior to the split-cane rods, lancewood, cedar, greenheart and bethabara woods all enjoyed varying degrees of popularity. Eventually, hard, powerful, responsive Tonkin cane became the preferred material for building split-cane rods. And with its use, fly rods eventually became lighter and shorter than anglers had dreamed possible. By the early 1900s they averaged less than 10 feet in length and 7 ounces in weight. Split cane remained the favorite fly rod material of the knowledgeable enthusiast until it became virtually unavailable during the early 1950s. By that time, hollow rods made of woven fiberglass were on the scene. Their resilience and toughness were comparable to split Tonkin cane and they captured the mass market for quality casting instruments. Fiberglass fly rods are by far the popular favorites today. And it's doubtful if split-cane rods will ever regain the popularity they once enjoyed, except among the most critical and romantic casting enthusiasts.

Fly lines began a parallel metamorphosis a couple of decades before the midpoint of the twentieth century. With the availability of relatively stiff, fast, powerful fly rods, tournament casters like Marvin Hedge and others began to splice and test-cast lines of weight-forward design that would fully utilize the distance-casting potential of the new rods. Today's weight-forward, bug-taper and saltwater-taper lines, coupled with powerful fiberglass and bamboo fishing rods, extend the fishing range of the flyrodder to distances exceeding 90 feet.

To take advantage of rod and line improvements, new casting techniques have evolved. Some of the most significant refinements include the casting-hand "squeeze" to assist the angler in firming up his wrist during the backward and forward casting strokes; full, free arm, elbow and shoulder movements that achieve a longer, more powerful stroke; and the double line-haul, to increase line speed for long-range casting. Each of these methods will be discussed in detail later in this chapter.

Line Control

No two persons are identically constructed physically, nor do they articulate in quite the same way. Although the ideal arc described by the rod tip, as it would be controlled by the ideal man, may in theory seem to be the best way to cast, in practice it serves merely as a guideline. Few of us are built ideally, and fewer yet possess ideal powers of concentration, muscular development or sense of timing. Our casting is limited by our natural talents, by our desire and ability to improve, and by physical limitations.

Fortunately, the fish couldn't care less if a back cast occasionally ticks the water behind the angler. What the fish is interested in is something to eat. And that primary consideration should give considerable encouragement even to the least polished caster, but it should not be taken to mean that negligent casting will be rewarded by success. Within the limits of individual ability, the fly fisherman must learn to maintain close control over the fly line, throughout the casting movements. It's possible to cast to distances in excess of 80 feet and still be a very sloppy fly caster. No doubt you'll recall the old story about the gorilla that putted a golf ball the same way he hit his drives . . . 400 yards straight down the fairway. The same principle applies to fly fishing. Truly effective casting is the product of both a degree of patiently developed muscular strength and finely tuned timing. The reason for the angler to work diligently toward developing both aspects of his casting is that by doing so he will achieve a greater degree of line control while fishing a wide variety of water types and under an equally large variety of climatic conditions. The angler who is in more or less full control of the fly line at both close and long distances, in dead air or still, chest high in the water or standing on the pitching deck of a skiff—that angler can concentrate on the fishing aspect of the sport, which is what this book is all about.

Basic Casting Principles

The primary principle influencing the behavior of an airborne fly line is incredibly simple: The fly line must flow along a path similar to that described by the rod; in other words, the line goes where the rod tip goes. If you swing the rod up, the line must travel in an upward direction. If the rod is thrust forward, the line must follow and flow forward. From that principle one could conclude that fly casting is ridiculously easy. And it is—provided one is willing to put a little concentration and effort into training the eye, hand, elbow, shoulder and torso until they work together in a coordinated fashion. From the beginner's standpoint, fly casting is most certainly much easier than hitting a golf ball with control.

Actually the term "fly casting" is inaccurate and misleading. For what is cast is not the fly, but the fly line. And what takes place during the cast is that velocity is imparted to the line through the various rod flexings and unflexings and line manipulations. Line speed and the ways in which it is imparted cause the line to flow up, down, back or forward and to drop to the water in a straight, curved or slack configuration.

Rod/Line Balance

Each individual fly rod delivers its optimum forward thrust under the influence of a specific amount of line weight, which is expressed as the weight in grains of the front 30 feet of the line according to AFTMA standards. The exact line weight that fully activates a rod's casting potential varies a little in supposedly identical fly rods—and varies a great deal between ultralight and heavy-duty models. There are similar variations in the actions of surf-casting, bait-casting, spin-casting and spinning rods.

Essentially, if a fly line is too light for a given rod, it will not bend the rod enough to develop full thrust for the casting movements. On the other hand, if the line is too heavy it tends to overstress the rod, altering its ability to deliver thrust at the right time and possibly causing it to break.

A rod and line are said to be balanced when the line weight develops the rod's best casting qualities, in terms of both power and control. Interestingly, some fly rods balance well with two or three AFTMA line weights, depending on the style of line employed and the distance and type of casting to be performed. I have one fine bamboo rod that will cast a light 9-weight shooting head about 100 feet, drive a 7-weight-forward line 80 feet into a headwind, and drop a dry fly delicately with a 6-weight double-tapered line at distances up to 60 feet—all without over- or under-stressing the bamboo fibers. Another of my favorite bamboo rods is most unforgiving. It doesn't balance well with any line that's more than five grains off the optimum weight.

Although an experienced caster can usually determine the correct line weight to balance a rod after a few minutes of test-casting with several different weights and styles of lines, novices are cautioned to note the rod maker's recommendations for suggested line weights, usually inscribed on the rod's butt section just forward of the cork grip. Unfortunately, not all rod manufacturers follow this practice and trial casting with several line weights is sometimes necessary. The Cortland Line Company makes available to its dealers a line/rod balancing kit that is extremely helpful in achieving a well-balanced fly-casting outfit.

Getting the Feel

After obtaining a correct balance between your line and fly rod, affixing a single-tapered leader to the point of the line, and spooling the line on a fly reel, go to a nearby park or playing field where there is at least 100 feet of unobstructed grass surface. Make sure there are no overhead power lines or tree limbs.

First, pull about 10 feet of fly line through the tip guide. Pull an additional 10 to 15 feet of line from the reel and allow it to lie in loose coils on the grass at your feet (Fig. 11).

Take a stance with your feet slightly apart, left foot a bit in advance of the right if you're right-handed. Grasp the cork grip of the fly rod lightly but firmly in whichever hand you elect to train as your casting hand. Most anglers prefer to cast with whichever hand is best coordinated. The thumb should rest on top of the rod grip (Fig. 12). This thumb position helps you maintain a firm wrist during the back cast and to apply power to the forward thrusting movement.

Employing a lifting backward movement and a thrusting forward movement, flip the rod tip back and forth several times, rod held upright (vertically), line

Fig. 11.

Fig. 12.

hand firmly holding the fly line at about waist level. Do not release your grip on the line. Hold it firmly in your line hand so that your casting hand can experience the feel of a little line weight working against the rod tip.

After flipping the rod up and forward a few times with the very short 10-foot length of line, extend about 20 feet of line on the grass in front of you and repeat the process (Figs. 13 and 14). This time watch the line as it flows up and back. Start the forward thrusting movement only when the line has almost straightened out in the air behind you. This will necessitate a brief pause between the up-and-back and forward rod movements. Allow the rod to pause long enough so that you can feel the weight of the line pulling against the tip section at the completion of both the backward and forward movements. Practice this until you can keep the line in the air

Fig. 13.

Fig. 14.

through several back and forward movements, with your eyes closed, strictly by feel.

The Basic Overhead Cast

Now that you're accustomed to the feel of the line working against the rod, assume a stance with your feet somewhat spread (Fig. 15). Face 30 to 45 degrees away from the direction in which you intend to cast. This body position will allow your arm, elbow and shoulder the freedom of movement that is most important in several of the modern casting techniques.

Start by holding the rod horizontally at about the 9-o'clock position in front of you. Your casting wrist should be firm, cocked slightly downward so that the rod extends in a straight line from the forearm. The forearm should be held parallel to the ground. The elbow should be bent at about 45-degree angle and the upper arm held away from the side of your torso so that the entire arm and shoulder can move freely (Fig. 16).

What comes next is very important: Begin the cast by firmly and swiftly accelerating the rod upward to a position approximating 12 o'clock (Fig. 17). Keep the wrist firm throughout the movement. An easy way to do this is to lightly squeeze the rod grip during the lifting movement. Squeezing imparts additional force and speeds up the flowing of the line.

It should be strongly emphasized that the back-cast movement is a *lift* employing the hand, wrist, forearm, elbow and upper arm and shoulder in a smooth, coordinated upward movement.

During the back cast, the casting hand travels about 2 feet or less, depending on the length of your arm. The direction the hand travels, as viewed out of the corner of your eye, should be upward and only *very slightly* backward. Try to stop the movement of the casting hand about even with your right eye or temple.

Visualize a large sheet of thin paper suspended flat overhead at rod's length. The object is to poke the rod tip neatly through the paper at as nearly vertical an angle as possible over your right shoulder. These

Fig. 15.

Fig. 16.

Fig. 17.

mental gymnastics may help you avoid back-and-forth flailing, a common and self-defeating fault.

The second important part of the basic overhead cast is the brief pause at the top of the back cast, during which the line flows in an upward and backward loop, ultimately straightening out in the air behind you (Fig. 18). Watch the line flow out and up throughout the back-cast movement. An instant before the line is fully extended you'll begin to feel its weight pull on the rod tip. Commence the forward casting movement at this point.

While waiting for the line to straighten, you'll probably notice the tendency of the rod tip to drift back to about the 1- or 2-o'clock position. That's fine. Let it drift. If your back cast has been a lifting one, you can allow the rod tip to drift behind you without unduly influencing the upward and backward unfurling of the line loop.

Fig. 18.

Allowing it to drift back to a more or less natural resting point at 1 o'clock will put the rod in position to apply the straight, forward thrusting movement that follows the pause at the top of the back cast.

The next stage is essentially a thrust, or throwing movement, similar to driving a nail with a hammer or throwing a ball. It is a smooth, accelerating movement of hand, wrist, arm and shoulder that drives the rod tip forward from the 1-o'clock position to the 10-o'clock position (Fig. 19). Maximum acceleration is applied between 11 o'clock and 12 o'clock, where the rod tip is snapped forward in what is commonly called the kick. It is roughly comparable to wrist snap in throwing a baseball. (Kick is also applied to the back cast to impart lift and line speed between 11 o'clock and 12 o'clock.) The same kind of squeeze that added control and momentum to the back cast is used again to accelerate line speed during this forward casting motion. As the

Fig. 19.

line straightens out behind you on the back cast, allow your casting hand to relax very slightly between 12 and 1 o'clock; but then commence the forward thrust with a second, firm, gentle, progressive squeeze. The rod will seem to spring alive in your hand. And you'll notice that line speed develops more or less naturally if the squeeze is a *progressive* one, timed to achieve its greatest intensity during the kick.

Now, if you've lifted the fly rod into the back cast and thrust it forward precisely as described, the line loops, both forward and backward, will travel precisely the same vertical plane. When this occurs there is a tendency for the fly to strike the rod during the forward cast.

So the first real casting refinement we'll work on is to separate the line-loop planes *very slightly*, starting the rod tip back and up a hair off the vertical and thrusting the rod tip forward in as nearly a vertical plane as possible.

If you were able to look down on the caster from directly overhead, you would note that the rod tip follows a somewhat oval pattern during the movements, as illustrated diagrammatically in Fig. 20.

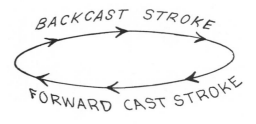

Fig. 20.

Fig. 21.

Practice separating the backward and forward line loops very slightly until the movements become habit.

Whether flowing back or coming forward, a line loop may be relatively narrow from top to bottom or quite wide. The depth of the loop, or bow as it's sometimes called, is one of the most important controls to be learned by the creative fly fisherman.

When the loop is narrow, or "tight," very straight casts can be made to considerable distances. A narrow loop does not promote especially delicate delivery of the fly, however. In order to present a very tiny fly with great finesse, you'll want to learn how to widen the loop a bit. Utilizing the basic principle that the line must follow the path described by the rod tip, it's easy to see that in order to widen the line loop you must widen the casting arc.

For a wide loop, stop the back cast a little farther back of vertical than usual—at about 1 o'clock. Allow the rod tip to drift back to about 2 o'clock. Apply power to both the back and forward casts more with the middle of the rod than the tip section. Start the forward cast by dropping the casting hand straight down a few inches during the pause, then apply the thrusting movement forward (Fig. 21). Impart less kick to both backward and forward movements than in the basic overhead cast.

If you want to tighten the line loops, follow the reverse procedure by narrowing the casting arc and accentuating the kick on both back and forward casts (Fig. 22).

One of the most common faults is overcasting—exerting too much effort during the forward thrust. Some instructors refer to the error as "shocking" the rod tip.

Applying more power than is needed for a cast of a given distance not only wastes energy but tends to make the rod tip vibrate at the end of the cast. When the tip vibrates up and down it imparts a wavy configuration to the line, making it virtually impossible to cast a straight line.

Fig. 22.

To be sure, a wavy configuration is desirable in certain fishing situations, but it is better to learn first how to cast a straight line before branching out into useful tricky refinement.

Shooting the Line

The next step is to learn how to extend your cast to 50 or 60 feet. Either double-tapered or weight-tapered fly lines may be employed for this exercise. First, cast to a distance of about 30 feet. Let the line fall in a straight line on the grass ahead of you. Pull an additional 10 feet of line from the reel and let it fall in loose coils at your feet.

Make an overhead cast. At the completion of the forward thrust and kick, as the line starts to straighten in the air over the target but before it completely unfurls, release your grip on the fly line. When you get the timing right, the weight of the unfurling line will shoot (pull) the additional 10 feet of line smoothly through the guides.

Once you've mastered the timing of the basic line shoot, pull 10 more feet of line from the reel and try another cast and shoot. Allow the weight of the 40-foot length of line to pull the additional line through the guides. No difficulty should be experienced with a weight-forward line. If you're using a very light double-tapered line, you may not be able to extend the cast to 50 feet without employing the maneuvers I'll describe next.

Single Line Haul for Long Casts

To cast distances approaching 60 feet with double-tapered lines (75 feet with weight-forward lines) it's necessary to ac-celerate the speed of the line in the air. Still longer casts will be covered in sections on the use of shooting-head fly lines. In addition to developing great line speed, you must deliver the cast at a high enough angle to allow for the gravitational pull exerted on the long length of moving line. You begin by fully loading the rod action with the weight of the line—i.e., the forward 40 to 55 feet of the line. Then you employ one of the two line-hand manipulations, the single line haul or the double line haul, to achieve acceleration.

The single line haul imparts additional speed to the line during the back cast. It is

Fig. 23.

accomplished by pulling down sharply on the line with the line hand during the back-cast kick, between about 11 and 12 o'clock (Fig. 23). Some anglers begin the hauling movement almost simultaneously with the start of the back cast in order to help break the surface tension of the water on the line. This is especially helpful when you want to lift an inordinately long length of line from the water into the back cast—say 50 to 70 feet of line—not too common a problem on trout streams, but frequently necessary in salt water or on large rivers and lakes.

A single haul usually imparts enough speed for casts of 45 to 60 feet with double tapers, 55 to 70 feet with weight-forward lines.

The line to be shot is pulled from the reel and held in large coils in the hand, coiled loosely in a stripping basket, or lightly held by the lips in long loops. The length of the downward haul varies considerably among casters, from a few inches to a foot or more, depending upon the length of the arm and the amount of line speed required to cast the desired distance.

Line haul is imparted with progressive speed, beginning slowly and at the same tempo as the rod lift and reaching its maximum intensity during the back-cast kick. The forward cast is made in the usual manner. The loops or coils of additional line are allowed to shoot out through the guides at the completion of the forward cast.

Double Line Haul for Longer Casts

When it's necessary to shoot a great deal of line or when casting directly into the wind, the double line haul is used. Its first stage duplicates the single haul. But as the rod hand drifts back between 12 and 1 o'clock, the line hand comes back and up, close to the butt guide (Fig. 24).

A second hauling movement is then imparted during the forward cast, as the rod is thrust forward into the kick (Fig. 25). The line is released and shot toward the target at the completion of the second haul as the line begins to straighten from the forward loop.

An especially high back cast is not desirable for really great distance because you have to aim well above the far-off target—to about 11 o'clock. And in order to achieve the necessary higher casting arc, you allow the back cast to drop to a point fairly close to the ground or water level.

Stop the back cast at about 1 o'clock and allow the rod to drift back to about 2 o'clock, maybe even a bit lower. Then, as the line begins to straighten behind you (it pays to inspect the back cast visually during long casts) start the forward thrust and downward haul, in that order. Double hauling is easy once you learn to coordinate opposing movements of your two hands. It requires a trick of timing, rather like patting your head and rubbing your stomach at the same time. But it works after a little concentrated practice.

Casting the Shooting Head

To cast a shooting head backed with monofilament or fine-diameter braided shooting line, you employ the double haul exactly as with conventional fly lines—but with one little refinement: a certain amount of overhang must be allowed between the butt end of the fly line and the tip of the fly rod (Fig. 26). Normally, three or four feet of separation is sufficient for casts up to about 90 feet. Competitive dis-

Fig. 24.

Fig. 25.

tance casts, which employ very long haul-ing movements with the line hand, usually require six or more feet of overhang to pre-vent the spliced loop at the butt of the line from striking the rod tip during the hauls.

In both single- and double-haul casting, especially with a shooting-taper fly line, the most satisfactory results are usually achieved by limiting the number of false casts to a bare minimum. Try to get the

|← OVERHANG →|

Fig. 26.

line loop to fall into a narrow, vertical configuration with no more than three false casts. After the third, casters who are less than expert tend to lose their sense of timing and, as a result, some of their ability to impart casting power correctly.

CASTING IN THE WIND

Wind is frequently an unwanted companion, a most unfriendly one that at times demands casting adaptations to accommodate its cantankerous disposition.

Wind driving directly from the rear is fairly easy to cope with except when blowing at near hurricane force. The main thing to remember in a tail wind is to throw the back cast with enough extra force to straighten the line out. Failure to do so can result in a hook being planted somewhere in your posterior. A single line haul is a great help in straightening out the back cast into a wind.

Wind blowing directly into your face is also easy to deal with. Make a high back cast, throwing as tight a loop as possible. Employ the double haul and shoot the line as low as possible over the water on the forward cast. Deliver the forward thrust and kick very firmly, following through aggressively with the rod tip. If the thrust is properly executed, the forward loop will slice neatly through the headwind in a very tight bow (Fig. 27), flowing rapidly to the target a few inches over the water, rising slightly toward the end of the cast. A headwind tends to lift the forward-moving line. If the cast is delivered at too high an angle, the fly will fall short of the target.

A crosswind is more difficult to handle. The "backhand cast" (see page 38) is a good way to deal safely with a crosswind at short distances. For long casts, deliver

Fig. 27.

Fig. 28.

the back cast with great firmness to the 1 o'clock position, allowing the rod tip to drift nearly to 3 o'clock (Fig. 28). Deliver the forward cast by progressively applying the thrusting power to the middle and butt sections of the rod. Rods with full, fairly stiff parabolic actions work best for this cast. Excessively tippy or soft rods aren't recommended where long distances and crosswinds frequently combine to frustrate fishermen. The line is rolled forward in a grossly exaggerated wide loop, with the fly well above head level. The technique takes considerable practice to really master. But once learned, it permits safe casting for considerable distances in crosswinds.

Directional Control

The sudden need to change the direction of a cast is practically a universal problem on streams, lakes or salt water. Changing direction while the line is in the air is a maneuver needed most often when fish are spotted feeding or moving at or near the surface.

To accomplish the directional change, allow the back cast to flow out along the normal path, but at the start of the forward thrust pivot your upper torso toward the new target and make the forward stroke in the usual manner. If a delicate presentation is indicated, it's usually advisable to make a false cast or two in the new direction before kicking the line into the final delivery.

EXTRA-HIGH BACK CASTS

High stream banks, trees and brush to the rear often necessitate an abnormally high back cast. Of the several ways to effect a high, or climbing, back cast, perhaps the most dramatic is called the steeple cast, or tower cast. Begin the back cast stroke with the rod tip held as close as possible to the water. Make a very swift vertical lift of the hand, arm and shoulder to 11 o'clock (Fig. 29). But instead of stopping there momentarily, as in the pause for a normal overhead cast, continue to raise the arm vertically until it is fully extended high over your head. Then, before the line can finally unfurl overhead, drop the casting hand to shoulder level, elbow bent. Aim the forward cast somewhat higher than normal, accentuating the thrust and follow-through. This cast is rather difficult while standing deep in the water, nor is it really practical for distances greater than 50 feet.

One of the best ways to make the fly line continue climbing throughout the back cast is a fairly complex maneuver usually known as the Belgian cast. Rotate your wrist to the right in an out-and-up direction during the back cast so that the rod tip travels an outward, upward path (Fig. 30).

Looking straight down on a flyrodder making a Belgian cast, one would observe the rod tip following a near-circular pattern, at the same time sweeping upward in an oval vertical arc. The rod is started back in a semi-horizontal plane. The line flows

Fig. 29.

back rather close to the water during the initial phase of the back cast. As the wrist is rotated outward in a progressive, accelerating movement of about 45 degrees, the line climbs until the start of the forward stroke.

Probably the easiest way to achieve a constantly climbing back cast is with the elliptical cast, during which the rod tip describes an oval pattern throughout the entire sequence of movements. No distinct pause is made at any time, so the weight of the line is constantly loaded on the rod throughout the cast, eliminating many timing problems inherent in conventional overhead casting.

If you're a right-hander, tip the rod a bit to the right during the backward stroke. Make the forward thrust in the vertical position. Because the line is brought back low and lifted into the ascending curve of an ellipse (Fig. 31), the back cast always rises—much in the same way as in the Belgian cast. The difference lies in the oval paths described by the rod tip, both vertically and horizontally, in the elliptical cast. In the Belgian cast the horizontal path is circular, whereas wrist rotation is not consciously employed in the elliptical cast.

The forward stroke of the elliptical cast more or less resembles the throwing of a baseball. Right-handed casters should stand with the left foot slightly forward. No pause is made between the backward and forward movements. The elliptical cast is especially useful with ultralight, short fly rods, and when casting large, weighted flies with light-action rods.

Casting a Slack Line

Varying speeds of current between the caster and his target area can create drag on the line making the fly race unnaturally past the fish. Drag can be counteracted to varying degrees by either mending the cast in an up or downstream direction, or causing the line to drop slackly to the water in a wavy configuration somewhat resembling the track left by a snake in the sand.

The most commonly used and simplest slack-line cast is called the Lazy-S cast. There are two ways to accomplish it with a minimum of difficulty. The first—and probably easiest—is to waggle the rod tip back and forth a few times at the completion of the forward cast before the line drops to

Fig. 30.

Fig. 31.

the water. The second is to stop the rod tip abruptly at the completion of the forward cast and impart a slight reverse tug on the line with the rod tip.

Both techniques can be employed in combination with the overhead, elliptical, backhand or horizontal casting described in this chapter. Either a double-tapered or a weight-forward line performs satisfactorily with conventional slack-line casting, though only the double taper is recommended in the case of the long-tippet technique, described below.

Bill Lawrence's Long-Tippet Technique

It's a rare privilege to become unexpectedly acquainted with an angling method that's truly innovative—truly new and creative. Such was my experience a few years ago when I had the pleasure of dry-fly fishing some of Montana's blue-ribbon trout streams with my friend Milt Kahl, of Los Angeles.

The method is called the long-tippet technique and, according to Milt, it was originated by Bill Lawrence, former owner of Hot Creek Ranch in California. It is without a doubt the most consistently effective way I've ever observed to present dry flies to large trout. I'll let Milt describe the method in his own words.

"First, I should point out that the technique is for anglers who are out after the larger fish. If they're merely after numbers regardless of size, they'll do almost as well with a 12-foot leader.

"This technique is the *only* way a perfect float of a dry fly can be achieved in difficult water. It takes a good caster and a hell of a lot of practice to achieve perfection with the method, and I suspect that's why some people are inclined to belittle it.

"The idea is to achieve maximum slack in the tippet without sacrificing accuracy or control of the fly. With this maximum slack a perfect float can be achieved in widely varying current speeds, and even through changes in current direction, as in eddies. It's been my experience that the larger fish do their surface-feeding in difficult water situations, more often than not protected by conditions that produce drag. (See Fig. 32 for three examples of such situations.)

"For small to medium streams I use a 7-

Fig. 32. The long-tippet technique
The long tippet employed in three difficult situations.

The first (Fig. 32a) was an actual situation in which a fish was coaxed into taking after several days of angling. The trout was 22 inches long and weighed about three pounds. The weed island was about four feet long and the channel between it and the bank about eight inches wide. The fish above him on the same bank presents another quite difficult situation common in presenting a fly to a large trout. Usually they won't move to a fly in the nearby faster current, so it's necessary practically to hit them on the head with the offering. The fish in the "V" is a little easier to get at. But it still takes the long-tippet method to achieve a long enough float to give him a chance to look

the fly over.

The second (Fig. 32b) is a situation very common on meadow water: This is very similar to the diagram showing the weed island. The fly must be floated down a narrow channel. The float is difficult because, quite often, just as the fly is about to reach the fish, the tippet will catch on weeds. The fly starts to drag and down goes the fish—frustrating situation that's easier to solve by employing the long-tippet technique.

The third (Fig. 32c, page 34) is a very difficult situation where the current is very turbulent and bubbly against the bank. To complicate matters, it's almost impossible for the angler to see the fly, and a fish in a place like this sometimes rises so quietly it may not be seen.

Fig. 32a

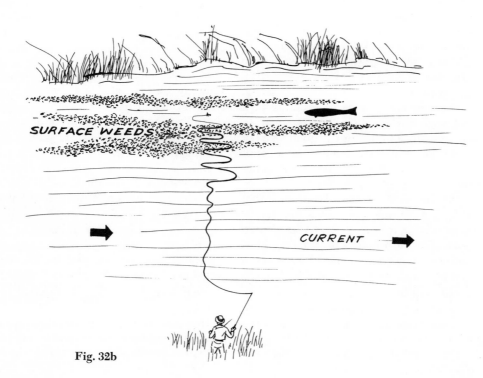

Fig. 32b

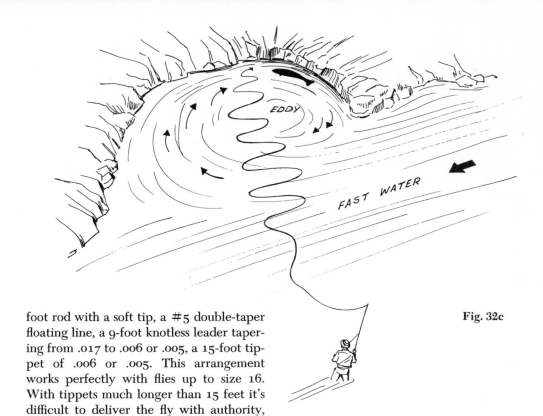

Fig. 32c

foot rod with a soft tip, a #5 double-taper floating line, a 9-foot knotless leader tapering from .017 to .006 or .005, a 15-foot tippet of .006 or .005. This arrangement works perfectly with flies up to size 16. With tippets much longer than 15 feet it's difficult to deliver the fly with authority, especially with a little wind blowing.

"If you cast properly, with a wrist-snap at the end of the forward movement (Fig. 33), about 10 o'clock, the tippet can be made to collapse on itself, resulting in a good deal of slack tippet in as small an area as you desire. With a great deal of practice, an angler can control the amount of slack he throws into the tippet quite well.

"On the larger streams I use an 8-foot rod with a #7 line, a 9-foot leader tapering from .022 to .010 and 15 feet of .010 tippet. The reason for this, of course, is that we're using larger flies. In passing, I should mention that the leader butt size is critical, and the terminal tackle used on a #5 line can't be used with a #7 line with this technique. You lose contact with the fly.

"I'd suggest that anyone trying this technique start modestly, with perhaps eight feet of tippet, and then lengthen out as he becomes more proficient."

Milt's statement that the long tippet is the only way to achieve a perfect dry-fly float in difficult water will stir up a storm of controversy among dry-fly enthusiasts. It is also probable that my support of that statement will subject me to the same criticisms, leveled by staunch advocates of more conventional deliveries. But that's fair enough. The long tippet is one of the more innovative stream-angling methods to be developed in this century. As with most new methods, general acceptance will take time. All I ask is that you reserve judgment until you become proficient enough with it to make an objective evaluation.

How deadly is it? I would make a conservative estimate that a skilled long-tippet artist can hook two to three times as many large trout, over the course of an entire season, as an equally proficient conventional caster. If you're willing to take

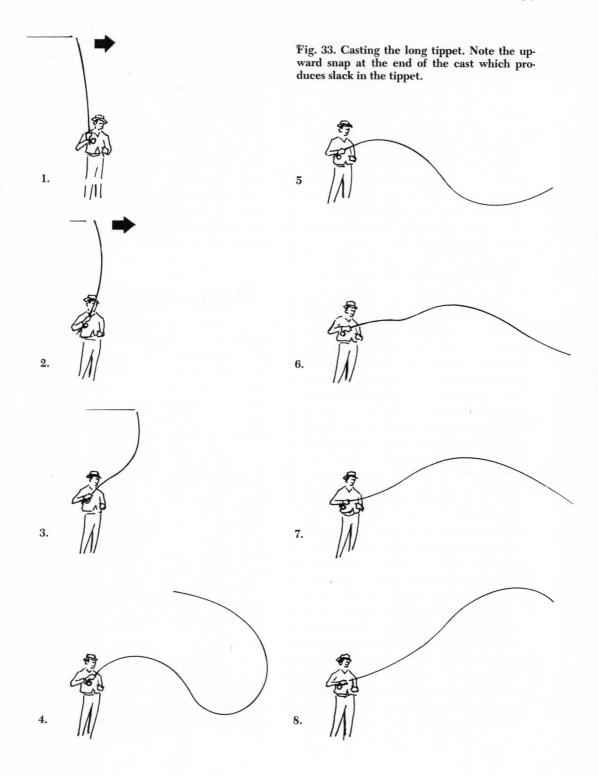

Fig. 33. Casting the long tippet. Note the upward snap at the end of the cast which produces slack in the tippet.

1.

2.

3.

4.

5

6.

7.

8.

on a casting challenge with a payoff in large trout, give long-tippet casting your best effort.

CASTING A MENDED LINE

Mending the line after the cast—making a correction when the line bellies with the current and drags a dry fly under or makes a wet fly race unnaturally fast—is one of the most crucial flyrodding maneuvers and, fortunately, one of the easiest. The basic method is to flick the rod tip in a little circle, flipping line upstream. There are times, of course, when you want to mend the line *down*stream. For example, the fly may be carried along in a fast flow while the line follows in a sluggish current that happens to prevail between your casting position and the tippet. You'll also want to mend downstream when using a shooting head on broad, fast rivers and trying for a deep, dead-drift run of the fly. I'll cover this shooting-head technique in Chapter 4, and will have more to say about mending the line for other purposes, too. It's easy once the line is on the water, but there are sometimes distinct advantages to having the line touch down in an already mended state. This is a casting technique which should be understood before we go further.

Casting a mended line is quite easy. It calls for a rolling movement of the casting wrist during the forward stroke. If you wish to mend the line to the left, the wrist is rotated to the left during the forward thrust, then rotated back to the normal position before the forward movement is finished. Rotation of the wrist early in the casting thrust puts the mend relatively close to you. Late wrist rotation locates the mend proportionately nearer the end of the line.

However, the technique is quite different when using a shooting taper in conjunction with braided or monofilament shooting line of fine diameter. At the completion of the forward cast and almost at the finish of the shoot, the rod tip is flipped sharply sideways in an up or downstream direction. This is done a split second before the head portion of the line lands on the water. Location of the mend can be somewhat controlled by wrist rotation when braided shooting line is used, provided the line is cast like a conventional weight-forward or double-tapered line and no great length is shot through the guides.

HORIZONTAL CASTING

The most frequent purpose of casting a fly line in a horizontal or semi-horizontal plane is to drop a fly under overhanging bushes or trees. To make a horizontal, or side-arm, cast, cant the rod tip to the right until it is horizontal to the water. Make the back cast with an up-and-back stroke, pausing at about 10:30 o'clock (horizontally) and letting the rod drift back between 12 and 1 o'clock. Deliver the forward stroke in almost the same horizontal plane (Fig. 34), taking care not to drop the rod tip at the end of either the backward or forward stroke. The line loop should describe a narrow arc. False-casting and delivery strokes should be firm but delicate. Very few situations require the use of an absolutely horizontal delivery. Usually a casting arc somewhere between vertical and horizontal will suffice.

CURVE CASTS

Casts curving either to the left or the right are normally attempted either to present the fly to the fish in advance of the

Fig. 34.

leader tippet, or to deliver the fly on the far side of some in-the-water obstruction such as a large rock. Wading or casting conditions often prevent a fisherman from getting into position for a more direct presentation.

A cast curving to the right of a right-handed caster is called a negative-curve cast. One bending to the left is a positive-curve cast.

To make a fly line curve to the left, perform the backward and forward casting strokes in either a semi- or fully horizontal plane, as described above. Use a double-tapered fly line and a tapered weight-forward leader.

Deliver the forward cast with more drive than usual. Check the rod slightly at the completion of the forward thrust (Fig. 35). The degree of curve will depend on

how much kick you put into the forward movement and how abruptly you check the thrust. The line's curve will also be affected by any wind, of course.

Negative-curve casts are more difficult. The easiest way is to employ the backhand cast, which will be described next. Take the rod back diagonally across your opposing shoulder at a semi- or fully horizontal angle. The forward thrust is delivered with about the same amount of kick as in the positive-curve cast (Fig. 36).

Another and more difficult negative-curve cast is made by utilizing the middle and butt sections of the rod for the power delivery during the forward thrust. Less thrust than is necessary to straighten the line is the secret of this cast. A little head-wind also helps. The objective is to make a very soft forward cast that causes the line

Fig. 35.   Fig. 36.

loop to lose velocity before the line is extended, causing the line to fall to the water ahead of the leader. A long, fine, tapered leader with a very fine tippet, used in conjunction with a double-tapered fly line, is the best combination for this cast.

THE BACKHAND CAST

Casting over your opposing shoulder, backhanded casting—is a highly useful method of coping with crosswinds and streamside bushes, and is also an easy way to achieve a negative curve.

The backward stroke is delivered diagonally across the chest at any desired angle between near-vertical and fully horizontal (Fig. 37). There's a tendency to let the back cast drop too close to the water, so care should be exercised to keep it fairly high.

The forward thrust is made in nearly the

Fig. 37.

same plane as the back cast. It is not especially difficult at short distances, but casts in excess of 50 feet are tricky and require superior timing and a considerable amount of development in the casting wrist and hand.

Roll Casts

Roll casts allow an angler to deliver the fly in situations where no backcast of any kind is feasible—for example, when wading very close to a bank lined with tall trees or overhanging bushes. Although a roll cast can be performed in a number of ways, perhaps the best and easiest is to start by raising the rod in a moderately slow, progressive lift to about 11 o'clock (Fig. 38).

Take care not to completely break the surface tension of the water with the leader and the forward section of the line. It's next to impossible to make a really good roll cast with a weight-forward line, so use a double-taper where such casting will be frequent. However, if your fishing requires a high percentage of long casts as well as some roll casting, you should probably purchase one of the new long-belly weight-forward lines which roll-cast exceedingly well.

The right foot is positioned somewhat forward of the left. Without breaking the slow, even tempo of the upward swing, pivot your torso to the right. This will cause the fly and leader to drag across the surface of the water.

Deliver the forward casting thrust in the

Fig. 38.

Fig. 39.

vertical plane and with enough force (to a point over the target) to extend the line and tippet fully while they're still in the air. The line and leader should roll forward over the surface, lift into the air (Fig. 39), straighten, then fall to the surface fully extended—in that sequence.

It's possible to shoot fly line with a roll cast, but there's a trick to it. As you lift the rod during the initial portion of the upward swing, make a single line haul. The amount of line you want to shoot should be coiled in the line hand. When the rod is about halfway through the forward stroke, allow your line hand (which is still holding onto the coils) to swing forward toward the butt guide. At this point the extra line is released, to shoot forward and extend the cast a few feet. Timing is critical when shooting line with a roll cast. Don't expect spectacular success until you've put in many hours of practice to learn the precise point at which the line must be released.

A technique called the roll-cast lift is used to pluck line, leader and fly from the water with as little disturbance as possible. First, make a roll cast in the prescribed manner. Following the forward thrust of the rod, and the instant the line lifts clear of the water, snatch it up and back into an overhead back cast. Make a false cast or two and the subsequent fishing delivery by whatever means is indicated at the moment. Again, double-tapered lines perform this maneuver more effectively than weight-forward lines.

Roll casting tends to drag a fly through the surface film, which is most undesirable with floating artificials. The "snatch roll cast" eliminates the possibility of drowning the dry fly.

At the beginning of the cast, use your line hand to hold onto the leader a foot or two from the fly. Line is extended before the delivery stroke by stripping it from the reel with the line hand and making roll-cast motions with the rod without releasing the grip on the leader. Get line out with false roll-cast strokes until the midpoint of the line loop is about half the distance to the target area. Then make a roll-cast delivery, releasing the leader from your line hand at the point when you would normally shoot the line.

Chapter 4

Fishing Moving Waters

F ISH-APPEAL in an artificial fly depends on its visibility to the fish, its shape, translucency, color, flash, behavior under the influences of current, the water clarity and temperature, the angle of the sunlight, and the movements imparted to the fly by the angler. Currents in streams, rivers and tidal flows may impart very definite fish-attracting movements to certain parts of nymphs, wet flies and streamers, as well as to the long, flexible tails on various types of surface artificials. On the other hand, currents can also interfere with the effectiveness of a presentation. For example, unequal speeds of current between angler and artificial can cause the fly to race unnaturally past fish, dramatically reducing the probability of a response.

The angler can influence the behavior of his flies in a number of ways, beginning with the choice of fly-tying materials. The strength of current tends to affect one's choice of materials. Generally speaking, the softer and more flexible the materials, the more mobile the fly will be under the influences of current or action-imparting presentations (Fig. 40). Another factor influencing fly behavior in moving waters is the relative sparseness or bushiness of the dressing. A fly's bulk tends to affect its ability to sink, float or wiggle enticingly in the water almost as much as the inherent buoyancy and flexibility of the materials themselves. Once the fly is on or beneath the surface, how it behaves depends not only on all of these qualities, but also on the weight of the hook, the style of the dressing and the mode of presentation.

Thus, when we speak of a "deadly fly," we refer not only to a particular com-

Fig. 40. Three exceptionally delicate, flexible flies.

bination of colors, form, sparseness or bulk, size and weight, but also to how we intend to make the fly *behave* in the water—the total effect, the ultimate, unified result of creative fly tying and fishing. Before tying some flies, let's examine certain proved presentation methods and attempt to comprehend the effects they produce on the feathers at tippet's-end.

UPSTREAM PRESENTATION

There are two readily apparent reasons to cast a fly upstream or markedly up and across the current. The most obvious is to offer a floating fly to the fish in a way that minimizes the probability of its being unnaturally influenced by currents. The other is to present a nymph, flymph, wet fly or streamer in such a way that it will sink very quickly as it drifts downstream toward the fish.

There is considerable logic in dressing nymphs for upstream fishing with as much built-in wiggle as possible and with fast-sinking qualities, since this mode of presentation somewhat reduces the angler's control over the actual run of the fly and limits his ability to make any really effective action-retrieve. Normally, the tying goal sought by the upstream nymph and wet-fly angler is an artificial possessing qualities of responsiveness to the current, qualities resembling those inherent in the living organism on which the fly is patterned. Such responsiveness is sought in impressionistic artificials as well as closely imitative types. The more inherently wiggly the materials, the more active they will be under the effects of a relatively free drift downstream (Fig. 41).

It is interesting to note the striking similarities between certain deadly nymphs

Fig. 41. Nymphs and streamers benefit from "wiggly" materials too.

designed for maximum wriggle in moving waters and some enticing feathered fakes originated for sub-surface angling in backwaters, lakes and ponds. The common element, in both cases, very frequently is mobility.

An effective fly is sometimes the offspring of inspirations. At least as often, it's the stepchild of necessity. Such was the case in the development of this writer's Marabou Leech. The fly came about while I was fishing a lake containing some exceptionally large rainbow trout. Normally the lake has massive hatches of caddis flies during the month of June. I had timed my angling to coincide with what I hoped to be the peak of the hatch.

After three days at this supposed still-water Shangri-la, I was thoroughly disappointed. The hatch was practically non-existent. There was almost no surface feeding activity, even at night. A friend and I fished until well after midnight to prove that point.

Then, on the fourth evening, a three-pounder somehow bungled and was hooked on a large nymph suggesting a caddis pupa. It was the first fish over a foot in length to come to net. Burning with curiosity as to what the fish were feeding on, I dressed the trout immediately. Out of its gullet tumbled five three-inch gray-brown leeches.

That evening I sat down at the tying vise and attempted to imitate the general colors and configuration of the leeches. My prototype was dressed on a size 2, 6XL hook. It was a very simple concoction with a slim, dun-colored spun-fur body, an overbody of gray-brown yarn and fine oval silver-tinsel ribbing.

The new fly stimulated our hopes but not many strikes the next morning. Only two fair-sized fish came to net in three hours of hard fishing. Again we checked their stomach contents and found leeches. Either my new fly wasn't quite right in configuration or color or we weren't employing exactly what was needed in the way of a retrieve, or possibly both.

During lunch, I sat on shore next to the water, nibbling a sandwich and watching a few caddis larvae inch their "mobile homes" along the lake bottom. Gradually I became aware of leeches undulating through the water. I watched their movements closely, mentally trying to formulate a way to imitate the undulations with a retrieve. I fed the last bite of breadcrust to a young ground squirrel and headed onto the water. I was satisfied that a different recovery technique would turn the trick. But it didn't. The long, stick-like "leech fly" wouldn't wiggle.

Back at the tying vise, I pawed hurriedly through feathers and furs, looking for some olive-brown marabou feathers that I remembered dying the previous winter. Once the marabou feathers were located, the new fly's configuration gelled rapidly. I tied on a 1½ inch tail, utilizing the tip of the feather. The butt end was not trimmed off; it would be retained for the overbody. The body was dubbed out of gray muskrat fur. Then, the overbody of marabou was wrapped down over the top of the body with a strand of fine, oval silver tinsel.

The resulting highly mobile marabou leech was an instant success—and I hooked a dozen heavy rainbows on it during the next two hours. Fished on a fast- or very fast-sinking fly line, it eventually proved to be deadly on three species of trout as well as largemouth and smallmouth bass. I vary the colors occasionally to resemble leeches in other regions, but the wiggly, slender configuration is the same.

Upstream presentations of artificial flies can be accomplished effectively with either floating, sinking-tip or sinking fly lines. But the floating and sinking-tip lines are the most popular among experienced flyrodders. They allow a fisherman to lift a good portion of his line completely off the water during the fly's run downstream, thereby reducing the probability of drag.

To make a straight upstream delivery, cast an appropriate length of line directly upstream from your boat or wading position in the current (Fig. 42). As the line, leader and fly drift back toward you, recover lengths of line with your retrieve hand (the left hand if you're a right-handed caster) fast enough so that you have sufficient control over the line to set the hook in case of a strike or rise. Keep the rod tip fairly high so as to lift as much line as possible from the surface.

Swimming action can be imparted to a submerged fly by recovering line faster than the current flows. On the other hand, if you want to suggest a relatively rigid-bodied nymph that has been swept free of

Fig. 42.

its foothold, you may prefer to let the fly drift without tension near the streambed, a technique usually called dead drifting.

The basic upstream presentation is varied quite easily by delivering the fly up and slightly across the current with a curve cast. A positive or negative curve (covered in the preceding chapter) lets you float a dry fly, nymph or flymph, fly first, over the fish (Fig. 43). This ploy can be very productive when angling for particularly wary, leader-shy game fish like brown trout.

It pays to set the hook at the slightest indication of a strike when fishing sunken flies upstream. Some of the signs to look for are a flash beneath the surface, a twitch or hesitation of line or leader, breaking of the water's surface by a fish and, of course, a noticeable tug.

One of the largest stream trout I have ever hooked on an upstream delivery mouthed a brownish-yellow nymph offered near the fish's lie spot on a positive-curve cast of less than 30 feet. The nymph stopped drifting almost the moment it landed in the water. But I didn't feel a tug,

merely a gentle resistance caused by the pressure of the water against my line. I set the hook almost instinctively and was fast to a rambunctious six-pounder.

Another very productive form of the upstream presentation of floating artificials can be enjoyed during the peak of the grasshopper season in late summer and early fall, when many stream banks abound with the insects. Approach the stream bank very low, on hands and knees if need be. Make your casts short and accurate, within inches of the upstream bank. And, don't be surprised if you hook a better-than-average number of normally cautious lunker trout while fishing this way. An abundance of grasshoppers seems to cause the big ones to lose some of their ingrained caution. Incidentally, if you have observed a good fish rise to examine your fake hopper only to refuse it and drift back to his lie, make another presentation and this time impart a little twitch to the fly as it approaches the fish's cone of vision. This trick will often bring an enthusiastic response from a shy or undecided trout.

When faster-than-normal sinking seems

desirable, it often pays to weight an artificial with wraps of lead fuse wire, underneath or outside of the body materials. Fuse wire is better for weighting casting flies than regular lead wire or cut strips of lead. It is very soft and easy to wrap on in larger sizes, and it doesn't discolor easily stained body materials like the flosses and synthetic yarns.

Some anglers won't go to the trouble of concealing the weighting wire inside their flies. When the unexpected need for a very heavy, fast-sinking fly arises, they wrap the wire right over the body of the fly. The result is a rather sloppy looking expedient, but it gets results when you desperately need a very deep-running nymph or streamer. Still other anglers weight their leaders instead of their flies by wrapping very fine lead wire or strips over the lower

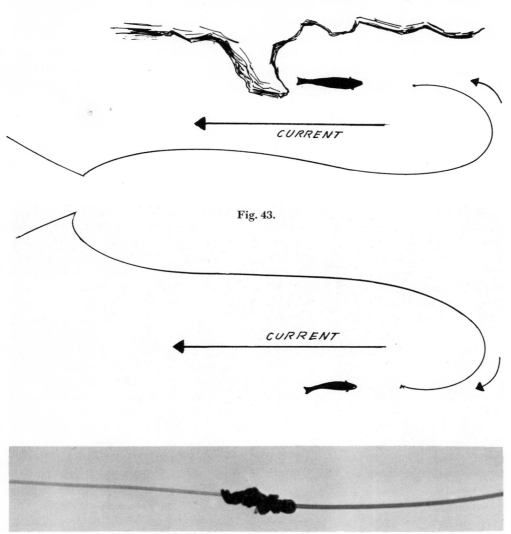

Fig. 43.

Fig. 44. Lead wire wrapped over a leader knot.

two or three leader knots (Fig. 44). Leaders weighted this way make for better casting than heavily weighted flies. The technique is fairly common among West Coast steelhead fishermen.

Up-and-Across Presentation

The reasons for an up-and-across-stream delivery are somewhat like those for a straight upstream presentation. This mode of delivery is excellent for fishing a sunken fly on a dead drift, deep beneath the surface. It's also one of the more useful methods of delivery for floating flies on certain types of current and behind rocks in waters too deep for wading. Floating, sinking-tip, sinking, shooting-head and lead-head lines all can be employed.

Up-and-across delivery is accomplished simply by casting the desired length of line at an angle up and across the current. Precisely how much the cast is angled depends on the nature of the currents, how deeply you want to offer a sunken artificial or how long a drag-free run you want with a dry fly. The farther upstream the cast (Fig. 45), the deeper a sinking line will submerge before swinging the fly back across the current. If your desire is to keep the silhouette of the artificial broadside to the current for as long a drift as possible, mend the line periodically during its downstream run using the methods described under "Greased-Line Fishing" in this chapter.

Fig. 45. Up-and-across delivery.

There are several schools of thought on whether to work a run upstream or downstream with a dry fly. Each method has some merits, depending on the nature of the water and the relative wariness of the species being sought. Brown trout in limestone streams are probably the most wary freshwater game fish, followed closely by largemouth bass, rainbow trout, smallmouth bass and very large Arctic grayling. When seeking these species in clear, flat, slow-moving stretches, it's sometimes a distinct advantage to offer the fly first from a position of concealment downstream.

However, it's the nature of certain rivers to defy wading in an upstream direction. In such instances, up-and-across casts delivered as you progress in a downstream direction can be very productive. Usually the angler is fairly well concealed by the turbulent, broken water associated with many of the better fast-flowing freestone streams.

With wet flies, nymphs and streamers, some of the more proficient anglers practically comb every square inch of water. They'll start at the head of a run or pool and sweep the water on consecutive presentations, making four or five casts, then moving a few steps downstream and repeating the procedure until they arrive at the lower end.

Very often, when fishing with a streamer fly suggesting a small fish, an angler will want the retrieve to have a swimming or darting action. This can be accomplished with a few twitches of the rod tip or with a stripping retrieve (Fig. 46). The action can be imparted both during the downstream drift of the fly and as it swings across the current at the end of the drift.

Rod-tip twitches resulted in a pair of 20-inch brown trout one morning not a month prior to this writing. The water level of the river was exceptionally low and clear for

Fig. 46. The stripping retrieve.

the season, but cold enough to practically eliminate the possibility of an insect hatch. I decided to fish a marabou-winged streamer fly as closely as possible to the river's deeper undercut banks.

Fishing with a high-density sinking-tip fly line, a short six-foot leader tapering to six-pound test and a heavily weighted streamer fly, I managed to hook only two small browns during the first hour on the river. I was fishing a stretch of water with which I was totally unfamiliar and didn't really expect spectacular results.

I waded around a bend and came upon a long, deep pool, at the tail end of which rested a submerged log. The opposing bank of the stream was deeply undercut and shaded by overhanging trees and bushes. My heart skipped a beat as I started working my streamer fly along the undercut bank in an across-and-downstream direction.

Halfway down the pool I felt a heavy tug. A brown trout of about three pounds rolled to the surface, then sounded and tore away downstream beneath the undercut bank. That fish became entangled in some sort of underwater obstruction and I was forced to break off.

At the tail of the pool the river shallowed a bit and then dropped into a very deep pocket under the submerged log, a good place to lose a fly, but also a good place for a big brown to select as a midday hangout.

On the first drift of the fly through the pocket beneath the log I felt a couple of hesitant, pecking tugs. The next cast produced the same result, two or three suspiciously gentle nips. By this time my heart was thumping again. The interested trout could possibly be a 10-incher, I thought, but in this location I doubted it. Chances were that the fish was a good one.

The third cast presented the fly in a slightly up-and-across direction. I wanted the sculpin-imitator to swing as deeply as possible under the log.

It swung lazily through the depths. I pulled in a couple of feet of line to assure a broadside delivery, and as the fly approached the depression, I payed out some slack. Again, two quick tugs greeted the presentation. But this time I twitched the rod tip twice, paused an instant and imparted two quick stripping recoveries. The fish hit so sharply during the second strip-in that the line was torn from my finger tips. This fish was indeed a good one. It was several anxious minutes before I could lead him away from the log and undercut bank, 19½ inches of glimmering brown trout. It was a pleasure to release the fish unharmed with the hope that someday soon I can return and once again test his ability to detect a flaw in my presentation. If I'm lucky, there'll be a hatch in progress and his response will be a vigorous rise.

Maximum mobility of the fly may or may not be an advantage on an up-and-across delivery. It depends on what kind of aquatic or terrestrial creature you're attempting to suggest. For example, if you're skating a floating-spider type of dry fly over the surface of a relatively quiet pool, it may be that you may want the fly dressed with extremely long, stiff spade hackles on a turned-down-eye hook that will keep the fly from burying itself in the surface film. In this case, soft, wiggly hen-neck hackles would work against the high-floating effect you hope to achieve.

On the other hand, you might want a fly that rides very low in the water in order to finesse a trout on caddis flies from a shore-line pocket on a slow-moving stream. You might, therefore, decide to use a tailless parachute-style dry fly, with the body dressed from buoyant spun fur or poly-propylene yarn so that it floats exceedingly well but low in the surface film like a live adult caddis.

On other occasions the quarry may be a salmon, steelhead or trout resting behind or adjacent to a boulder in water of moderate speed. Here the objective will very likely be to make the fly visible to the fish for as long as possible. The angler decides to present the fly, which will probably be a fast-sinking bucktail or streamer, broadside to the fish's field of view by means of an up-and-across-stream cast. Because of the fish's holding position, it's quite likely that the mode of presentation in this instance will be a major factor, perhaps the most important one, influencing the fish's response. It is crucial to consider a fly's visibility to the fish before attempting any type of presentation.

Two variations of the up-and-across delivery rate special mention at this point. They are the slack-line drift, also known as the patent method, and the greased-line techniques for fishing Atlantic salmon wet flies and nymphs. In addition to being effective on salmon, both methods are frequently productive ways to use nymphs, wet flies and streamers for trout, steel-heads, small- and largemouth bass and a few saltwater fishes in streams, rivers and tidal flows.

The Patent Method

The purpose of the patent method of fishing a wet fly is to achieve a free drift without imparting any swimming or other action to it.

Current speed, water depth, relative turbidity and the species of fish will affect your judgment in deciding whether to use a floating, sinking-tip or sinking fly line. In the patent method of delivery, the line is cast across and upstream. Before it lands on the water, during the end-portion of the forward cast, the line is stopped abruptly so that some slack falls on the surface. Allow the fly to complete its downstream drift without exerting any tension on the line.

When employing this method it is important to remain alert for any indications of a fish taking the fly below the surface. If you see a flash, feel a light tug or see the drifting line hesitate in its drift, set the hook very solidly with a downstream sweep of the rod tip.

As in other methods of dead-drifting submerged flies, artificials with relatively active hackles, tails and wings are frequently more productive than the more rigid ties.

Greased-Line Fishing

Greased-line fishing, originated by the late British angler A. H. E. Wood, derives its distinctive name from the fact that it was necessary to grease the old silk fly lines in order to make them float. The buoyancy of modern floating lines practically elimi-nates the need to use line flotant. They'll float of their own accord if kept free of dirt and algae. Periodic washing in mild detergent solution or a rubdown with line cleaner is the only care needed to keep most floating nylon fly lines riding high in the water. The specific gravity of the present-day floating fly line is less than that of water. It can't sink unless the specific gravity is altered by accumulated debris.

The purpose of greased-line fishing is to attain a uniform drift of the fly broadside to the current on a slightly slack line. When an angler wants to work his fly directly in or only slightly beneath the surface film, the fly is dressed on a relatively light-wire hook (in the case of salmon flies the hook style is called "low-water") and the leader is rubbed with line flotant to within an inch or two of the fly.

Long fly rods and double-tapered fly lines are preferred for greased-line fishing when the distances to be cast are not excessive. It's easier to mend line effectively with a long rod than a short one, and double-tapers mend somewhat better than weight-forward lines. The recent availability of floating shooting heads and floating shooting line has resulted in a considerable number of converts to this very long-casting combination, but I prefer the casting qualities of a weight-forward line over a floating shooting head for distances up to about 85 feet. Beyond that range a shooting head is the only practical solution for the caster of moderate proficiency. Most of the time it pays to fish within 70 feet, at least when using the greased-line technique. Longer casts are difficult to mend properly.

Several types of flies are employed in greased-lining, although the preference among Atlantic-salmon and western-steel-head anglers leans to flies dressed in the low-water style; the fly is proportioned to a hook two sizes smaller than that actually used, and the hook is somewhat finer in the wire and longer-shanked than normal for a given size. My opinion is that the fly is far less important than the presentation— which is broadside to the current and, in that attitude, becomes highly visible to fish as they view the near-surface waters ahead of them.

To present a fly on a greased line, make a very straight cast up and across the current. If the current is faster toward the tip end of the line than around your casting position, make downstream mends as the line bends off a straight trajectory near the tip. If the current is faster near you than at the tip end, make upstream mends whenever a bow forms and causes the fly to pick up speed (Fig. 47). Keep two or three feet of slack line coiled in your retrieve hand during the early stages of the fly's run. If the current suddenly quickens, you can maintain relatively constant drifting speed by paying out some slack. Recovering a bit of line will speed up a fly's drifting rate if the current suddenly slows down.

There's some controversy about whether or not to set the hook when greased-line fishing for Atlantic salmon. But it is virtually a necessity to plant the barb firmly in a steelhead's mouth when fishing in slow to moderate currents. Unless you've hooked or missed enough fish to form an educated opinion, let me suggest that when an Atlantic salmon rolls to meet the fly you drop your rod tip toward the surface of the water. Then set the hook lightly once the fly has been taken in and the fish turns upstream. When steelhead fishing, sock the hook home with a firm sweep of the rod tip as soon as possible after the fish hits. That may be immediately, or you may not have an opportunity until the fish stops momentarily after a characteristic, deceptively short first run. Like all large rainbow trout, steelheads have very tough mouth parts. The big sea-run 'bows don't

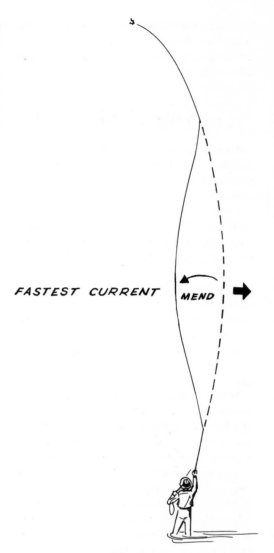

FASTEST CURRENT   MEND

Fig. 47.

take flies fished on a greased line with the same degree of solid assurance they display when taking deeply sunk wet flies. When the fly is riding on or barely beneath the surface, the strike is frequently very quick or slashing. A fair percentage of fish will come unbuttoned before you have time to set the hook. The most knowledgeable steelheaders try to set it a couple of times, as insurance, if they estimate a fish's weight at over 12 pounds.

Greased-line methods are very deadly on game fish other than salmon and steelhead, including most of the stream-bound trouts and basses. It's frequently advisable to vary the broadside drift of the fly with some sort of action-inducing manipulation, like a stripping retrieve. A few lifelike movements by the artificial sometimes prove to be the clincher in provoking a strike from a marauding old bass or trout.

Straight-Across Presentation

Depending on the whims of current, a straight-across-stream delivery can be used with telling effect to fish both floating and sub-surface flies. Floating, sinking-tip, sinking, shooting-head and lead-head lines are all compatible with this delivery, a major advantage of which is that it affords the angler an excellent view of a fish rising to meet the fly.

Dry-fly buffs frequently employ a slack-line cast. A little slack in the line allows a longer drag-free float than a fly cast on a perfectly straight, taut line (Fig. 48).

Across-and-Down Presentation

This popular form of wet-fly and nymph delivery is used primarily to comb every bit of a run, in an exploratory manner, when the precise lies of the fish are not known. It is also used as an aid in an inter-

Fig. 48. Straight-across delivery with slightly slack line.

esting and effective method of fishing floating caddis flies described by Leonard M. Wright, Jr., in his recent book *Fishing the Dry Fly as a Living Insect* (E. P. Dutton & Co., 1972). All types of fly lines can be employed, depending on the desired depth for the sweep of the fly and, of course, the speed of the existing current.

When implemented with a sunken fly, the across-and-down delivery is one of the more popular and effective methods of locating trout, salmon and steelheads. Practically any type of fly will catch fish when used this way, but I'm of the opinion, based on over 30 years of experience, that flies with the broad, cross-sectional density afforded by collar-type hackles are the most killing. This delivery presents a fly more end-first to fish than broadside presentations. Collar hackling makes the fly more visible from the tail end than does a sparse beard of hackle fibers.

Start fishing by wading (or anchoring your boat) at the top of the run or pool (Fig. 49). Make a cast of appropriate length down and across the current—on a straight line. Throughout the cross-stream sweep of the fly, maintain just a light tension on the line. The tension will cause the fly to swim in a lifelike manner. If a fish takes the fly solidly, chances are he'll hook himself, provided you've honed the hook point needle-sharp. If the take is light, or occurs in very slow-moving water, you'll probably have to set the hook.

Extend a few feet of line on each subsequent cast until you've reached your maximum fishing distance, whatever that may be in a given piece of water. Even if you wade reasonably well, longer casts than 70 feet are not recommended. For one thing, it's much easier to set the hook in a fish on a short line than on a long one. Casting accuracy and line control are also much better on shorter casts.

Once you're convinced you've presented your fly to most of the fish within casting distance, move a few feet downstream and repeat the procedure until you reach the end of the drift. The searching, probing, down-and-across sweep of a run is one of the surest ways to locate outsized brown trout during their fall spawning runs. It's also a fine way to explore unfamiliar salmon and steelhead waters and those trailing riffles off points of land adjacent to

Fig. 49. Trout solidly hooked after down-and-across delivery.

Fig. 50. Downstream delivery.

backwaters where smallmouth bass sometimes feed during the summer months.

In the case of Leonard Wright's technique, designed to simulate the inch-long
lurching movements of adult caddis flies,
the cast is usually made slightly down and
across the stream. Wright suggests throwing an upstream curve into the cast before
the line or leader can sink. Slack is fed into
the line following the twitch. According to
Wright, the twitching movement imparts a
sudden lifelike action to the stiff-hackled
dry fly he recommends, and this proves
highly motivating to the trout in a manner
similar to the way the "Leisenring Lift" affects the behavior of a mobile-hackled
flymph or wet fly.

Whether you're fishing dry or wet with
down-and-across deliveries, it's a good idea
to hold a little slack line in the retrieve
hand to help control the speed of the drifting fly. With a dry fly, a little hand-held
slack line also gives you a few extra feet of
drag-free downstream drift.

STRAIGHT DOWNSTREAM PRESENTATION

Straight downstream delivery can present a floating or submerged artificial to
fish whose feeding stations cannot be
reached by other casting means, and it en-
ables you to run a fly straight downstream
through narrow channels in weeds or bedrock ledges. Any type of sinking or floating
line can be used.

Cast straight downstream, stopping the
line abruptly at the end of the forward cast
so that some slack falls on the water (Fig.
50). Hold several feet of additional line in
your retrieve hand and pay it out as the fly
drifts toward the target area. Fish very often hook themselves when flies are presented in this manner. If there's still a considerable amount of slack on the water
when the fish hits, you may have to set the
hook with gentle firmness.

Trailing the Fly

Trailing a wet fly or streamer directly downstream from your casting position will often prompt a strike. Seasoned fly-fishers commonly use this stratagem for a few moments at the end of each across-stream sweep. You can simply let the fly float away with the current for some distance, but any number of variations can be added to the basic technique, including jiggling the rod tip, stripping in a few lengths of line and then letting the fly drop back downstream, or slowly raising and lowering the rod tip. As in the case of the straight downstream presentation, fish sometimes savagely rip into a fly fished this way.

Recently I was fly fishing for steelhead on Idaho's Clearwater River when a big one belted my trailed fly. I've developed a habit of checking the behavior of my wet flies and streamers after knotting them to the tippet, and that morning, after knotting a size 2 low-water steelhead fly to my tippet, I assured myself that it was riding properly in the water. Then I began to wade across the calf-deep shallows to my planned casting position. As I waded along, the fly trailed downstream at a distance of no more than 20 feet. My rod tip was suddenly and violently yanked downward. Almost instantly, a fish close to 15 pounds sailed out of the water, the sparse little bucktail flashing white and crimson at its lip. Moments later the fish came unbuttoned. No doubt in my state of shocked amazement, I neglected to set the hook. It was the second time in the last eight years that I'd hooked a fish that way. The first time it happened I somehow managed to land the fish after falling flat on my rump in the middle of a riffle on the Kispiox River. If it weren't for incidents like those,

proving that there's a big element of luck to the game, a fellow might tend to take his fly fishing too seriously.

Riffling the Fly

Riffling is a technique used to skate or swim a wet fly on or through the surface film. A properly riffled fly does not sink; it leaves a well-defined V-shaped wake in the water, believed by some to attract a fish's attention.

A riffled fly can tantalize several freshwater and anadromous game fish, most notably Atlantic salmon and steelheads. Two half-hitches of the tippet applied immediately aft of the fly's head produce the desired action. The knot is called the Portland, or riffling hitch (Fig. 51).

First tie the fly to the tippet with a return knot or another positive-holding knot, such as the improved clinch knot (Fig. 52). This tie-on knot will have little or no bearing on the fly's performance in the water, because the position of the tippet in relation to the hook eye will be dramatically

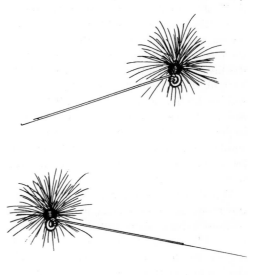

Fig. 51. The riffling hitch.

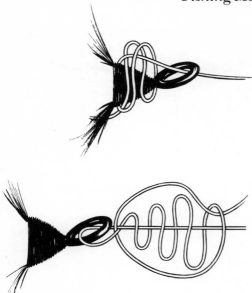

Fig. 52. Either the return knot (top) or the improved clinch knot is the beginning of the riffling hitch.

altered from what is considered normal once the riffling hitch is applied.

To add the hitch, hold the fly so that the eye of the hook is directed upstream, and half-hitch the tippet twice around the head of the fly. Align the tippet so that it extends from the half-hitches on the side of the fly facing you.

Paul Kukonen of Worcester, Massachusetts, recently showed me another excellent riffling method that relies on a fly-tying trick instead of the two half-hitches. Before dressing the fly, you simply doctor the hook by fastening along its side the eye and a portion of the shank of a second hook (Fig. 53). The dressed fly is knotted to

Fig. 53. The Kukonen riffling method. A second shank is fastened to the hook before the fly is tied.

the leader by the eye extending from the side, so there's no need for the half-hitches over the head. Paul points out that some of your flies should have the extra eye extending from the right side and some from the left side. A fly with the extra eye protruding to the right (as viewed from the rear) will riffle properly in current flowing from the angler's right, while a left-eyed fly will riffle in a left-hand current.

Some authorities believe that flies dressed on double hooks swim more upright when riffled than those on single hooks. You really should give each type a fair trial to see which type performs better for you—that is, which gets you the most strikes.

Use of the Shooting Taper

Shooting-head fly lines are generally best adapted to fishing broad, relatively fast-flowing rivers where casts in excess of 70 feet are the rule rather than the exception. With the aid of a shooting head, a fly can be directed up and across, straight across or down and across. To accomplish a dead drift with a shooting-taper line, make an up-and-across cast. For the deepest possible run of the fly, make a downstream mend of the shooting line just as the line and fly are about to land on the water. Continue to mend line as the fly drifts downstream (Fig. 54). As the line approaches the end of its downstream drift, and before it starts to pull the fly across the current, strip out a few additional feet in order to extend the run. At any time during the run, sock home the hook if the floating portion of the shooting line hesitates or behaves unnaturally. Chances are good that a fish has taken the fly in its mouth to examine it.

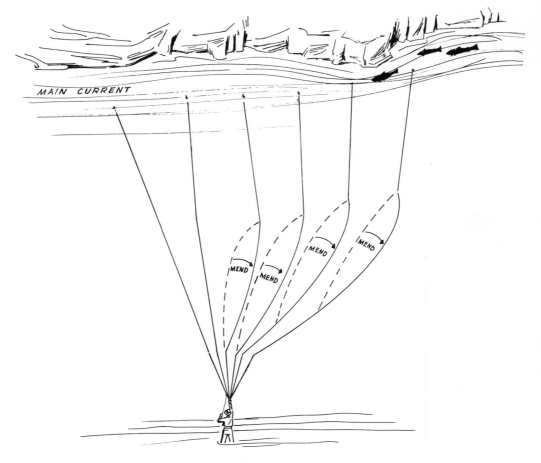

MAIN CURRENT

Fig. 54. Mending line following up-and-across delivery.

When the fastest currents are nearer to the fly than to you and you want the fly to swim instead of drifting freely, throw a quick downstream mend into the shooting line an instant before the shooting head lands on the water. It may also be necessary to make additional mends in order to keep the line straight enough to maintain light tension on the fly. The tension causes it to work against the current with a swimming action.

To rig a shooting-head line for fishing, first reel on from 150 to 300 yards of 20-pound-test Dacron or nylon backing. (Dacron stretches less than nylon and for that reason is preferred by most salmon and steelhead flyrodders.) Next, affix 100 feet of 30-pound-test monofilament or floating braided shooting line to the backing. Use "low-memory" monofilament—in other words, a line that is neither too limp nor too wiry, one that can be easily straightened by stretching and will not spring back into a series of tight little coils upon contact with cold water. The best monofilaments I've found for this purpose bear the trade names Maxima and Kroic, but undoubtedly there are other brands that will serve equally well.

Finally, knot the spliced loop at the terminal end of the shooting-taper line to the mono or braided shooting line. Most anglers use an improved clinch knot, though some splice the shooting line directly to the head. The splice runs through the guides far more smoothly than the knot but will probably need resplicing several times each season. After a day or two of continuous casting, the shooting line tends to wear noticeably at the point of contact with the tip guide of the fly rod, necessitating frequent inspection and removal of the worn sections. The knot runs through the tip guide well enough, even when a heavy fish is being played prior to tailing or beaching.

Virtually any type of dry fly, nymph, bucktail or streamer can be fished effectively on a shooting head. The important thing to remember when dressing flies for fishing on any type of fly line is how you want them to behave under the influences of manipulation and current. It should be mentioned that factory-made shooting heads are available in floating models as well as the more popular sinking models.

Skittering the Fly

Skating, or skittering, a stiff-hackled, lightweight dry fly across the surface of a stream or lake can sometimes be a highly effective way to coax a fish into rising even when there is no evidence of surface feeding and your nymph or streamer offerings have been refused.

Almost any fairly long-hackled dry fly can be skittered well enough to prompt some sort of response. But the method is frequently most killing when accomplished with spider-type dry flies dressed with very stiff, glossy hackles up to 2½ inches in diameter. Flies dressed on light-wire hooks with turned down eyes are preferred by most expert proponents of the method. Both line and leader are treated with flotant. Excessively fine tippets are to be avoided with the same care as one avoids contact with poison oak. They get twisted as the skittered fly corkscrews along over the surface film.

On streams, the fly is usually presented with an up-and-across-current cast. The fly is cast on a straight line and immediately started skating back toward the angler with a series of stripping recoveries, or rod-tip jerks, or a combination of both. The objective is to cause the fly to skate enticingly over the surface on its long, stiff hackles.

It pays to start fishing with several well-siliconed spider-type flies ready in your box. Once these flies become waterlogged, they usually require thorough drying and a fresh treatment with fly flotant before they are fishable again.

Dapping

Dapping amounts to delicately and repeatedly dropping a fly onto the surface directly from the rod without benefit of a cast. The technique is useful for fishing small, brushy creeks where casting is impossible and for drifting a fly very close to overhanging banks on the near side of a stream when casting is impossible from the opposite side of the current flow.

The angler creeps cautiously to the edge of the brook, most often on hands and knees, then extends his rod out over the bank and drops the fly on the water for a short float or run. He may lift the fly from the water and redeposit it for repeated floats over the same lie or he can skitter it along like a newly emerged caddis.

Dapping is a great way to introduce a youngster to stream tactics. And youngsters over 40 sometimes find that dapping not only engenders moments of pleasant nostalgia but also produces some sporty activity at the tippet's end. I recall once as a youngster of 14 when I dapped a fly with my very first fly rod over a mysteriously intriguing pool behind a snag. A big, spawning Dolly Varden of about six pounds surged out of the depths and almost yanked the rod out of my hands. Thunderstruck, I pointed the rod tip at the fish and held on for dear life. It was a good thing, too. If I'd reacted in any other way, the fragile tip of the bamboo rod would have broken. It was probably just as well I lost the fish almost immediately.

IMPARTING ACTION

Very frequently a strike occurs because the flyfisher imparts some sort of lifelike action to the artificial apart from the movements caused by vagaries of current.

These angler-imparted movements (Fig. 55) can be controlled to emulate the swimming and darting of fishes; the crawling, creeping, rising and skating of insects; the wriggling of leeches and other annelids; and the scuttling, swimming and jumping antics of certain crustaceans.

Most, though not all, of the enticing movements are accomplished with variations on four basic retrieve techniques: the

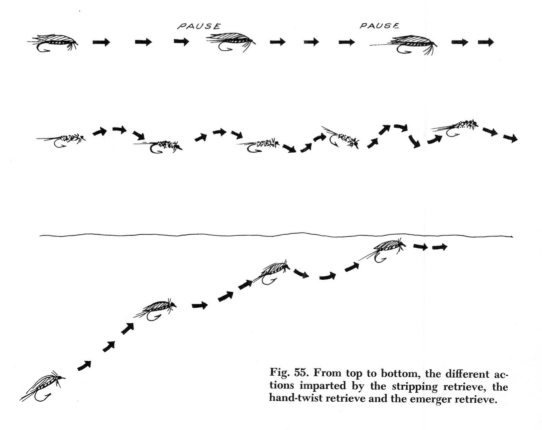

Fig. 55. From top to bottom, the different actions imparted by the stripping retrieve, the hand-twist retrieve and the emerger retrieve.

"stripping" retrieve, the "hand-twist" retrieve, "rising" movements suggesting
those of an emerging aquatic insect and
the twitched or skated fly. Most of the action-imparting maneuvers can be used effectively on both still and moving waters,
and there are almost limitless possibilities
for varying the basic stratagems. Now let's
look at each of the four action-retrieves in
more detail.

The Stripping Retrieve

Probably the most familiar of all fresh
and saltwater recovery methods, the
stripping retrieve—also known as the strip-
in or long-loop retrieve—is especially useful to suggest swimming bait fishes, darting
nymphs, undulating leeches, swimming
frogs and jumping shrimps and scuds, as
well as rodents and other small terrestrial
animals.

The stripping retrieve also maintains a
light tension on the line while swimming a
submerged fly broadside to the current,
and it provides a degree of control over the
fly line as it drifts downstream after an upstream presentation.

The stripping tempo may be slow, moderate or fast. In some situations the most
strikes can be had by accelerating the recovery or slowing it progressively. Line recovered during each strip-in may vary
from a few inches to over a foot and a half,
depending on the typical movements of
the organism being simulated. More about
this when we deal with tying and fishing
flies suggesting specific types of nymphs,
crustaceans and forage fish.

In order to strip-in a fly, simply pull in
lengths of line with your retrieve hand,
grasping the line between pulls under the
index finger of your casting hand. That

way, if a fish grabs the fly between pulls,
you have enough line control to set the
hook solidly. Look again at Fig. 46 for the
correct hand position during a stripping
recovery.

Game fish frequently nail a stripped-in
fly with jolting gusto. The hardest strike
I've ever experienced in fresh water came
about as a direct result of stripping a large,
bedraggled fur nymph rapidly up from the
lake bottom in about 20 feet of water. It
happened on Arthur Lake, in British Columbia, back in the early 1950s when that
relatively small body of water contained a
few Kamloops rainbow trout in the eight-
to 15-pound class.

I had rowed to the far end of the lake
and mooch-trolled my nymph several
times through a favorite hot spot, to no
avail. It was a cold, bleak rainy day, and
after a couple of unsuccessful hours I'd decided to call it quits. I shipped the oars and
began to rapidly strip-in the line, which
had sunk almost to the bottom. Apparently
a fish had been following with interest. A
little earlier I had felt a couple of gentle
taps. Suddenly, as the fly began to rise, my
rod tip was yanked down so savagely that
the five-sided bamboo tip fractured at the
male ferrule. The huge Kamloops surged
away in a powerful run. I was amazed that
the tippet held. But the fish was too much
for even that formidable a leader point
without the full benefit of a flexible rod tip.

Hand-Twist Retrieve

The hand-twist retrieve, also known as
the Figure 8 and the line-hand zigzag retrieve, is ideal for emulating the crawling,
creeping and darting of aquatic nymphs
and the movements of fallen adult insects,
as well as certain minnows, crustaceans,
annelids and mollusks. As in a stripping recovery, the tempo, rhythm and length of

Fig. 56. The hand-twist retrieve.

and at the completion of the downstream swing. Starting wth a very slow tempo, about six or seven twists a minute, I increased the frequency with each successive cast.

The first trout to respond took the nymph on a retrieve of medium speed, about 15 twists a minute. Five more browns, averaging between one and two pounds, all made the same mistake within a half-hour or so. By that time a hatch had started. I soon switched to a dry fly.

the retrieve-imparted actions are infinitely variable. And the hand-twist is often employed to enhance the appeal of a strip-in retrieve in both still and moving waters.

Grasp the line between the thumb and index finger of the retrieve hand. Rotate the wrist, pulling in a few inches of line with the remaining fingers (Fig. 56). Repeat, varying the frequency and tempo of the twisting until you develop a killing combination.

Hand-twisting movements are usually imparted after or during the across-stream swing of a submerged fly. I recall one occasion on a favorite little brown-trout stream when this technique turned a mediocre session into an exciting one.

It was toward the end of June and the gray drakes were hatching sporadically, but when I started fishing no hatch was in progress. After about an hour I located several fair-sized brown trout nymphing actively in a slow-moving run near the shoreline. Several down-and-across-current casts with a brownish-gray, nondescript fur nymph resulted in not a strike. I was reluctant to change flies because I'd hooked and released several trout on the nymph during the first hour by fishing it blind in slow stretches of water that had been productive earlier in the week.

I began to experiment with hand-twists as the fly coursed near the feeding trout

Emergent-Action Recoveries

There are several effective methods by which the stream fisherman can suggest the rising movements of soon-to-hatch aquatic insects. One good way is to fish a nymph on a floating line with an up-and-across stream cast; as the nymph approaches the fish's feeding station, tension is put on the line, causing the fly to rise in the current. This technique is frequently enhanced by giving the rod tip a series of short lifts, making the fly rise erratically toward the surface like a live nymph swimming up to hatch. The intricacies of this technique are described by James E. Leisenring and Vernon S. Hidy in *The Art of Tying the Wet Fly and Fishing the Flymph* (Crown Publishers, Inc., New York, 1971).

A frequently effective little variation of the "Leisenring Lift" is to drop the rod tip abruptly as the fly approaches the fish's cone of vision. The lifting movements of the rod tip, followed by the sudden drop, · cause the fly to drop back in the current a few inches and seem to suggest a nymph that has momentarily tired from the exertion of swimming. It's a deadly ploy on trout in free-stone and limestone streams when the fish are feeding on rising nymphs.

I also recall numerous occasions in the extreme shallows of lakes when a weighted nymph used with a floating line in this fashion, proved to be deadly. And probably the premier moment of stream fishing I've enjoyed in the past three years resulted from Leisenring's technique of simulating the rise of hatching nymphs.

A massive flight of tiny *Tricorythodes* spinners was in progress when I arrived at the spring creek. Larger dun-colored mayflies, which I couldn't positively identify, were hatching simultaneously with the spinner flight. Surprisingly, the trout didn't seem to be feeding on the abundant spinners. The rise forms suggested nymphing trout. And it didn't take more than a few minutes of casting with dry flies to confirm that conclusion.

I selected a size 12 dun-colored flymph and tied it to a very long, fine tippet testing about 1½ pounds. So many trout were active that the stream looked like a hatchery pond at feeding time. By manipulating the fly so it drifted under virtually no tension until it approached the trout's cone of vision, then giving the rod three or four short lifts to make the fly rise in the current, two companions and I hooked and released more than 150 trout in four hours. That means each of us averaged one fish about every five minutes, which is about as fast as the action can be and still leave time to cast and play the fish.

Twitching the Fly

Rod-tip twitches make a fly behave like a struggling insect or a darting forage fish.

Delicate, erratic twitches that cause a floating fly to struggle and rock gently in the surface film as it drifts downstream will frequently bring slashing strikes. One of the best times to twitch a dry fly or otherwise cause it to scurry over the surface is when caddis flies are hatching on lakes or streams. Leonard M. Wright, Jr. treats this subject in detail in his recent book. Serious fly fishermen are urged to study, learn and practice as wide a variety as possible of such action-imparting methods, which very often mean the difference between a delightful angling experience and a disappointing day.

Rod-tip twitches enhance the appeal not only of floating artificials but of marabou or splayed feather-wing streamer flies in moving waters. Once, on a biting-cold early-October afternoon, my companion walked upstream to work his streamer along a deep run near an undercut bank while I used a size 1 sculpin-imitator to probe a deep pocket under a partially submerged snag. As the fly coursed through the pocket on its first pass I felt a couple of nipping, hesitant tugs. I made a second cast and waited breathlessly for a more determined take that never materialized. On the third run I gave the streamer a couple of energetic short twitches with my rod tip. Suddenly, the fly stopped with such finality that I assumed I'd overcast and hooked the deadhead. I slammed home the hook anyway. The "snag" yanked back and surged away in a deep run toward some underwater debris. A few minutes later a 26-inch brown trout had been carefully released, to provide a thrill for another angler some day.

CHAPTER 5

Fishing Still Waters

S INKING FLY lines were developed in the late 1940s, and they were rightly considered revolutionary. Their introduction greatly amplified the fishing possibilities in deep tidal channels, slack reaches of streams and rivers, food shelves in lakes. At last the angler had a line whose specific gravity was greater than that of water—a line that would sink without the application of graphite or any other treatment. Now he could really prospect the depths between 10 and 30 feet where a high percentage of feeding activity takes place among game fish. And the more recent development of floating lines with sinking tip sections has fostered seductive new action-retrieves that make artificial nymphs rise toward the surface remarkably like live ones about to hatch. The depths are being fished more efficiently than ever before.

Although the subject of fly fishing in lakes is treated at considerable length in my book *Fly Fishing the Lakes* (Winchester Press, N.Y., 1972), I believe a brief review of slack-water fishing will be helpful to the angler who hopes to dress flies that will consistently entice fish in lakes, ponds, reservoirs, impoundments, sloughs and the slowest part of rivers and streams.

Line Selection

The factors to consider in choosing lines for still-water fishing are water depth, the speed of the current or tidal-flow (if any) and the type of action to be imparted to the fly.

Slow-sinking fly lines, designated I in AFTMA terminology, are designed for use with wet flies, nymphs and streamers at depths ranging from a few inches to about six feet. Fast-sinking lines, designated II in the AFTMA code, perform best at depths ranging from six to 15 feet. Extra-fast-sinking lines, designated III in the code, allow an angler to probe effectively as deep as 30 feet.

Fly lines with tip sections that sink are called sink-tip lines, and their main function is to facilitate a retrieve that suggests the rising of an aquatic creature toward the surface. In streams, of course, a sink-tip line is extremely useful for fishing submerged flies because the floating portion allows the angler to mend his cast during the downstream run of the fly.

Flies for Still Waters

Still or slow-moving clear waters afford the fish extraordinary opportunities to scrutinize feathered offerings closely. Clear lakes and ponds are as much a test of an artificial fly's inherent allure as the slowest stretches of a limestone stream, for in still waters there is seldom enough current to impart fish-enticing movements to flexible tails and hackles, translucent body-dubbing furs or mobile marabou, saddle-hackle or bucktail wings. Most strikes will result from an angler's ability to approach fish without frightening them, to make frequently long casts and retrieves and to dress artificials that will be responsive to those recoveries.

There are two theoretical approaches to the art of fly tying. Extremists of one persuasion often strive for near perfect imitation of the forms and movements of live nymphs, adult insects or minnows. Their flies are often distinguished by meticulously trimmed and joined legs, extended or articulating bodies, painted parr marks or body segments, delicate setae, tints and hues of the subtlest colors. The other school strives to suggest certain dominant physical characteristics of aquatic creatures that distinguish them to the fish in a more or less impressionistic way, in terms of shape, color, translucency, size and flash. Both types of flies catch fish.

Regardless of one's theoretical approach to fly tying, it is fishability—a fly's inherent ability to be worked in a way that triggers a game fish's response—that is the most important aspect of fly design for either still or moving waters. With flies dressed for still-water angling, fishability can frequently mask a multitude of sins in tying technique and presentation.

In designing nymph and streamer flies for lake fishing, the angler must consider whether he wants the fly to sink slower, faster or at the same rate as the sinking line. He must also consider the degree of mobility he must build into the fly so that it will respond to his retrieve manipulations, and the form, flash, color and translucency of the particular fish-food organism he's trying to simulate.

Flies dressed for fishing on the surface of still waters sometimes require an accuracy of proportion, shape and color seldom needed in flies intended for fast-moving streams. Some of the more effective lake dry flies for trout and landlocked salmon,

for example, are dressed on the lightest possible hooks with a minimum of hackle or none at all. The Canadian-originated Tom Thumb dry fly, which is constructed of buoyant deer-body hair and suggests a newly emerged caddis or mayfly, and the Swisher-and-Richards no-hackle dry flies are characteristic of types now in use. Examples of relatively mobile nymph flies designed specifically for slow or still water include the Carey Special, the Big Ugly Nymph and the damselfly nymphs designed by Jack Hutchinson and the author.

Still-Water Fishing Technique

Successful still-water fly fishing hangs precariously upon two contingencies: finding the fish and causing the fly to behave in a tantalizing fashion. Locating game fish in large bodies of still water can at times be an excruciatingly difficult exercise, a major test of an angler's knowledge of aquatic life, his intuition, perception, persistence, casting and retrieving ability. Consistently finding fish in expansive tidal flats, large lakes and impoundments takes a lot of experience and know-how, but the beginner should bear in mind that the ultimate key lies in discovering the fishes' food organisms. Find the natural foods and you'll more often than not pinpoint the fish.

Certain areas of the waters (whether tidal or fresh) attract or promote the production of prey species that in turn attract the fish. These organisms include aquatic and terrestrial insects in their nymphal, larval or pupal forms, plus minnows, crustaceans, mollusks, waterworms, leeches, plankton and a host of other creatures. Productive areas include drop-offs, inlets and outlets, weed beds, channels, holes, flooded trees and brush, and a wide range of bottom types. Additional hints at locating fish will be found in Chapters 9 through 13 of this book and in Chapter 1 of my book on fly fishing the lakes.

RETRIEVE

Lake and saltwater recovery techniques attempt to simulate several very distinctive types of insect, animal and forage-fish locomotion: the swimming of small fish, annelids, nymphs, animals and snakes; the darting of minnows, larger forage-fish and nymphs; the creeping and crawling of aquatic insects, crustaceans and mollusks; the jumping movements of both aquatic and terrestrial creatures, like scuds and frogs; the rising of nymphs and pupae toward the surface, preparatory to hatching; the emergent contortions of insects hatching at the surface; and the struggles of hatched insects and terrestrial creatures on the surface.

The most essential basic retrieves around which you can devise more refined methods are listed in the preceding chapter under "Hand-twist," "Stripping" and "Emergent Action" retrieves.

Stripping retrieves are good for emulating the darting and fast swimming of small fish and insects. Slow-swimming aquatic insects and the wealth of creeping, crawling, bottom-inhabiting aquatic creatures are often most effectively suggested by the hand-twist method. The rising movements of emergers, on the other hand, can frequently be simulated in still waters by the hand-twist retrieve coupled with a floating or sink-tip fly line and weighted nymphs that sink faster than the leader or line.

The swimming of forage fishes can be simulated either by the retrieve after a cast or by trolling methods. Depth of the trolled fly and trolling speed are regulated to approximate the natural behavior of the bait fish being simulated. They are also influenced by the retrieve clarity of the water and the presence or lack of algae bloom, seasonal variations of water temperature and stratification.

CHAPTER 6

Fly-Tying Tools & Accessories

VISES

THE ROLE of the fly-tying vise is purely one of convenience, not necessity. Some tiers much prefer to hold the hooks in their fingers throughout the tying operations. For the average individual, however, the vise is a definite aid in holding the hook rigidly and, in conjunction with accessories like hackle guards and thread clips, it reduces the degree of manual dexterity required (Fig. 57).

Because of their high quality, ease and

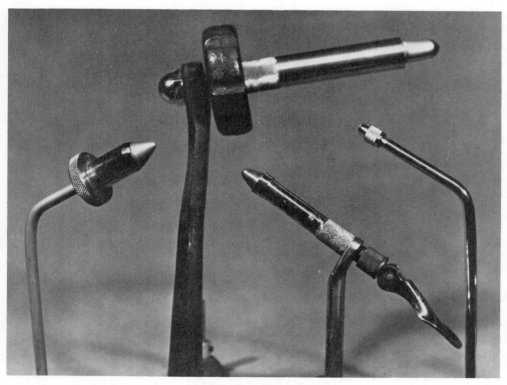

Fig. 57. Four vise models.

speed of operation, vises of the finger-lever, collet-and-sleeve-jaw design are highly popular among American fly tiers. Half a dozen of the better vises of this design are described below.

Thompson Ultra: The main features of this sturdiest vise in the Thompson line are adjustable collet angle, adjustable height, and a double cam embracing the collet.

Thompson A: This vise has been one of the most popular for many years. It is very similar in construction and appearance to the Ultra model, but it lacks the collet-angle adjustment. It is available with a pedestal base as an option to the normal clamping base.

Herter's Model 9: Available with either a clamping or pedestal base, Herter's Model 9 is of excellent quality. It resembles the Thompson A in appearance.

Herter's Model 9D: The advantage of this vise, which is similar to the Model 9, is that its ball-and-socket base allows it to be turned to virtually any position.

Veniard Cranbrook: This is a high-quality vise similar in appearance to the Thompson A and Herter's Model 9.

Supreme Vise: Made by Crest Tool & Supply, Inc., the Supreme is a beautifully crafted tool distinguished by a round, palm-conforming device at the end of the cam lever and by large heads on the base-clamp and height-adjustment screws.

Another highly popular design features collet-and-sleeve jaws operated by a threaded hand-nut. Vises of this type are usually less expensive than the finger-lever models. I'll describe some good ones here.

Thompson B: This fine, moderately priced vise has a collet and sleeve of the same size as the Thompson A. It's an excellent choice for the uncommitted beginning tier.

Thompson Short B: This one is just like the B model, but only half as high. It

makes an excellent choice for a compact, portable fly-tying kit.

Herter's Model 3: This fine vise resembles the Thompson Model B.

Herter's Model 4: Here is another compact model, rather similar to the Thompson Short B vise. It stands 6½ inches from jaw tip to table top.

Herter's Model 6: A very sturdy utility vise, the Model 6 is intended for work on large hooks and for special operations such as soldering and wire-forming. It features a wide-gaped table clamp and large, sturdy jaws. A four-compartment, revolving cast-metal tray can be affixed to the upper base of the clamp arm.

Veniard Salmo: A revolving head makes this beautifully machined vise an excellent choice for work on double-hook salmon flies. It is strongly constructed and well finished.

When a tier dresses a lot of flies in the smallest sizes—ranging from 18 down to 28—he generally gets the most satisfactory results from a vise with very finely pointed jaws. I'll list a couple of the best vises for tiny, wet and nymph flies.

Swisher-Richards Super Vise: An excellent-quality, pedestal-base vise designed to hold hooks as small as size 28, this model has jaws with very positive clamping action and cadmium-plated steel construction.

Veniard Coulsdon: Featuring tiny jaws of simple collet design for holding the smallest hooks, this one is a fine choice for the beginning limestone-stream angler.

SCISSORS

Four kinds of scissors are most commonly used by fly tiers. Those with long, straight points and stout blades are ideal for heavy cutting and trimming operations, as in shaping deer-hair bass bugs, cutting the center quills of feathers, and trimming and shaping sheet Mylar and sponge-rubber body material. Every fly-tying bench should be equipped with at least one pair of heavy-duty scissors with 3- to 4-inch blades (Fig. 58). Professional barbering shears are ideal.

Straight, fine-pointed fly-tying scissors with lightweight 1½ to 2-inch blades are the workhorses of the trout-fly tier. Their tiny, sharp points are perfect for trimming butts of tied-in materials close to the hook shank and for cutting feather sections, tapering tinsels and snipping chenille, floss, herl and a host of other materials soft and light enough not to spring the blades.

A more durable type of like size is made of spring steel and features adjustable finger loops and crossing points. The loops are easily adjusted to fit a hand of virtually any size. This type can be retained in the hand during wrapping and knot-tying operations.

Those who tie very tiny flies, ranging from size 16 down to 28, will appreciate having a pair of very fine, curved-blade cuticle scissors. They are ideal for cutting the tying thread close to a finished head, shaping feathers for wing cases and snipping off unwanted feather flues and hairs.

LANCE

To slit bass-bug corks, to trim tying thread very close to the head of a fly, or to remove herl-flues from peacock eye quills, many veteran dressers employ a single-edged razor blade or a surgical-steel fly dresser's lance.

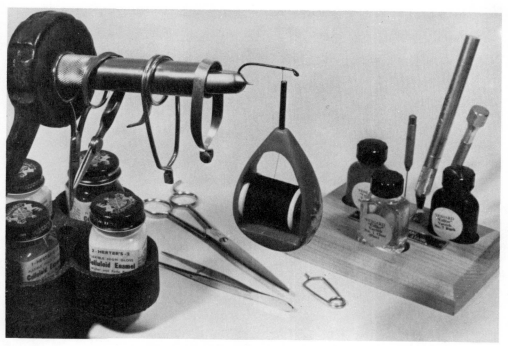

Fig. 58. The fly tier's battery.

When stripping the herl from a peacock eye quill grasp the quill by its tip. Angle the blade firmly on top of the quill against a wood surface. Then, draw the quill firmly and smoothly beneath the blade several times until all of the flues are peeled off.

A faster, simpler way to remove herl is to soak the peacock tail-feather eye in a solution of Clorox and water until the herl disappears. With a strong solution, the process takes only a few minutes, but bear in mind that Clorox will bleach the eye quills a shade lighter than you may desire. I use a Clorox solution to remove herl, then tint or dye the feather to a proper shade with Rit or acid-vat dye.

Hackle Pliers

Hackle pliers serve three main functions: to grasp the ends of hackle while winding them around the hook shank, to hold material and thread ends to prevent their unwinding and to grasp the ends of certain body materials during wrapping operations. This last function is especially important when wrapping materials like chenille, that tend to pick up natural oils from the fingers.

Three main types of hackle pliers are commonly used. Heavy-duty, or English-type, pliers have very strong spring-coil construction. They are available in standard and miniature sizes. Jaw tension is adjusted by the tier to suit his preference. Non-skid hackle pliers feature jaws covered with corrugated rubber pads, one on each jaw face. The pads protect the material being wound from damage by sharp metal edges. Duplex hackle pliers have a rubber cushion on one jaw facing against a sharply grooved metal jaw on the opposing side. They provide a very positive grip, yet

are relatively gentle on hackles and other feathers.

Some fly dressers make their own hackle pliers out of spring-type clothes pins. The jaws are either serrated with a knife blade or covered with rubber. Home-made pliers are really pretty good for jobs like holding thread and material, winding large hackles and grasping chenille during the wrapping operation.

Virtually every major American supplier of fly-tying material offers a selection of hackle pliers.

Hackle Guards

Hackle guards are thin metal cone-shaped holders, to keep hackles out of the way while a tier winds and finishes a fly head. They're not as essential as scissors but are most helpful to a beginner—and to all of us when we tie very tiny dry flies.

Tweezers

Tweezers are extremely useful in handling tiny hooks or dubbing fur, positioning small feathers and holding wing sections in place while tying them onto the hook, as in the dressing of compound wings on certain highly complex Atlantic-salmon patterns. The most useful tweezers are straight with square tips, straight with pointed tips, or curved with pointed tips. If your wife will let you have an old pair of eyebrow tweezers, they will do fine.

Bobbin

The fly-tying bobbin holds a spool of thread under moderate tension during wrapping and tying-down operations. It has the benefit of keeping the fingers clean when using waxed tying thread, and it's an extremely useful tool for anyone with very large hands, broad finger tips and rough nails.

Several types of bobbins are available commercially. Some are relatively expensive, others quite cheap. Most hold the tying thread under tension quite well. The style you select (if you decide to use a bobbin) will be pretty much dictated by the size of your hand, the cost and your personal judgment. I prefer to tie most flies without a bobbin, but I must say that Thompson, Herter's and Veniard all market excellent models.

Thread & Material Clips

Like bobbins, thread and material clips are a help to some tiers and a hindrance to others. Let me suggest that you start tying with a single material clip on the sleeve of the vise, positioned to hold unwound ribbing and body materials out of the way. A large rubber washer screwed to the edge of the tying table will serve as an excellent thread holder.

Dubbing Needle

A small needle affixed to some sort of handle is virtually indispensable to every fly tier for teasing and blending dubbing furs, picking out wound-down hackle fibers, separating sections of wing feather, applying head cement to finished flies and removing dried cement from hook eyes. Dubbing needles are easily made in the home workshop and are also available in a variety of sizes and styles from material suppliers. The well-equipped tier will find at least two sizes useful.

Additional Tools

Apart from the essential or common fly dresser's gear listed here, numerous tools are available for special purposes. They include a gallows tool used to assist in the construction of parachute-style dry flies, a whip-finish knot-tying tool, a half-hitch tool, hackle-trimmers, wing-formers, pliers with special jaw grooves to help form nymph bodies, etc.

Most of these tools are very useful, but not essential. Whether you eventually decide to employ them will probably depend on how skillful you become at manually performing some of the trickier tying operations and how well you like to collect tools that are only occasionally employed.

Chapter 7

Fly-Tying Hooks & Materials

Hooks

FLY HOOKS are usually made of round or oval wire that is bent, formed and tempered into the final product. Round wire is most commonly employed in the manufacture of hooks for tying trout, panfish and freshwater-bass flies. Oval wire is used for hooks requiring great strength, such as those made specifically for Atlantic salmon and steelhead. The oval-wire hooks are said by some to be 20 percent stronger than round-wire hooks of comparable quality. Some styles of hooks are forged to a semi-rectangular shape—a flat-sided oval—to enhance the strength at barb and point. Fly dressers refer to such hooks as "forged" or "forged flat." The three styles are shown in Fig. 59.

In selecting hooks for a specific type of angling, it is extremely important to choose sizes, styles and strengths that will contribute to a fly's fishing potential. For example, no sensible tier would dress dry flies on heavy-wire hooks that would sink them, nor would he tie a tarpon fly on a hook that lacked great strength. Let's examine qualities that affect hook performance and, therefore, hook selection.

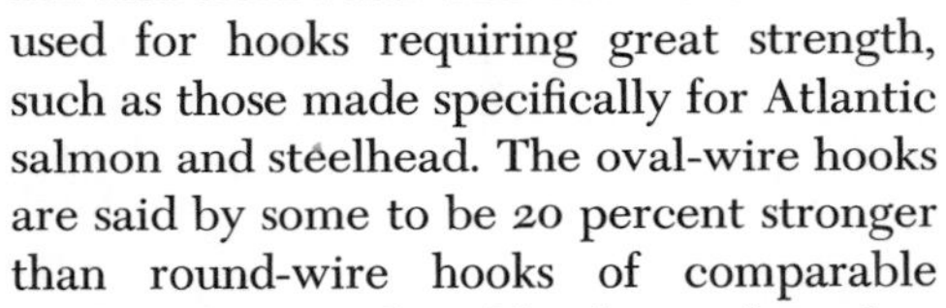

Wire Size

Fly-tying hooks are made in wire sizes that are designated to be standard, extra-fine or extra-stout for a particular size of hook. From a practical standpoint, standard wire hooks in sizes 8 to 18 are usually adequate for dressing both floating and sinking flies. But for optimum performance, extra-fine hooks are usually preferred by experienced flyfishers for dry flies and for some nymphs and wet flies to be used near the surface. Extra-stout wire increases hook strength and weight for a given size, and is normally used only on flies intended for sub-surface fishing.

The terminology for relative wire size utilizes the designator "X" preceded by a numeral which indicates the weight of that hook's wire compared to standard wire in a hook of the same size. For example, a "2X fine-wire" hook is made from wire that is standard on a hook two sizes smaller than the one in question. Conversely, a "2X stout" hook is made from wire that would be standard on a hook two sizes larger (Fig. 60).

Fig. 59. Cross sections of round, oval and forged-flat hooks.

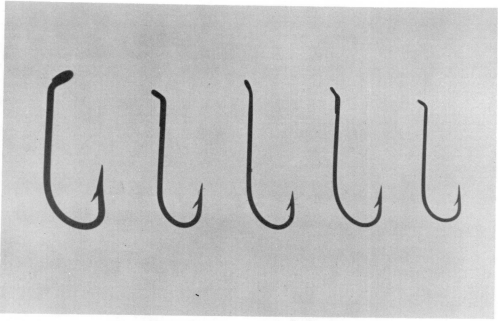

Fig. 60. Hooks ranging from about 5X stout to 2X fine.

Fig. 61. Four popular hook shapes.

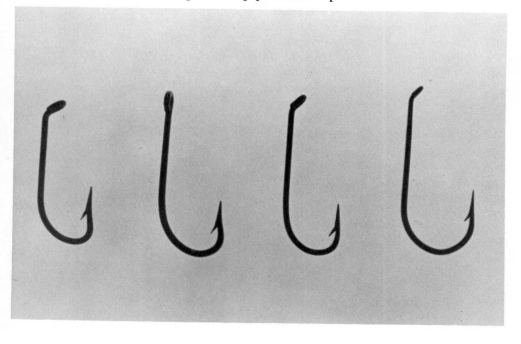

Shape

A hook's shape affects both its hooking and holding qualities. With regard to hook design, the word "shape" refers to the pattern of the hook, commonly called the bend. (The word "bend" more properly describes the lateral offset between a hook's point and shank, but through common usage it has also become synonymous with shape.) Four very popular hook shapes are most commonly used by American fly tiers: Model Perfect, Sproat, Limerick and O'Shaughnessy (Fig. 61).

Model Perfect hooks, also known as Perfect, Round Bend or Viking Bend, are most popular for freshwater flies dressed for trout, bass and panfish. The uniform, round bend characterizing this design allows the hook to bite very deeply and hold well in the mouths of small to moderately large fish. Some of the very highest-quality extra-fine-wire dry-fly hooks are made in this pattern, as are some very useful extra-stout-wire hooks for nymph, streamer and wet-fly fishing. The pattern is also available in some saltwater models.

Both the Sproat and the Improved Sproat designs are very popular for dressing dry flies, nymphs, wet flies, streamers and steelhead flies. The Sproat, characterized by a slightly parabolic return bend, has bite and holding qualities similar to that of the Round Bend. Sproat hooks are available in a wide range of shank lengths, sizes and wire weights. They are usually a little less expensive than Perfect Bend hooks.

It should be noted, however, that the difference in cost between the most expensive hooks and cheap ones is negligible. The finest hooks for freshwater fly tying rarely exceed three cents apiece. Most cost much less. It pays to use the best hooks. They usually have sharper points, more

strength at the barb and wire tempered to reliable but not excessive hardness. Some of the cheap ones break or bend too easily and have poorly crafted points and eyes.

Limerick or Pennel's Limerick hooks are markedly parabolic shapes that have gained great popularity for trout, steelhead and landlocked-salmon flies in some parts of the country. There's a lot of variation to the abruptness in the return bend of Limerick hooks crafted by different manufacturers. Those with the most abruptly parabolic shapes have poorer holding qualities than those with a moderate return bend closer to the Sproat design. Some of the best Limerick hooks are made by Veniard, Hardy Bros. and O. Mustad & Son for Atlantic-salmon flies. They bite deeply and hold heavy fish very well indeed.

Dramatic Limerick Bend hooks have achieved a degree of popularity, perhaps unearned, among dressers of brook-trout and landlocked-salmon streamers. The exaggerated Limerick neither bites nor holds as well as the Perfect or Sproat.

O'Shaughnessy hooks, in tinned, stainless steel or bronzed finish, are excellent for tying most saltwater flies as well as streamers and surface bugs for northern pike and muskellunge. The O'Shaughnessy shape resembles both the Sproat and Limerick families, except that the point is usually a bit longer than that of the Sproat and the barb is somewhat higher.

Some anglers, seeking record-class steelheads in British Columbia's Babeen, Dean and Skeena river systems, prefer stainless steel O'Shaughnessy hooks. Having hooked numerous steelheads on them myself, I can report that they do hold heavy fish very well. On the other hand, some saltwater flyrodders do not advocate stainless steel for hard-mouthed species like tarpon. They say stainless steel won't hold a sharp point, and they prefer harder-wire hooks that have been corrosion-proofed with a process called tinning. Tinned hooks in various shapes and sizes can be purchased in turned-down-eye models for fly tying. Some of the stainless-steel hooks are available only in straight, ring-eye models. Turned-up or turned-down eyes aren't necessary for most saltwater, bass, pike and muskie flies.

A discussion of some of the other available shapes (like the Sneck, Aberdeen, In-Turn and Centripetal designs) would serve no real purpose. They're not really designed for fly fishing and can't offer comparable performance. However, some anglers may be interested in trying out the relatively new "Keel Hook"—a brand name for a hook of modified centripetal design suited for fishing stumpy, brushy, rocky or weedy parts of lakes, rivers and sloughs. A little way behind the eye, it turns down abruptly to form a dropped shank with a form somewhat like a boat's keel and the point on a level with the eye. The fly is dressed literally upside down,

and the weight is distributed so that the point rides up rather than down in the water, greatly reducing the number of hang-ups (and lost flies) on rocks and snags.

Bend

Bend is the proper term for the lateral offset between the hook's point and shank. Offset to the left is known as a "kirbed" bend. When the offset is to the right (looking down at the hook from above) the hook is said to have a "reversed" bend.

Shank, Gape & Spear

The shank is the straight part of the hook, beginning behind the eye and extending to where the shape begins. Hook shanks are designated by their relative length compared to the manufacturer's standard for a specific pattern and style. When the shank is longer than normal for a particular size and model (Fig. 62) the hook is said to have an extra-long shank.

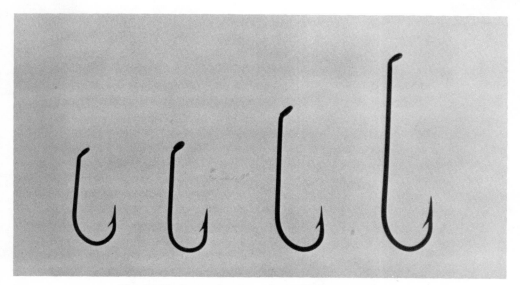

Fig. 62. Hooks ranging from about 2X short to 4X long.

This is described by the designator "XL" preceded by a numeral showing that the length would be about standard for a hook so many sizes larger. For example, a size 10, 4XL hook has a shank approximately equivalent to one four sizes larger—a size 6 hook of normal length. Long-shanked fly-tying hooks range in length from 1XL to 8XL. They are used for dressing a wide variety of nymphs, wet flies, dry flies, bucktails and streamers. Fine- and extra-fine-wire hooks in 1XL and 2XL versions are very popular for tying mayfly imitations. Nymph fishermen usually tie their sub-surface artificials on hooks ranging from 1XL to 4XL. The 3XL and 4XL shanks are also the most popular lengths for dressing streamers and bucktails for casting, while 6XL and 8XL hooks are favored in some areas for tying trolling streamers for trout and landlocked salmon.

With short shanked hooks, the length is designated by "XS" preceded by a numeral indicating that the shank is normal for a hook so many sizes smaller. Short-shanked hooks usually run from 1XS to 5XS. They are primarily used for tying shrimp-shaped wet flies and special dry flies like spiders and variants.

Two unusual shank styles (Fig. 63) are of special interest to bass, pike, muskie and saltwater flyrodders. One is the bentdown shank, of which a popular version is the previously mentioned Keel Hook. It allows the fly to be dressed upside down on a hook that rides point up in the water. The other is the humped-shank hook, used in dressing cork-bodied bugs for both fresh

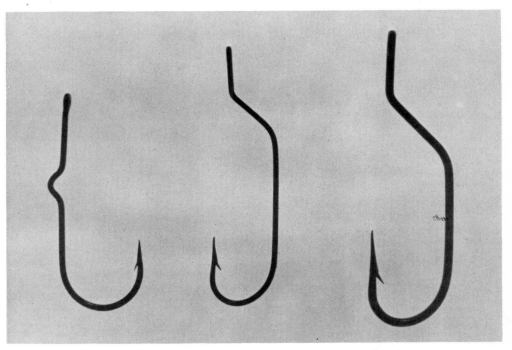

Fig. 63. Two keel hooks and a humped-shank hook.

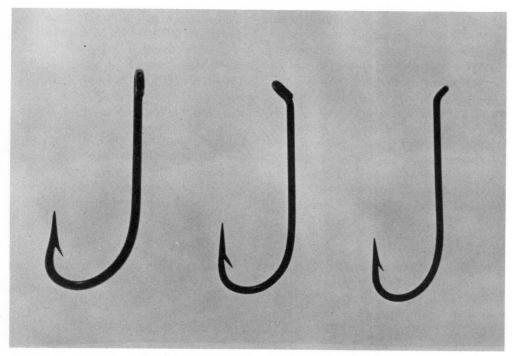

Fig. 64. Straight, turned-up, and turned-down hook eyes.

and saltwater surface fishing. It's available with a single or an S-shaped hump. The Model Perfect bend is generally preferred in hump-shanked hooks because of the wide gape inherent in the design.

The term "gape" refers to the distance between the inside of a hook's shank and point. Generally speaking, the wider the gape is, the deeper the hook will penetrate the fish's mouth. Special wide-gape hooks are available to fly dressers, but hooks with extra-short shanks achieve similar penetrations.

It is important to remember that if you intend to dress a very bulky bug or fly, a portion of which will fill or partially fill the gape, hook size should be scaled proportionately upward in order to prevent a loss of penetration.

The spear, or return bend of the hook, is measured from the point to the extreme edge of the shape. Some tiers refer to the spear length as a hook's "bite." Spear length, like gape, influences the hook's depth of penetration. Hooks with relatively long spears and points are recommended for fish with tough mouth parts. Short spears and points often hold poorly after a fish is hooked.

Eye

Although eyed hooks—with rings at the ends of their shanks—have been on the scene a little less than a century, they have practically eliminated the use of snelled flies tied on plain, tapered or marked-shank hooks. The three types of eyes currently popular with American fly dressers are shown in Fig. 64.

Hooks with eyes in the same plane as the shank—neither turned up nor turned down—are very popular for flies to be used behind spinners, for cork-bodied surface bugs and for saltwater flies.

Turned-down eyes—turned down from the plane of the shank—are popular for all types of dry, wet, nymph and streamer flies, except in sizes 16 through 28. In those small sizes a turned-down eye is said by some to reduce the gape of the hook. In fly-tying nomenclature, hooks with turned down eyes are designated by the abbreviation TDE.

When the wire in the eye has the same diameter as the rest of the hook, it's called a "ball eye," and when the wire in the eye is tapered, it's simply called a tapered eye. A hook with a turned-down ball eye is abbreviated TDBE; one with a turned-down tapered eye is shortened to TDTE.

A hook whose eye angles upward from the plane of the shank is called a turned-up eye hook—TUE. This style is popular for everything from dry flies to salmon wet flies. Anglers seem to prefer the TDE for wet flies and streamers. Loop-eyed hooks, available in both turned-up and turned-down versions, are popular for landlocked

salmon, Atlantic salmon and steelheads because of the strength of the design and the fact that it presents no sharp edges to the leader tippet. They are designated by the abbreviation TULE. The eye wire is tapered and looped back parallel to the shank, the tapered loop being wound under the forward parts of the fly. Such hooks are also available in standard, heavy-oval wire, light-wire "low-water" and extra-fine-wire dry-fly styles. Most models have a Limerick bend and can be had in both bronzed and japanned (lacquered) finishes.

Points

Hooks are available with several common types of barbed point (Fig. 65). Probably the best grades of hooks for freshwater fly fishing feature hollow points which are first shaped, then hand-ground to an interior curvature up through the barb. Some authorities claim that hollow grinding a point reduces its strength, and they're probably right. But in over 30 years of fishing I can't recall more than a couple of instances when the point on a high-quality hollow-ground hook failed while I was handling a heavy fish. And in both cases

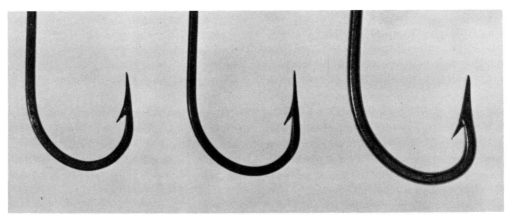

Fig. 65. Left to right, hollow point, needle point and spear point.

the point broke only after repeated sharpening.

Needle-pointed hooks are very fast-penetrating and can be excellent if an adequate barb is sliced and the point is long enough. The style is found mostly on British-made hooks. The best dry-fly hooks I ever used were made in France prior to the Second World War and, as far as I know, have been unavailable for over 20 years. They featured very long, incredibly sharp needle points and long, fairly low barbs. Some of the better oval-wire salmon-fly hooks are made with needle points, as are many of the highest-quality English dry-fly and wet-fly hooks.

The spear point, sometimes called a filed point or a Dublin point, is machine-made and usually not equal in quality, sharpness or uniformity to needle or hollow-ground points. It is suitable for bass, pike, saltwater and salmon flies, provided the angler is willing to devote the necessary time to hand-filing or honing each point to fishable sharpness.

Spear-point hooks are best sharpened by filing them to a triangular shape with a fine point- or hook-file (Fig. 66). Filing a hook to triangular shape provides three

sharp cutting edges which definitely assist in driving the barb home in hard-mouthed species.

Experienced flyrodders are careful to check the sharpness of every hook to which they dress a fly, regardless of its quality. They also usually check their hooks for malformed eyes or eyes with sharp cutting edges. Virtually every box of fly hooks contains one or more that should be discarded. Careful inspection at the tying bench is your cheapest insurance against losing a trophy fish to a faulty hook.

In addition to the conventionally barbed point, there is also, of course, the barbless hook. Its purpose is to allow easy release of fish that have been hooked and played for purely sporting purposes. Two styles are available, one with an unbarbed hump located in the normal barb location, the other without a hump. Because of the limited number of hook styles and sizes available in barbless models, many anglers simply bend down or file off the barbs when barbless hooks are required.

Hook Finishes

Of the variety of hook finishes most commonly employed by manufacturers in America and abroad, bronzing enjoys the greatest popularity among freshwater fly fishermen. However, bronzed hooks do not resist saltwater corrosion particularly well. Because of resistance to such corrosion, the japanned (black lacquered) hooks enjoy solid popularity among salmon and steelhead flyrodders who fish tidal stretches of coastal streams.

Fly fishermen who utilize their artificials exclusively in salt water usually prefer nickeled, tinned or nickel-chrome-finished hooks. All three are very corrosion-resistant. But it should be noted that veteran saltwater fishermen usually wash their flies

Fig. 66. Triangular filing pattern for spear points.

following each use to prevent corrosion, not only of the hooks but also of tinsel parts of flies.

Expensive and beautiful gold-finished hooks are available only in limited quantities for fly-tying purposes. Most professional as well as amateur tiers utilize them only for dressing exhibition quality flies, although gold hooks are not uncommon in the dressing of certain West Coast steelhead flies such as the popular Golden Demon, a summer-run pattern in very wide usage throughout California, Oregon and Washington. The gold finish has been applied to certain dry-fly hook styles from time to time. But it has never attained much popularity except in the case of some short-shanked models primarily used for spider ties. Certainly the value of a gold-finished dry-fly hook is open to question.

Recommended Hooks

There follows a listing of various hooks with which I've had personal experience and which, in my opinion, meet acceptable standards of quality for a majority of North American fresh and saltwater fly-fishing conditions. (The recommendations do not, of course, preclude the possibility that other brands and models are equally suitable.)

Nymph & Wet-Fly Hooks

Mustad
- 3906 Sproat, TDE, reg. weight
- 3906B Sproat, TDE, heavy wire
- 7948A Viking, TDE, heavy wire
- 7957B Viking, TDE, heavy wire
- 7957BX Viking, TDE, 1X stout, 1XL
- 9671 Viking, TDE, 2XL
- 9672 Viking, TDE, 3XL

Veniard
- Round Bend, TDE
- Forged Salmon Hook, TULE

- Low-Water Salmon Hook, TULE, light wire, long shank

Herter's
- 7029 T Gaelic Supreme, TDE
- 7029 3XL Gaelic Supreme, TDE
- 777 Wet-Fly & Nymph Hook, TUE, 2XL, 1X stout

Allcock's
- W170 Model Perfect, TDE, straight bend
- S219 Sproat, TDBE, 2X stout
- S216 Sproat, TDBE, 2X stout, 1XL
- S217 Sproat, TDBE, 2X stout, 1XL, nickel
- S218 Sproat, TDBE, 2X stout, 3XL

Dry-Fly Hooks

Mustad
- 94833 Viking, TDE, 3X fine
- 94840 Viking, TDE, extra-fine wire

Allcock's
- S220 Model Perfect, TDE, extra-fine wire

Orvis
- Orvis Premium, TUE, 4X fine, Perfect Bend
- Orvis, TDE, 3X fine, Perfect Bend

Veniard
- 61441 Dry Fly, TUE
- Wide Gape Dry Fly, TDE
- Wilson Dry-Fly Salmon Hook, TULE, extra-fine wire, extra long

Herter's
- Custom No. 3029T May-Fly Hook, TDE, 2XL, 1X fine
- 5029T, Scotch Dry-Fly Hook, TDE, 1XL, Round Bend

Streamer Hooks

Herter's
- 7029 3XL Gaelic Supreme, TDE, Perfect Bend

- 7029 4XL Gaelic Supreme, TDE, Perfect Bend
- 7029 6XL Gaelic Supreme, TDE, Perfect Bend

Allcock's
- S218 Sproat, TDTE, 3XL

Mustad
- 9672 Viking, TDE, 3XL
- 79580 Viking, TDE, 4XL
- 79582 Viking, TDE, 6XL
- 94720 Viking, TDE, 8XL

Saltwater, Pike & Muskie Hooks

Mustad
- 3407Z O'Shaughnessy, Duranickel finish
- 34015ST O'Shaughnessy, tinned, TDE, hump-shank
- 9659 Viking, bronzed, TDE, hump-shank
- 7048A Viking, TDE, heavy-wire

Herter's
- 39RMXC O'Shaughnessy, stainless
- 7029RK, Gaelic Supreme, hump-shank

Shakespeare
- L126C, long-shank, fine wire, Round Bend

Wright & McGill
- 254 SS. Round Bend, reg. shank length, stainless

Salmon & Steelhead Hooks

Allcock's
- S216 Sproat, TDBE, 2X stout, 1XL
- S217 Sproat, TDBE, 2X stout, 1XL, nickeled

Mustad
- 7970 Viking, TDE, 5X stout
- 3123B Limerick, TDE, 4X stout
- 3658B Limerick, TULE, oval wire, japanned

- 36890 Limerick, TULE, oval wire, Dublin point, japanned

Veniard
- Forged Salmon Hook, TULE, japanned
- Low-water Salmon Hook, TULE, fine wire, extra-long, japanned
- Wilson Dry-Fly Salmon Hook, TULE, extra-fine wire, extra long, japanned

Sealey
- S1937 Forged Salmon Hook, TULE, bronzed

Herter's
- 3718 Limerick, TUE, 2X stout, japanned

Bass-Bug Hooks

Herter's
- 7029RK Gaelic Supreme, TDE, hump-shank

Mustad
- 9659 Viking, TDE, hump-shank

THREAD & THREAD Colors

Silk and nylon threads are utilized in a wide range of sizes, twists and colors. The thread used to wrap various materials to the hook shank is called the tying thread. Various threads are also used to rib fly bodies with contrasting colors and to strengthen fragile feathers, like peacock, emu and ostrich herls, once they are wound in as bodies, butts or heads. Creative fly dressers have discovered that certain cotton and buttonhole-twist threads are excellent for making effective nymphs and wet flies.

Silk tying threads were once the most popular type. They're still favored by some tiers and are available in a wide range of sizes, from size A to gossamer-fine 8/O Silk threads made expressly for fly tying have a special twist that prevents their unraveling during the winding operations.

Twisted nylon threads, though very strong, were excessively stretchy when first introduced to the market. Modern twisted nylon is usually excellent and no longer has the disadvantage of excessive stretchiness.

Untwisted synthetic threads, under trade names like Nymo and Monocord, are rapidly gaining loyal adherents. They're probably the best of the present-day threads for all-around fly-tying purposes. The untwisted nylon threads have very little stretch, are tremendously strong for their diameters, and allow the tier to fashion very smooth heads because of their relatively flat configuration. They also are available in a wide range of useful colors.

Fly-tying threads, like sewing threads, come in standard sizes. Sizes E, EE and D are sometimes preferred for tying operations requiring a maximum pressure such as in dressing certain very large saltwater flies and hair-bodied bugs.

Size A is the normal preference for large steelhead, salmon and streamer flies when the patterns are simple, and for hair-wings involving heavy wrapping tension.

Size OO is the most common thread for large flies requiring a few more tying-in operations than the simplest patterns. It's also a good size for dressing dry flies larger than size 8.

Size OOO and OOOO are the all-purpose threads for dressing medium freshwater flies of all types. They work well on almost any hook from size 12 to 6.

Size OOOOO is a good choice for small flies from 18 to 10, dry or wet. The same is true of size OOOOOO, but OOOOOOO (called 8/O requires a very delicate tying touch and is used mostly on the smallest artificials, ranging down to size 28.

A lot of fly-fishing experts say that the color of thread makes little difference in a fly's effectiveness. Just as many experts contend that thread color does make a difference in a fly's ability to attract fish, especially in the case of small, delicately hued dry and nymph flies for trout. A third group, taking a moderate stand, says that sometimes thread color does seem to influence a fly's effectiveness, and sometimes it doesn't.

After 30 years or so, I still haven't drawn a hard conclusion on the subject of thread color. I probably never will, because of the near-infinite number of variables affecting a fly's performance. All I can say is that if you keep an open mind you may someday create a fly as deadly as the Royal Coachman, a fly that doesn't really suggest to the human eye any specific food organism, but probably accounts for more total poundage of hooked trout, bass, steelheads and panfish than any other dozen patterns combined.

It's been my experience that an angler's confidence in his artificial flies often has as much bearing on how effectively he fishes them as does their size, color or shape. It's confidence in a fly that sometimes makes the difference between a man who merely fishes with flies and a genuine fly fisherman.

Tying threads are available in a considerable range of standard colors, including black, white, red, orange, fluorescent orange, yellow, gray, brown, tan, green, purple, blue, gold, olive, bright green, wine and light blue. Additional shades are available in Belding dye colors at most sewing-supply stores. Some of the Belding threads make excellent tying silks for delicately hued dry flies, nymphs and streamers.

If a desired color is not available commercially, the tier can mix dyes and tint white thread to the precise shade desired.

Nylon threads require special dyes, but silk and cotton are quickly and easily dyed or tinted with Rit.

Fly-Tying Waxes

Various waxes are used to waterproof the tying thread, promote its adherence to the hook and materials and make it tacky enough so that fur can be spun or dubbed to it. The better waxes used on the tying thread proper are reasonably hard and slightly tacky. Most experienced tiers prefer a clean, colorless wax on the tying silk to prevent color bleed-through on floss and other soft body materials in hot weather. The tying thread can be waxed by drawing an appropriate length through a small piece of wax that's been kneaded between the fingers until slightly softened (Fig. 67) or it can be soaked in melted wax right on the spool. And some of the more popular brands of tying thread can be purchased pre-waxed.

Wax used for dubbing or spinning fur bodies should be very soft and tacky. One of the best commercially available waxes for dubbing is made with turpentine for a solvent. When it becomes too hard, a drop or two of turpentine can be added to soften it. When I was dressing flies commercially, I made an excellent dubbing wax from a mixture of pure beeswax, a drop of castor oil, and a small piece of tacky bootmaker's wax. The ingredients were melted, thoroughly mixed, then solidified by pouring into a container of ice water. Fly tying literature is well sprinkled with tying and dubbing wax formulae, most of which work very very well. Pure beeswax alone is hard to beat as a general-purpose wax for tying thread. Mixtures of beeswax and paraffin are also quite good. How hard or soft one prefers his waxes is a matter of personal preference, influenced by the temperature of the region where he lives and fishes. A fellow may take pleasure in experimenting with such things, but it's difficult to improve on the commercial products.

Cements, Varnishes, Resins & Lacquers

A considerable array of lacquers, cements, resins and varnishes can be used for fly tying. Some are ideal for adding permanence to the thread windings that lash down hair wings and certain types of body materials. Others are designed primarily to finish the thread-wrapped heads. And others are useful chiefly to finish cork-bodied bass, pike, muskie and saltwater popper bugs. A few can be used for multiple purposes.

Substances referred to as head cements are usually, though not always, relatively fast-drying lacquers requiring special thinners supplied by the manufacturers. True head cements can be employed to finish completed heads, to cement the butts of hair wings and to add permanence to critical tying-in operations.

Fig. 67.

Generally, you need only one or two coats of good head cement to firmly seal and waterproof the thread wrapping at the head. But for really professional-looking results, several very thin coats of head cement should be applied, allowing adequate drying time between coats. Out on the stream bank, when you are trying desperately to match some hatch in rapidly failing light, head cement isn't worth the wasted fishing time. A firm whip finish will hold the head more than well enough to hook a few fish before darkness falls. Most popular brands of head cement are available in both clear and black.

When the object is to finish a large fly head or the cork surfaces of a bass bug with a shiny, tough covering, celluloid-base enamel is an excellent choice. Celluloid enamel is available in several basic colors.

Relatively thick, fast-drying cement is generally the best choice for cementing the butts of hair wings, streamer wings and cheeking and eyeing materials. Some tiers simply let a bottle of head cement thicken up a bit for the purpose. Others purchase special hair and cork cements. I like Duco Household Cement that's been slightly thinned with acetone or methyl ethyl ketone.

Many old-time tiers still prefer to finish the heads of their flies with varnish. Marine spar, polyurethane, Bakelite and British fly-tying varnishes all make excellent, slow-drying head finishes. Several thin coats are preferred. A full day's drying time should be allowed between coats for best results.

There's been a recent trend toward the use of epoxy cements for finishing the heads of steelhead, salmon and streamer flies. A single coat of epoxy dries overnight into a glass-hard, smooth, shiny finish. The epoxy can be colored with a drop of India ink after mixing the two parts of the cement (a binding element and a drying element) in equal portions. A minimum amount is applied, just enough to cover the thread wraps. Epoxy is also excellent for cementing line splices and spliced loops in fly lines, and it makes a good finish for the splice-wrappings. Its tremendous bonding strength allows shorter-than-normal splices.

Fluorescent lacquers are lure and plug paints that offer interesting and effective alternatives for finishing and eyeing streamer and bucktail heads. They're most effectively employed over a coat of white base lacquer and finished with a coat of sealer for a glossy, durable finish. The same is true of subtle luminescent and opalescent finishes available from fly-tying supply houses and commercial paint outlets.

Cork-bodied bugs should always be prepared with a sealer coat and a white base coat prior to application of colored enamels or lacquers. If an exceptionally high gloss is desired, the color should be topped with a coat of clear enamel or lacquer. Make certain your cork-finishing materials are compatible with one another. Enamel is preferable. You can ruin a finish by mixing coats of enamel and lacquer, because the solvent in a lacquer will lift the enamel finish.

Fly Anatomy

Standard nomenclature for the various parts of dry, wet, nymph, streamer and salmon flies are shown in Figs. 68a and 68b. This diagram is also intended to show the standard proportions of the different types of fly. The most commonly used materials for dressing each portion of a fly are listed below in their proper categories.

TIP: fine flat or oval tinsel, floss, fine silver or gold wire.

EGG SAC: dubbin, yarn, chenille.

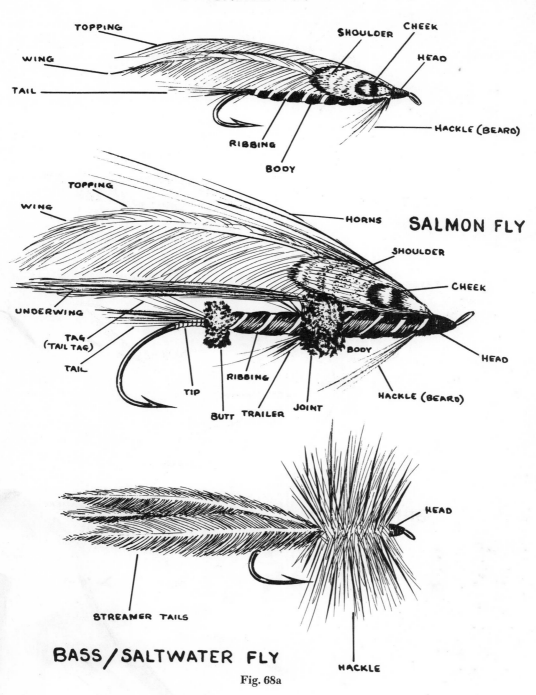

STREAMER FLY

TOPPING

SHOULDER   CHEEK

WING

HEAD

TAIL

HACKLE (BEARD)

RIBBING

BODY

SALMON FLY

TOPPING

WING

HORNS

SHOULDER

CHEEK

UNDERWING

TAG
(TAIL TAG)

TAIL

HEAD

BODY

TIP

RIBBING

HACKLE (BEARD)

BUTT   TRAILER   JOINT

BASS/SALTWATER FLY

HEAD

STREAMER TAILS

HACKLE

Fig. 68a

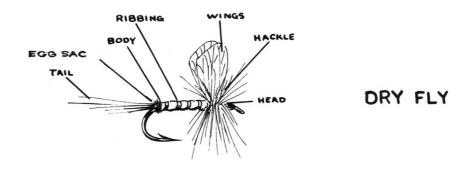

DRY FLY

WET FLY

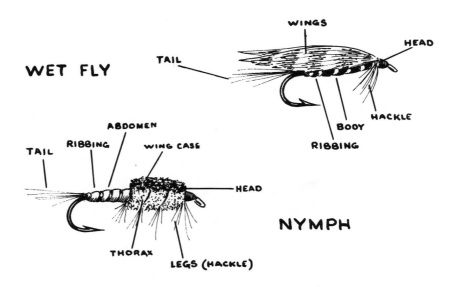

NYMPH

SHRIMP FLY

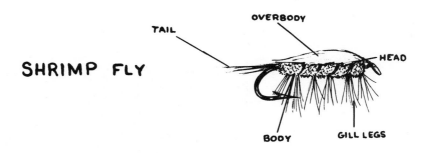

Fig. 68b

TAIL: hackle wisps, guard hairs, body hairs, moose mane, stripped hackle stems, marabou, herl, sections of duck or goose primary feathers, sections of waterfowl and upland-bird plumage, nylon "hair," exotic pheasant crest and tippet materials (Fig. 69).

TAG, OR TAIL TAG: yarn, various types of plumage, tinsel.

BUTT: herl, chenille, dubbed fur, yarn.

BODY: floss, chenille, spun or dubbed fur, yarn, wrapped guard hairs or feather sections, spun and trimmed body hairs, braided hairs or nylon, raffia grass, hackle.

RIBBING: flat, round and oval tinsels, thread, monofilament, yarn, floss, guard hairs, tail hairs, mane hairs.

JOINT: chenille, herl, yarn, floss.

TRAILERS: crest feathers, hackle.

HACKLE: hen or gamecock neck, spade or saddle hackle, breast or flank feathers from upland birds or waterfowl, spun-on body hairs, woven hair, pheasant-rump feathers (Fig. 70).

THROAT: various types of hackle fibers, exotic-pheasant tippet, wing-feather sections, tufts of yarn or floss.

WING: sections of wing and flank feathers, bucktail, hackles, tail-feather sections, artificial hair, guard and tail hairs from many fur-bearing animals, Mylar strips, whole flank feathers (Fig. 71).

SHOULDER: hackle tips, body feathers, Mylar strips.

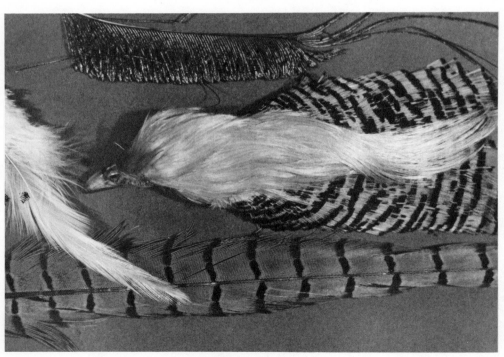

Fig. 69. Tail materials.

Fig. 70. Hackle materials.

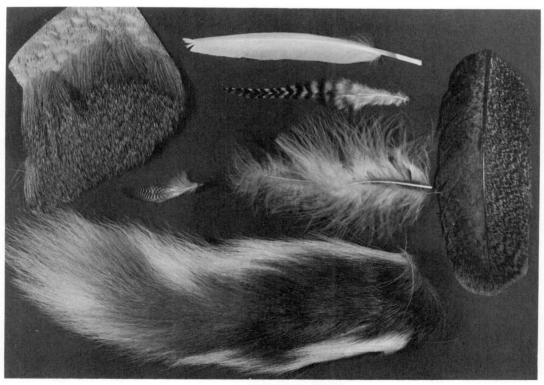

Fig. 71. Wing materials.

CHEEK: hackle tips, jungle-cock "eye" feathers, small body feathers, small wing feathers.

TOPPING: herl, marabou, crest feathers.

HORNS: pairs of feather fibers, hairs.

OVERBODY: feather sections, bundled hairs, floss, yarn, chenille, marabou.

THORAX: chenille, dubbed or spun fur, yarn.

WING CASE: feather sections, raffia grass, yarn, floss.

WING STUBS: feather tips, hairs, trimmed feather sections.

LEGS: hackles, trimmed hackles, rubber bands or strands.

HEAD: wrapped thread, herl, chenille, split brass beads.

EYES: lacquer, pull-chain beads, glass eyes.

SETAE: hackle fibers, hairs.

Every effort should be made to select the most buoyant materials available for floating flies. Stiff, glossy hackle fibers and buoyant hairs, like bucktail, are highly recommended for the tails. Spun or dubbed fur and polypropylene yarn are ideal dry-fly body materials. The stiffest, least webby gamecock neck, saddle and spade hackles afford optimum floating qualities, as do hackle-tip and bucktail wings.

Highly absorbent body, tail and wings are often desired for sub-surface flies. Hen-neck feather fibers, marabou feathers, and rump- or flank-feather sections make flexible, absorbent tails. Very absorbent bodies can be fashioned from wool yarns, thoroughly washed and dried underfurs, chenille and floss. Tinsels add additional weight to flies dressed for deep-water fishing. Sparse wings promote the fastest sinking. Absorbent flank- and wing-feather sections, and non-buoyant hairs like polar bear, skunk, badger and squirrel tail are all excellent wet-fly winging materials. Marabou feathers are among the most mobile and absorbent for nymph wingcases and streamer wings.

Chapter 14 will disclose dozens of feather, fur and material combinations known to perform well on both sinking and floating lines. Your own imagination should take over from there.

CHAPTER 8

BASIC FLY-TYING OPERATIONS

THE FLIES described and illustrated in Chapters 8 through 13 were chosen because of certain tying techniques used in their construction and because, in my opinion, they incorporate design principles that may be helpful to tiers throughout the country as prototypes for the development of their own killing patterns. If the next chapter, on trout, salmon and grayling, seems to be somewhat dominated by Western fly patterns, bear in mind that they were not chosen for reasons of regional favoritism, and that 69 of the 175 killing patterns described in Chapter 14 are useful throughout the United States, while 62 are of greatest interest to Eastern anglers. The dressings listed in Chapter 14 and in the Appendix on regional fly patterns were selected for their general usefulness and to some extent for simplicity of construction. Thus, regardless of where you do your angling or how much experience you have, you should find some valuable suggestions here.

I was sorely tempted to include George F. Grant's unique, remarkably life-like and effective stonefly designs, dressed with woven-hair bodies and hackles. However, they are complex and difficult to tie, and at the end of the last chapter, I referred interested tiers to Grant's own treatises on the use of woven hair.

I was also tempted to illustrate Harry Darbee's Stonefly Nymph (imitative of the *Perla capitata*) in this chapter. It's a very useful tie for Eastern trout streams. But I relegated it to the Chapter 14 listings because of its use of jungle-cock eye feather for the wing cases. Importation of jungle cock from India is now banned, and supplies of these gorgeous, waxy feathers are practically exhausted. I do list some patterns calling for jungle-cock—mostly designs in which the scarce feathers are optional—because imitation (plastic) jungle-cock eye feathers are available from various suppliers, and because creative tiers have devised substitutes such as dyed and lacquered feathers of quail, guinea hen, starling and barred wood duck.

PREPARING THE HOOK

Some of the most important fly-tying procedures should be clearly illustrated as well as described. It's not that the basic operations are complicated; on the contrary, they're quite simple. But a demonstration will clear up any doubt as to the order of the operations and the best way to perform each of them. Then, too, the pictures will later serve as instant references or reminders. With the aid of photos, let's go through the procedures, step by step.

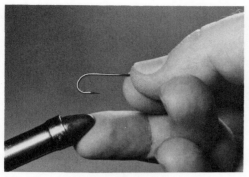

Fig. 72. Examine the hook for flaws, such as a faulty point, open eye or kinked shank. Discard any defective hook.

Fig. 75. Before the cement dries, wrap a tight, even thread base on the shank with the tying silk, finishing with a half-hitch knot (also see Fig. 80) except in the case of a fly to be dressed with a tip, tag and butt. If you intend to wrap a floss body on the fly, use white, unwaxed thread for the base.

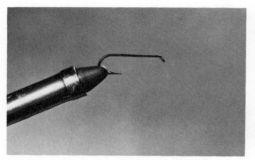

Fig. 73. Place the hook in the jaws of the vise, with the point of the hook covered if possible.

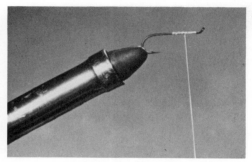

Fig. 76. If you intend to dress a winged dry fly, wrap the thread base only in the winging area, as shown.

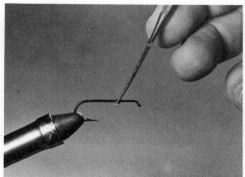

Fig. 74. Spread a thin layer of fast-drying cement on the hook shank from immediately behind the eye to the beginning of the shape.

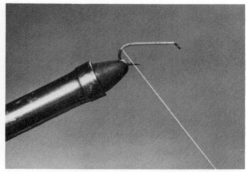

Fig. 77. For a shrimp-shaped wet fly, you need a long thread base, wrapped all the way to where the body will end.

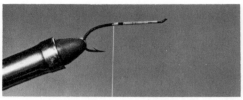

Fig. 78. For patterns involving tip, tag, butt and tail, wrap a divided thread base, as shown. This leaves room for neatly tying down the many materials. *Do not* half-hitch the rear thread wrappings. Cement the windings and hold the thread in place with hackle pliers or a clothespin— or, even simpler, tie it with a bobbin.

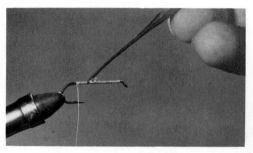

Fig. 79. Saturate the completed thread base with thin cement and allow it to dry while preparing other materials. You now have a firm, solid base on which to affix the materials without having them turn on the shank under pressure of the tying thread.

KNOTS & HITCHES

Half-Hitch: This is the basic knot for completing most tying-in and wrapping operations (Fig. 80).

Scotch Hitch: This is a positive locking knot, slightly bulkier than the half-hitch, useful for knotting the windings on bulky body materials like yarn and for completing wing windings on materials like

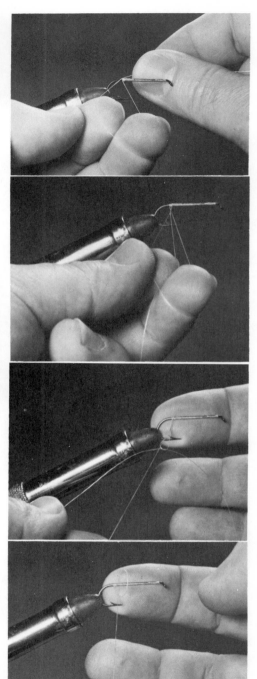

Fig. 80. Half-hitch.

polar bear hair that otherwise might have a tendency to pull loose (Fig. 81).

Whip-Finish Knot: This is the smoothest, most permanent knot for finishing the heads of flies (Fig. 82). It can be tied by hand, as shown, or with a special tool.

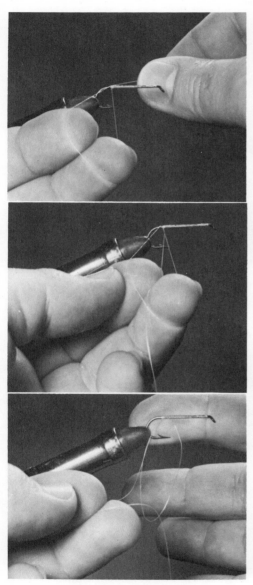

Fig. 81. Scotch hitch.

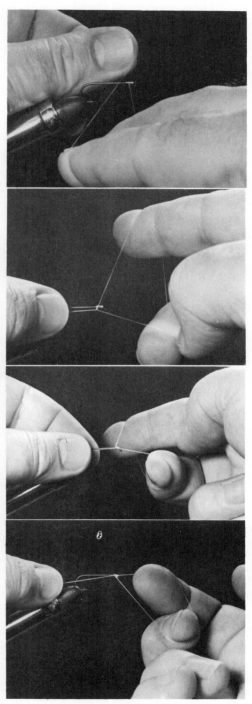

Fig. 82. Whip-finish knot.

Tying the Basic Wet Fly

Bucktail Coachman

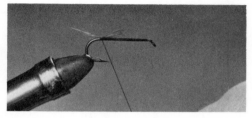

Fig. 86. Firmly draw the thread loop tightly down on the hackle wisps, maintaining pressure on the thread loop and materials between your finger tips.

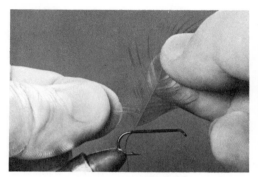

Fig. 83. Snip or strip about six or eight fibers from a scarlet saddle hackle.

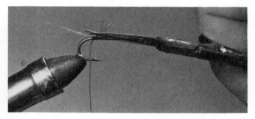

Fig. 87. Remove the fingers holding the material and take two more tight turns over the butts of the hackle fibers. Finish with a half-hitch.

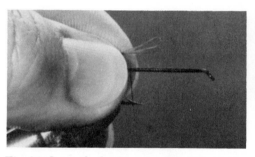

Fig. 84. Grasp the hackle wisps firmly between thumb and forefinger, holding the fibers close to the top of the shank.

Fig. 88. Trim the butts of the tail feathers with scissors, as close as possible to the windings.

Fig. 85. Loop the thread over the held material inside your finger tips.

Fig. 89. Tie in and half-hitch three peacock-herl flues by their tips, concave sides down.

Fig. 90. Grasping the butts of the herls between thumb and forefinger, wrap them forward in close, even turns to form a full, fluffy body. Tie off with three or four turns of thread and half-hitch winding. Trim the herl butts close to the windings.

Fig. 94. Snip off the excess hackle stem close to the windings. Place a drop of thin, fast-drying cement on the windings.

Fig. 91. Select a soft, webby hen-neck hackle. The fibers should reach almost to the hook point. Grasp the hackle by its tip and gently stroke the fibers toward the base of the stem.

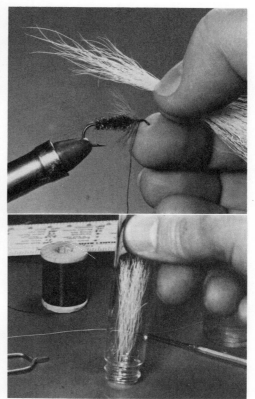

Fig. 92. Tie in the hackle by its tip, making sure the concave side faces down, and half-hitch the winding. Trim off the wound-down tip of the feather.

Fig. 93. Grasp the hackle butt with hackle pliers and wrap forward in two or three close turns. Finish this operation with three turns of thread and a half-hitch.

Fig. 95. Cut a small bunch of fine white bucktail, about two-thirds the size of a matchstick for a size 10 hook. If you want to even the ends of the hairs, drop the bunch, cut ends first, into a ½-inch-diameter glass tube and tap the mouth of the tube lightly on the table until the hair ends are even.

Fig. 96. Grasp the bucktail by the tip ends and work a drop of thick cement into the butts.

Fig. 99. Trim off the hair butts in a neat taper down toward the eye.

Fig. 97. Hold the bucktail firmly over the hook. Then take two loose loops of thread over the hair butts, holding bucktail and thread loops firmly between your fingers. Snug down the thread loops firmly until they compress the hair solidly against the thread base.

Fig. 100. Wrap a thread head tightly and neatly until no hair butts are visible.

Fig. 98. Remove your holding fingers and take three more very tight turns of thread over the hair butts, finishing with a Scotch hitch.

Fig. 101. Finish the head with a whip-finish knot and apply your first coat of head cement.

Tying
the Basic Dry Fly
Quill Gordon

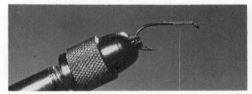

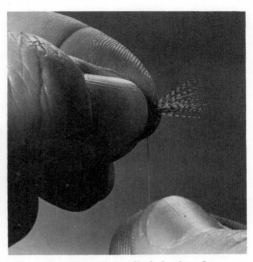

Fig. 102. On a size 12, fine-wire hook, wrap a dry-fly thread base as in Fig. 76.

Fig. 103. Select a symmetrical, barred lemon wooduck-breast feather with a minimum of curve. Strip off the down and short fibers at the base of the feather. Then clip out the tip section at the stem, leaving two matched sections attached.

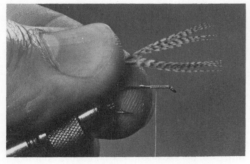

Fig. 104. Gently roll the trimmed feather between your palms or fingers until the fibers are reasonably straight.

Fig. 105. Grasp the rolled feather between thumb and forefinger and hold it in place over the shank, concave side up. Take a double loop of tying thread over the feather inside the finger tips and pull tight. Take several more thread wraps over the wound-down feather and tie a half-hitch.

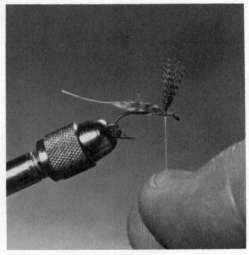

Fig. 106. Wind thread in front of the wing feathers until they stand erect, then divide the feathers into two equal bunches with criss-cross thread windings and half-hitch behind the wing. Place a drop of thin, fast-drying cement on the windings.

Fig. 107. Strip the soft, webby fibers from the butts of two stiff, glossy blue-dun gamecock-neck hackles. Spread the fibers gently with your fingertips.

Fig. 109. Tie in a stripped peacock-herl quill by the tip and wrap in close winds to immediately behind the wings. (The quill should be soaked in water before winding.) Tie it off with a few thread wraps and a half-hitch. Trim off excess quill. Lightly cement the quill body with thin, flexible lacquer for added durability.

Fig. 108. Tie in the hackles by their butts between the wings, facing forward. One hackle should be tied in with the concave side up, the other with the concave side down. Trim off the hackle butts close to the shank and neatly taper-trim the wing-feather butts down toward the shape. Wind your tying thread to the beginning of the shape and hold it there with the bobbin or a hackle pliers. Tie in a tail of a few very stiff blue-dun gamecock-neck or spade hackle fibers. The length of the tail should be about the same as that of the body.

Fig. 110. Using hackle pliers, wind each hackle separately. You want about two turns of each hackle, closely behind and in front of the wings.

Fig. 111. After tying off, hitching and trimming the hackle ends, wrap a neat head and secure it with a whip-finish knot. Finish the head with a couple of coats of fast-drying head cement.

Tying the Basic Nymph

Martinez Black Nymph

Fig. 112. On a size 8, 2XL hook, wrap a wet-fly thread base. Tie in a tail of a few black and white spotted guinea-hen feather fibers.

Fig. 113. Tie in a four-inch length of fine oval (or flat) copper or gold tinsel. Tie in an equal length of pre-spun black fur. Wrap a body with the fur approximately two-thirds the length of the shank, then rib the body with the tinsel in neat, evenly spaced turns. Five turns of tinsel will usually suffice.

Fig. 114. After fur and tinsel are tied down and hitched and unwanted ends are snipped

off, tie in a one-inch or longer strip of green raffia grass approximately ⅛-inch wide after soaking it in water for a few minutes. (The raffia will later be folded forward over the thorax to form wing cases, and only a short section of it will remain after tying it down and snipping off the excess, but it's easier to handle if you begin with a longer strip.) Tie in a three-inch length of medium-small black chenille, half-hitching the windings. Wrap a chenille thorax, leaving room near the head for two more tying-in operations.

Fig. 115. Tie in a beard hackle with a few light, speckled-gray partridge-breast feather fibers. To accomplish this, turn the hook over in the vise and tie down the fibers as a bunch. Then reverse the hook again to the normal point-down position. (With practice, you can tie in a beard hackle without inverting the hook.)

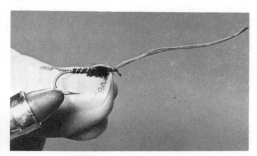

Fig. 116. Pull the section of green raffia forward over the thorax and tie it down at the head. The photo shows the nymph at this stage, but to complete the job you'll snip off all the excess raffia, forward of the tie-down at the head, as the green strip is intended only to represent wing cases over the thorax. Finish the head with a few thread wraps, a whip-finish knot and a couple of coats of cement.

Tying
the Basic Streamer Fly

Male Dace

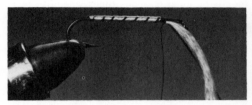

Fig. 117. On a size 10 long-shanked hook, dress a tapered, cream floss body. Rib the body with medium-narrow flat gold tinsel.

Fig. 118. Tie in a throat hackle from a small bunch of orange hackle fibers. Here again, you'll probably find the operation easier if you temporarily invert the hook in the vise. The hackle should be equivalent in length to the gape of the hook. Before proceeding, return the hook to its normal position in the vise.

Fig. 119. Match two olive-green and two golden-badger saddle hackles, concave sides facing inward, with the badger hackles on the outside. Trim the hackle butts to proper length so that the overall wing length extends slightly beyond the bend of the hook. Trim the hackle fibers close to the stems, back from the butts where they will be wound down with thread, probably a hair more than ⅛-inch.

Fig. 120. Place a drop of thick cement on the hook shank and firmly tie down the wing hackles on edge, employing the finger-held initial loops described earlier.

Fig. 121. Tie in natural or artificial jungle-cock cheeks on each side, one at a time. The butts of the cheek feathers should be trimmed close to the stem in the area where they'll be tied down. A drop of cement helps hold them in place during the tying-in operations. Finish the head with neat thread wraps and a whip-finish knot. At least three coats of head cement will be required to achieve a smooth, glossy finish. A single coat of black epoxy cement will achieve even better-looking results.

Some Special Techniques

Tip, Tag, Tail & Butt for Salmon Flies

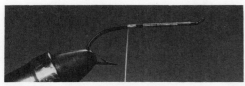

Fig. 122. Wrap a divided thread base as in Fig. 78. The space between the two wrapped areas allows room to make numerous wraps and tie-offs without building up bulky windings.

Fig. 123. Wrap in a piece of fine flat tinsel at the end of the rear base-windings. Two turns of thread is usually enough. Place a drop of thin, fast-drying cement on the wraps and allow to dry momentarily.

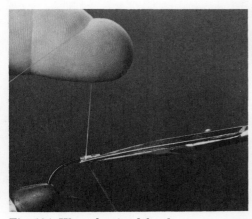

Fig. 124. Wrap the tinsel for three turns rearward and three turns back toward the thread tie-down. Tie off the end of the tinsel with two turns of thread. Cement the winding and snip off the excess tinsel.

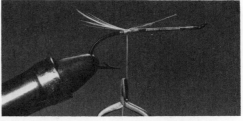

Fig. 125. Tie in the tail material with two or three turns of thread. Cement the windings and snip off the excess material.

Fig. 126. Tie in the tail tag from a short piece of feather, floss or yarn, using the same technique as above.

Fig. 127. Wrap a herl or chenille butt and tie it in as above.

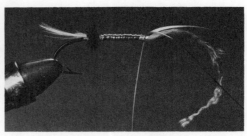

Fig. 128. Tie in body and ribbing materials in the gap between the base sections and complete the fly as in wet-fly methods.

Palmered Hackle

Fig. 129. With a normal thread base, tie in the tail of the fly and finish the operation with a half-hitch knot.

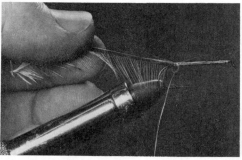

Fig. 130. Strip the fibers from the left side of a neck or saddle hackle, held by the tip, concave side down.

Fig. 131. Tie in the hackle by the tip, then tie in and wrap the body.

Fig. 132. Spiral the hackle up the body and tie it off, finishing with a half-hitch. The thickened, fuzzy effect gives the impression of a caterpillar's body; indeed, the term "palmer" is an old English word for a caterpillar.

Fig. 133. Complete the fly by tying in wings and hackle in accordance with wet- or dry-fly styles. An alternative style of palmer-hackling will be illustrated for the Schneider Stonefly Nymph in Fig. 181 in Chapter 9.

Overbodies

Fig. 134. Tie in the tail at the end of the thread base. Then tie in the overbody material, usually a bunch of hairs or a section of feather.

Fig. 135. Dress and rib the body of the fly.

Fig. 136. Pull the overbody material forward over the top and tie it off. Some patterns call for ribbing to be wrapped after the overbody is completed. Finish the fly according to pattern.

Parachute-Type Dry Flies

Fig. 137. Form a dry-fly thread base and cement it thoroughly. Then, if the pattern employs a bucktail tail and wing-post, cut a bunch of hairs as thick as a matchstick and long enough to form both the tail and the post. Tie in the bucktail, starting at the normal wing position, spiral-wrapping back to the bend and returning to the wing-post. Cement the windings.

Fig. 138. Wrap thread in front of the hair butts until they stand erect. Then solidly thread-wrap the base of the upright butts to stiffen them. Saturate the wrapping with thin cement and let it dry thoroughly.

Fig. 139. Tie in a high-quality gamecock-neck hackle (or hackles) at the base of the post concave side down, tip pointing forward over the eye. Then wrap the thread back to the bend of the hook and tie in the body material.

Fig. 140. Wrap the body and tie it off at the base of the post. *Do not trim* the end of the body material.

Fig. 141. Wrap several turns of the hackle around the post and tie it off in front of the

wing. Wrap the remaining body material in front of the wing to form the thorax. Trim the bucktail, form a neat head and whip-finish.

Weaving Hair Bodies & Hackles

The techniques involved in weaving hair bodies and hackles are relatively complex. It would take a very long chapter to illustrate them properly. But fortunately there is a book on the subject, written and published by one of America's finest tiers, George F. Grant.

His methods are described in *The Art of Weaving Hair Hackles for Trout Flies* (George F. Grant, 1971). The 81-page manual is virtually a must for serious, advanced tiers or students of authentic Western hair flies. (Grant is also author of another interesting book, *Montana Trout Flies*, published in 1972.)

Chapter 9

Flies for Trout, Landlocked Salmon and Arctic Grayling

A NY STUDY of flies and fly fishing must hinge on the feeding traits and habitat preferences peculiar to the major game fishes. Therefore this chapter and the next three will begin with brief descriptions of the more commonly sought fresh- and saltwater game species.

The Fishes

Brown Trout (*Salmo trutta*)

Brown trout, also known as browns, Loch Leven, Von Behr trout or German brown trout, range throughout North and South America, the British Isles and northern Europe. Anadromous brown trout are called sea trout.

In North American waters, browns range in size from a few inches to over ten pounds in weight. They inhabit lakes, streams and rivers. In moving waters they often prefer the slower parts of runs and pools, and they like the shelter of undercut banks, rocks, boulders, stumps and fallen logs. Very large brown trout are noted for their predominantly nocturnal feeding habits. Their primary food organisms include other fishes, aquatic insects and their nymphs, larvae and pupae, crustaceans, mollusks and small terrestrial and aquatic animals.

Because brown trout feed on such a wide variety of naturals, anglers generally use dry flies, wet flies and nymphs in sizes 28 to 2, depending upon local conditions and hatches. Streamers ranging from size 12 to 1/0 may be needed, their sizes and colors again depending on the region's predominant forage fish. Lists of popular regional fly patterns are included in the Appendix.

Nymph or streamer flies usually offer the best hope when the browns can't be observed feeding on nymphs near the tails of runs or on adult insects that have hatched or fallen onto the water's surface. Long leaders with fine tippets are the rule rather than the exception when these fish are feeding on or very close to the surface film. Outsized browns are easier to lure to flies during their fall spawning runs than during the low, clear-water periods of late spring and summer. During late fall, when the biggest browns are relatively concentrated in portions of their spawning streams, they respond readily to large streamers fished near the river bottom on a fast-sinking line and relatively short leader.

Incredible wariness, great fighting ability and a tendency to jump when hooked make brown trout superior fly-rod opponents.

Brook Trout (*Salvelinus fontinalis*)

Brook trout are found in most of the United States and Canada, in South America, Labrador and some other foreign lands. Some of the local names for the species are speckled trout, brookie, squaretail and Eastern brook trout. In its native North American habitat the fish usually averages under a foot long, but some waters contain specimens weighing five pounds and more.

Inhabiting lakes, streams and rivers, brookies show a decided preference for clear, cold waters. In lakes they feed chiefly on underwater organisms but will respond to surface artificials during periods of maximum insect hatching. In streams, they feed on whatever is available at the moment. The largest specimens seem to prefer habitat similar to that inhabited by outsized brown trout. Their main food organisms are small fish, crustaceans, mollusks, aquatic insects, annelids and small terrestrial animals.

Flies in the same range of colors and sizes as used for brown trout are generally effective on brookies. But in lightly fished waters and where their main foods are forage fishes, they do tend to show a preference for brightly colored bucktail and streamer flies. Yellow-and-white and yellow-and-red are two of the more killing color combinations.

In lakes, brookies seem to respond most avidly to streamer or nymph flies fished with fairly fast stripping recoveries alternated with pauses in the retrieve. Dry flies and nymphs are usually fished as indicated by the type of food organism represented. In streams, a broadside drift of the fly, followed by a stripping retrieve, is usually as deadly on brookies as on browns and rainbows.

Brook trout are strong, tenacious fighters, and the larger ones are capable of short, powerful runs. They're excellent table fish when taken from most of their native waters.

Cutthroat Trout *(Salmo clarki)*

The range of the cutthroat trout covers most of the western U.S. and Canada as well as southern Alaska. There are numerous strains of cutthroat, some highly insectivorous in their feeding habits, others relatively piscivorous. Sea-run cutthroats rank among the West Coast's sportiest fly-rod game, despite the fact that they rarely exceed 19 inches in length.

Montana black-spotted and another strain known to biologists as Eastern-Slope cutthroats are renowned for spectacular surface-feeding binges that endear them to dry-fly buffs during heavy mayfly and caddis hatches and mating flights.

Because of the cutthroat's tendency to hybridize with other trout species and because of the great number of cutthroat strains, their favored habitats are quite varied. In lakes, cutthroats can usually be caught by methods that would provoke strikes from rainbow or brook trout, although they're rarely as finicky as either browns or rainbows. Much the same is true of stream-bound cutthroats, which are gullible by comparison with brown trout.

Except for the sea-run strains, most cutthroats are relatively weak, unspectacular fighters. They fight about like Arctic grayling but without the jumps. Most cutthroat trout are exceptional table fish, however. Many Western anglers consider them the finest eating of all the region's freshwater game fish.

Special fly patterns are seldom, if ever, required to tease cutthroats into action. Simple, brightly colored bucktail or palmer-hackled wet flies provide consistent results on sea-run fish during their fall migrations upstream. Lake- and stream-bound cutthroats respond to virtually any nymph or dry fly that would interest a rainbow trout of the same region. The

Trout nymphs, wet flies and dry flies.
Row 1 (top to bottom): PKCK, Hutch's Dam-
selfly Nymph, March Brown Nymph, Big Ugly
Nymph, Stonefly.

Row 2: Bread Crumb, Breadcrust, Omnibus
Nymph (Gerlach).

Row 3: Kahl's Gray Sedge, Hendrickson Dun,
Hatch Matcher, Flot-n-Fool, Andrie Damselfly.

Trout, bass, salmon and steelhead streamers and bugs.

Row 1 (top to bottom): Little Brown Trout Streamer, Blue Charm, Skunk, Chappie Streamer, Kokanee (Engle), Pilkey's Mouse, Calcasieu Pig Boat.

Row 2, center: Male Dace Streamer, Colonel Bates Streamer, Montreal Streamer, Brown Bomber, Snollygoster, Hornberg Special (Eastern version).

Row 3: Dobson, Black Knight, Herb Johnson Special, Marabou Muddler (white), Louisiana Mickey Finn, Gray/Yellow-Striped Bass Bug.

Saltwater flies.

Row 1 (top to bottom): Stu Apte Tarpon Fly, Kukonen Bluefish Bucktail, Brooks Honey Blonde, Cockroach Tarpon Fly, Beer Belly (yarn variation), Bristle Back.

Row 2 (single fly top middle): Brine Shrimp.

Row 3: Phillips Pink Shrimp, Bonefish Fly (Keane), Roostertail, Beer Belly, Lefty's All-Purpose Deceiver, Whitney rolling and shooting fly (big-game version).

A few freshwater insects. At top left, two caddis cases of cemented pebbles. At top right, an adult mayfly spinner, its life cycle nearly complete. At bottom left, a three-tailed mayfly nymph, and at bottom right, two stonefly nymphs.

Bucktail Coachman, in both wet and dry versions, is one of the most regular producers over the cutthroat's entire range.

Rainbow Trout *(Salmo gairdneri)*

Although originally native to Western coastal streams, the rainbow trout today is distributed throughout North America, South America, Europe and New Zealand. The sea-run rainbow trout—the steelhead or steelhead trout—is one of the world's premier fly-rod species as is a fast-growing freshwater strain of rainbow known as the Kamloops trout. Although the average weight for steelheads is probably somewhere around 6 pounds and is somewhat less for Kamloops trout, both have been known to exceed 30 pounds.

In lakes, rainbows often feed actively on forage fish where they're abundant. Other favored foods include crustaceans, aquatic insects, mollusks and annelids. Streambound rainbow trout often prefer haunts somewhat faster than those of brown trout—for example, to the sides and in front of boulders, or along edges of the main flow of current, swift runs, riffles and broken-water rapids. In freshwater, steelheads tend to travel nocturnally and on dark days, then hold, or rest, behind large rocks or boulders at the tops of rapids and in long runs of moderate speed. During the periods of lowest water, summer-run steelies sometimes rest in surprisingly shallow, well-oxygenated riffles. Winter-run steelheads most often are located following age-old travel routes very close to the river bottom. As a rule, the colder the water temperature is during the winter, the more likely it is that steelheads will rest in deep pools and slow-moving runs.

Angling techniques for rainbow trout closely parallel those commonly effective for browns, cutthroats and brookies in both lakes and streams. Dry flies range from size 28 to 6, nymphs from size 18 to 2, and bucktails and streamers from size 12 to 2/0, depending on the predominant food organisms in a given piece of water.

It is debatable if even the high-jumping Atlantic salmon surpasses the sporting quality of a prime, fresh-run summer steelhead. Pound for pound, the rainbow trout has no battling peers in freshwater lakes and streams. It is surpassed in wariness only by brown trout and largemouth bass.

Landlocked Salmon *(Salmo salar sebago)*

On the North American Continent, these superbly fly-responsive fighting fish are found mostly in New England, Labrador, Newfoundland and the Maritime Provinces. They are also distributed through parts of South America, Europe, the British Isles and the Soviet Union. Although the average size of the landlocked salmon is probably under three pounds, it isn't too uncommon to hook a 10-pounder in highly productive salmon waters.

Cold lakes are the fish's primary habitat. Where forage fishes are abundant, the salmon tend to follow bait schools. In lakes where their primary foods are aquatic insects and crustaceans, the fish are more likely to be near submerged weed beds or in other locations associated with such prey.

Angling methods for landlocked salmon vary seasonally and regionally, depending largely on the abundance and relative availability of food organisms. In the Northeastern states and provinces, many anglers who seek the salmon in early spring prefer to troll streamers rapidly along shorelines and near inlet-stream mouths where bait fish are schooled. Landlocks tend to move to deeper waters when the shallows warm in late spring and summer.

On lakes experiencing substantial hatches of mayflies, caddis flies and chironomids, dry-fly fishing for landlocked salmon can provide stupendous action. A high-jumping, hard-running salmon hooked on a dry fly affixed to a 6X tippet is more than a handful, testing even the veteran flyrodder to the utmost.

Effective streamer patterns are numerous and varied, ranging from black through very bright combinations of colors. Most of them suggest primary forage fish of certain lakes or lake regions. Dry flies emulating existing hatches are normally quite killing when the fish are feeding on floating naturals. The same holds true for nymphs, sometimes used when the fish are gobbling up emerging nymphs.

Landlocked salmon are sensational jumpers. They're also capable of very long, high-speed runs that melt backing line off a fly reel at a frightening rate. And they're excellent table fare.

Arctic Grayling
(Thymallus Arcticus)

Arctic grayling are found in parts of Montana and Wyoming, in Alaska, the Yukon, the Northwest Territories and the northern parts of British Columbia, Alberta, Saskatchewan and Manitoba. They inhabit cold, clear lakes and streams. Throughout their range, they average about 10 inches in length. But trophy-class grayling up to about five pounds are sometimes found in the northernmost, remote waters.

These fish subsist primarily on aquatic insects, though they have been observed consuming annelids, shrimps and eggs deposited by others of their species. In lakes, grayling are commonly found near inlet or outlet streams and in gravelly or rocky shallows where aquatic insects abound. Large, stream-inhabiting grayling usually feed and hold in locations similar to those favored by brown trout. The smaller ones are likely to be hooked virtually anywhere in a stream.

Fly patterns and sizes, as well as angling techniques, are about the same as for brown trout. If you want to catch large grayling, exercise caution in your approach and care in your casting delivery. A sloppily presented dry fly isn't likely to fool a trophy-sized grayling any more than a hefty brown or rainbow trout.

The grayling is an exceptionally beautiful fish with a high, sail-like, colorfully marked dorsal fin. It jumps exceedingly well when hooked but is a relatively weak fighter, more or less comparable to the cutthroat trout. It is not tenacious and subdues quickly under steady pressure from the rod.

Lake Trout
(Cristivomer namaycush)

The lake trout's range extends from the Northwestern U.S. and Canada across the northern provinces and territories down into New England. Large lakers run to well over 40 pounds, but the average fish probably weighs less than five pounds.

Also known as Mackinaw trout, togue and gray trout, lakers prey mostly on other fishes. But they do feed periodically on insects at the surface and when this happens they can be taken readily on dry flies. Their primary habitat is in large, deep, cold, clear lakes, although at times they are found in streams where lakes form parts of river systems.

Although lakers spend most of their time in waters where conventional casting and retrieving methods are impractical, they are readily caught on bright streamer flies for a short time following spring ice-out and again late in the fall when they're spawning in the shallows. Slow trolling or a slow, stripping recovery usually will prove to be the most effective technique. It often pays to vary the speed of the retrieve or trolling speed considerably.

Lake trout are determined but unspectacular fighters. The outcome of a battle with a fly-hooked laker is usually predictable, if the fish is solidly hooked and played with reasonable competence. Depending on the waters, the season and the size of the fish (outsized lakers are sometimes very oily), lake trout are fair to excellent table fare. They're great when smoked with alder or hickory smoke after a proper curing in salt brine. Dry-curing with coarse salt, celery salt, garlic salt and brown sugar, prior to the smoking, provides a delightful variation.

The Flies

Midges (Order: Diptera)

Midges (Fig. 142) are aquatic insects that undergo complete metamorphosis. Larvae of this tremendously important fish food are cylindrical. They're found in mud and debris at the bottoms of lakes and in the slower-moving parts of streams and rivers. Pupae of the midges are also cylindrical but somewhat enlarged in the thoracic region and head. Filament-like gills at the head readily distinguish pupae from larvae.

Adults hatch periodically throughout the year, including the late fall and winter months, a characteristic that has given them the name "snow fly" in some regions. During hatching, the larvae usually lash their tail ends violently. Once hatched, adult midges often rest motionless on the surface until their wings have dried. Clouds of midges can be observed hovering near shore-line bushes close to the water's surface on lakes and streams. Pupal and adult midges are easy prey for sharp-eyed, fast-moving fish.

When dressing artificials to resemble midge pupae, the tier must consider important anatomical characteristics, the slim, cylindrical body and the filamentous gills at the head. Adult midges are tailless, and they hold their wings flat over their bodies when at rest. They ride very low in the surface film, which suggests the use of dry flies without hackles or with the hackle fibers trimmed close to the shank under the hook.

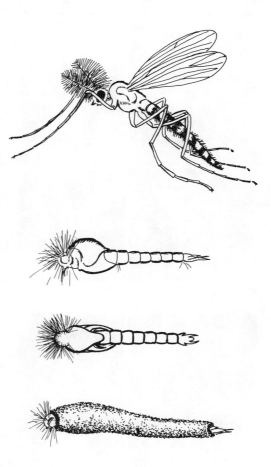

Fig. 142. The three stages of the midge: cased larva, pupa, and adult.

Tying and Fishing a Midge Pupa

Pattern: PKCK (Powell-Kilburn Chironomid Killer)

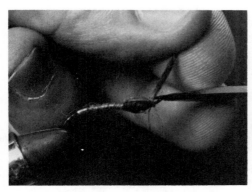

Fig. 143. On a wet-fly hook ranging in size from 16 to 8, wrap a wet-fly thread base. Wrap a flat silver-tinsel tip and a slim, round body of dull green wool. Rib the body with a stripped peacock eye quill.

Fig. 146. When using a midge pupa on lakes, look for cruising fish. Cast well ahead of working fish on a long, fine leader. Fish with a dead-drift if there's a riffle. If not, employ a dead-slow hand-twist retrieve or gentle rod-tip twitches when you figure the fish can see your fly.

Tying and Fishing a Midge Pupa

Pattern: Gray/Cream Midge Pupa

Fig. 144. Dress a thorax of dark brown yarn with an overbody of light brown turkey-wing feather section.

Fig. 147. On a size 20 or smaller fine-wire hook, wrap a wet-fly base with dark gray or black thread. Dub a slender, well-tapered body of cream-colored fur. Then tie in underneath the hook a few soft wisps of cream-colored hackle to suggest legs.

Fig. 145. Affix a short section of emu herl to protrude on each side of the head. Finish the head with a whip-finish knot. Apply two or three coats of head cement, allowing each coat to dry thoroughly before applying the next.

Fig. 148. Dub a well-enlarged thorax out of dark gray fur and finish the head in the usual fashion. This basic configuration, varied in color to suit regional needs, is excellent to suggest the tiniest midge pupae. Minuscule midges are common on many important trout streams and lakes throughout the United States. This tie, one of my favorites, resembles a form used by a number of Eastern and Midwestern anglers. There isn't much pattern standardization in midges as among the highly imitative mayfly dressings. Size is usually as critical as color in determining their effectiveness. If you fish where there are frequent midge hatches, it pays to carry a portable tying kit in your car for on-the-spot tying of any desired size.

Tying and Fishing a Midge Adult

Pattern: Godfrey Brown Ant

Fig. 149. On a size 14 fine-wire hook, wrap a wet-fly base with tan or brown thread. Tie in a very short, sparse tail of brown calf-tail hairs and wrap a thin, round body of brown floss, nylon thread or polypropylene yarn.

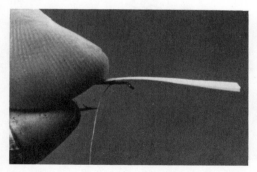

Fig. 150. Tie on a flat wing of gray mallard-primary feather, as shown. Then bend it back, tie it down, and trim it round at tip and the same length as the body (see Fig. 151).

Fig. 151. Wrap three turns of a stiff, glossy brown gamecock-neck hackle. Trim the underside of the hackle as shown in Fig. 152. Finish the head with a few thread wraps, a whip-finish knot and a couple of coats of cement. Fish the midge adult on lakes or streams the same way as a midge pupa but on the surface. Trout tend to sip these flies very delicately, sometimes with a dimpling rise that scarcely disturbs the surface.

Fig. 152. Clipping the midge hackle.

Mosquitoes (Order: Diptera)

The life cycle of the mosquito (Fig. 153) closely parallels that of the midge. The mosquito pupa is another with a pronounced thoracic enlargement. The adult rides a bit higher on the surface than a midge so trimming the underpart of the hackle may not be to your advantage.

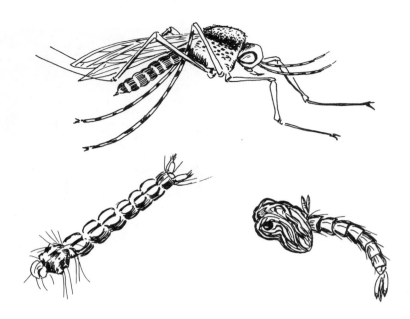

Fig. 153. Mosquito larva, pupa, and adult.

Tying and Fishing a Mosquito Pupa

Pattern: Mosquito Larva

Fig. 155. Tie in a few badger-hair tips beneath the hook to form a short beard. Wrap a fairly large head of medium-gray emu herl. Finish the head with a whip-finish knot and cement it. Fish it the same way as a midge pupa on lakes or streams. This type of fly is sometimes very deadly when fished deeply, near a lake or stream bottom on a sinking fly line. Originated by the late Terry Bryant, a Western professional tier, the pattern is useful anywhere there are mosquitoes.

Fig. 154. On a size 12 wet-fly hook, wrap a gray or black wet-fly thread base and wrap a body consisting of one dark and one light moose mane quill, or a stripped eyed peacock quill.

Tying and Fishing a Mosquito Adult

Pattern: Allen Mosquito

Fig. 156. On a size 14 fine-wire hook, wrap a gray or black wet-fly thread base. Tie in a very short tail of finely speckled mallard-breast feather fibers. Wrap a well-tapered body using the thin, membranous quill stripped from the face of a mallard primary's stem. Before wrapping, soak the quill membrane in tepid water.

Fig. 157. Tie in two slightly divided flat wings from grizzly hackle tips. Lightly wind a criss-cross between the wings so they'll remain divided during fishing.

Fig. 158 (next column). Add three or four turns of a high-quality grizzly gamecock-neck hackle and finish the head in the usual manner. On both lakes and streams, fish this mosquito like an adult midge imitation. It's a good fly virtually everywhere.

Fig. 158

Tying and Fishing a Crane-Fly Adult

Pattern: Orange Crane Fly

Although crane flies (Tipulidae) don't bite, they look like large, very long-legged mosquitoes; they belong to the same order and seek the same kind of habitat. But a crane-fly imitation has longer hackles than a mosquito, plus a bigger thorax and different wing configuration.

Fig. 159. On a size 8, 3X fine-wire hook, wrap a dry-fly thread base. Tie in two dark grizzly gamecock hackle tips, concave sides out, then divide them laterally with criss-crossed thread wraps so the wings lie flat, horizontal to the shank in spent-wing fashion. Place a drop of cement on the windings.

Fig. 160. Tie in a cree-variant or ginger-dyed grizzly hackle in standard fashion by the butt between the wings. The radius of the hackle fibers should be two or three sizes over normal for the hook.

Fig. 162. Wrap three or four turns of the hackle behind and in front of the wings and finish the head in the normal way.

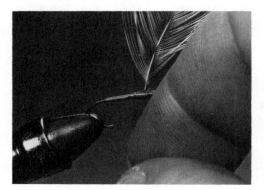

Fig. 161. Form a well-tapered body out of true orange floss or polypropylene. Wrap a very bulbous thorax with the body material.

The long-legged adult crane fly in Fig. 163 clarifies the need for an oversized hackle radius. The insect's life cycle more or less parallels that of midges and mosquitoes. Crane flies hatch sporadically throughout the season from swampy areas of lakes and slow-moving parts of streams, usually near sundown. When they're hatching in numbers the fish take them in avidly. The artificial is usually fished on a floating fly line with a long, fine leader. Occasional rod-tip

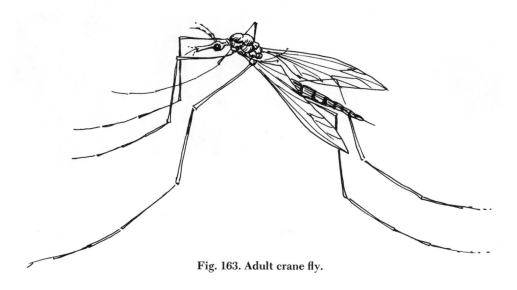

Fig. 163. Adult crane fly.

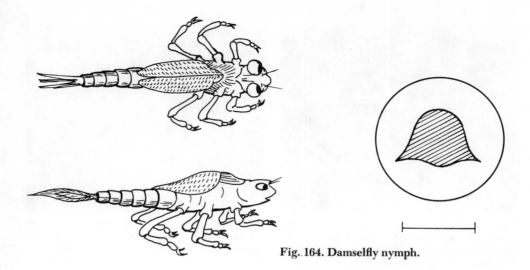

Fig. 164. Damselfly nymph.

twitches add enticement, especially when the naturals are whirling erratically in the air in their fascinating reproductive dance. Crane flies are widely distributed in both the East and West.

Damselflies (Order: Odonata)

Damselflies, like their cousins the dragonflies, undergo an incomplete metamorphic development. The nymphs (Fig. 164) are roundish, slender-bodied, inch-long creatures distinguished by the presence of three, paddlelike tracheal gills at the posterior end of the abdomen.

Adults always lay their eggs in aquatic plant tissue, unlike dragonflies which sometimes ovate on the water's surface. Whereas dragonflies prefer still waters, damselfly nymphs are sometimes found in moderate current as well as in still-water lakes and ponds.

In lake or stream, damselfly nymphs usually cling to or clamber about on aquatic plants. The adults are weak in flight. It's quite easy for a sharp-eyed, fast-moving game fish to pick them out of the air as they hover over the surface. At rest, they hold their glassy wings folded over their backs.

The heaviest hatches usually occur in the spring. Damselfly nymphs and adults provide an important source of food for game fish, particularly in rich, hard-water lakes where they are especially abundant.

Tying and Fishing a Damselfly Nymph

Pattern: Gerlach's Damselfly Nymph

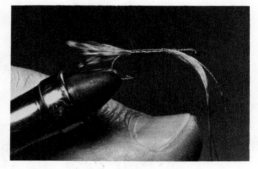

Fig. 165. On a size 10, 3XL hook, wrap a wet-fly thread base. Tie in three long cree-variant hackle tips on edge to form a tail of the same length as the body, or slightly shorter. Wrap a body of natural raffia grass or very pale tan floss and rib it with dark tan thread.

Fig. 166. Tie in a 3/16-inch width of oak-colored turkey-wing feather so that a 1/4-inch tip extends back over the body to form emergent wing stubs. Do not trim the butt ends; they'll be used to form the wing case later.

Fig. 168. Pull the spread hackle over the thorax and tie it down. Pull the turkey feather over the legs and thorax and tie it down trimming off the excess. Finish the head with a whip-finish knot and cement.

Fig. 167. Gently spread the fibers of a cree-variant hackle and tie it in by the tip. Do not trim the stem. The remainder will be used to form the nymph's legs after the thorax is wrapped. Wrap the thorax of dark tan chenille.

In lakes, look for damselfly nymphs wriggling toward the surface to hatch (Fig. 169), and also watch for nymphing fish. Use a sinking or sinking-tip fly line with a long, fine leader and an erratic hand-twist or stripping recovery. Try to suggest a nymph's rising movements from the lake bottom prior to hatching. A few jiggling lifts of the rod tip, interspersed with the regular retrieve motions, will probably enhance the effectiveness of the retrieve. Originated by the author in 1969, this fly is primarily useful in lakes, ponds and river backwaters and has national application as a design prototype.

Fig. 169. Emerging damselfly nymph.

Tying and Fishing a Damselfly Adult

Pattern: Andrie Damselfly

Fig. 170. On a size 10, 3XL or 4XL hook, tie a black wet-fly thread base. Tie in a ⅜-inch tail made with four pieces of peacock herl, trimmed at the ends.

Fig. 171. Tie in and wrap three or four turns of quality grizzly hackle immediately in front of the tail. Wrap a thin, round, blue floss body. Rib it with fine flat silver tinsel.

Fig. 172. Tie in two pairs of medium blue-dun hackles on edge, in splayed-V fashion to form two divided wings, concave sides of each pair facing out.

Fig. 173. Wrap three or four turns of grizzly neck hackle immediately in front of the wings. Wrap a large head of peacock herl and finish it in the usual way. Fish this fly on a floating line and long leader after a damselfly hatch is well advanced and numerous adults have fallen to the surface. Occasional rod-tip twitches that gently rock the fly on the surface film sometimes excite fish into striking. This pattern is useful mostly on lakes for trout and bass.

Dragonflies (Order: Odonata)

Dragonflies undergo incomplete metamorphosis. The nymphs (Fig. 174) can be identified by their relatively large size, hinged hooks on the lower mouth parts and distinctive, well-segmented abdomens. They vary in color from pale olive to brownish-black and vary from half an inch to two inches in length.

Adults of the species are characterized by powerful, rapid flight and wings that remain rigidly extended to the sides when at rest. Dragonflies are also known as "darning needles" in some regions.

Emergence begins in the spring and continues sporadically throughout summer and fall. Dragonfly nymphs are usually found sprawled or crawling slowly along the weeds, silt and litter at the bottoms of lakes and ponds. They are an important

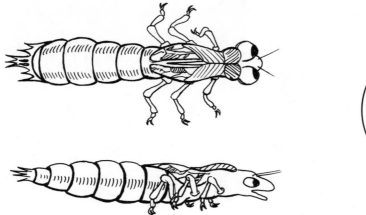
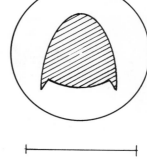

Fig. 174. Dragonfly nymph.

food item for trouts, basses and certain panfish. I've noted that dragonfly nymphs in my nymph aquarium undergo a dramatic color change prior to hatching. Most of them crawl toward the surface on water plants, turning a peculiar, almost translucent light green several hours before hatching. Experiments with very light green artificial nymphs during periods of maximum hatching activity are incomplete and inconclusive at this writing, but there are indications that such flies can be effective on those occasions.

Other characteristics to be considered include the ovate configuration of the abdomen and the large head of the nymph. Mobility of the hackle or leg materials is not as important as in damselfly and mayfly nymphs, at least when the artificials are being fished with fast stripping recoveries. The natural nymphs frequently dart about rapidly by forcing water through their tracheal chambers. However, when an angler employs slow retrieves to suggest an ambling insect, relatively mobile legs are an asset.

Tying and Fishing a Dragonfly Nymph

Pattern: Dragonfly Nymph

Fig. 175. On a size 6, 3XL hook, tie a wet-fly thread base. Tie in a short, stiff tail from a bunch of greenish-brown pheasant-rump feather fibers. Wrap a large, tapered body out of insect-green or olive-green chenille.

Fig. 176. Tie in a medium-sized pheasant-rump feather by the tip and wrap two turns, hackle fashion, finishing the head by the conventional method.

Fish a dragonfly nymph near the lake or stream bottom on a sinking line. Try both stripping and hand-twisting recoveries to suggest crawling and darting movements (Fig. 177). Game fish usually take these nymphs with great determination. Overly fine tippets are not recommended, and four-pound test is considered a minimum for trout. The flight of the dragonfly is so rapid that the adult is rarely taken by most game fish unless it has fallen to the surface of the water. Floating versions are not really practical for casting on light trout rods. Hair-bodied bass bugs with the general configuration of the dragonfly are practical for bass, pike and muskie fishing.

Dragonfly nymphs of this type are not yet in broad general use except in certain lake regions where the natural nymphs constitute a significant food for game fish. The pattern enjoys tremendous popularity in the Northwestern states, both as a trolling fly and for casting on sinking lines. The natural nymph that it suggests, most probably *Anax junius*, ranges from one to two inches in length.

It is most commonly dressed on a size 6 hook ranging in length from 2XL to 4XL. Although insect-green is by far the most popular body shade, some tiers vary the color, using medium and dark olive, as well as tan through dark brown.

References in angling literature to the tying and fishing of dragonfly nymphs are rare. Ernest Schwiebert's new book, *Nymphs* (Winchester Press, N.Y., 1973) contains excellent illustrations and descriptions of the more important Anisoptera, as well as some good-looking patterns with which to imitate them.

Stoneflies (Order: Plecoptera)

Stoneflies (Fig. 178) are aquatic insects that undergo an incomplete metamorphosis. The nymph of this stream-bound insect can be identified by its two short, bristlelike tails and by its clawed feet with which it clings to rocks. The size of the nymph varies up to two inches long for some species. Usually found clinging to the undersides of rocks, stonefly nymphs vary in color from mottled yellow and black to yellowish-orange to brownish-black.

Adult stoneflies are distinguished by their clumsy, wandering flight patterns and their strongly veined wings, held flat on their backs when at rest. Stream-bound game fish usually take in both the nymphs and the adults eagerly.

Fig. 177. Fishing the dragonfly nymph.

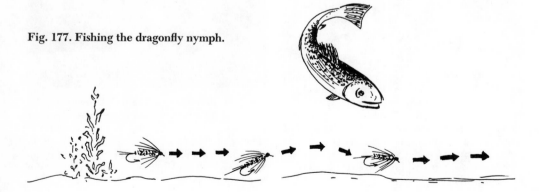

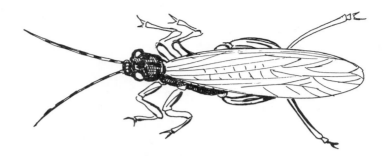

Fig. 178. Stonefly nymph and adult (different species).

Tying and Fishing a Stonefly Nymph

Pattern: Schneider Stonefly Nymph

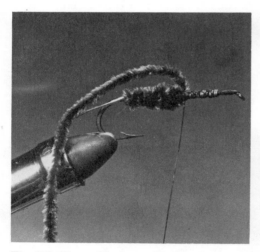

Fig. 180. Strip the fibers from one side of a black saddle hackle. Tie it in by the tip. Wrap a large thorax out of yellow or true-orange chenille.

Fig. 179. Wrap a black wet-fly thread base on a size 4, 4XL hook. Tie in a short, divided, V-shaped tail from two fibers taken from the leading edge of a gray Canada-goose primary. Wrap a fully tapered body out of large-sized dark brown chenille. Allow plenty of room for a long thorax. Do not cut off the remaining brown chenille; it will be used over the thorax as a wing case.

Fig. 181. Palmer-wrap the hackle over the thorax. Pull the piece of dark brown chenille over the top of the thorax and hackle, then tie it down at the head to form a wing case. Trim all material butts and wrap a large, smooth head, finishing with a whip-knot and several coats of head cement.

Fig. 182. Weighting the stonefly nymph.

Fish this nymph on an extra-fast- or fast-sinking fly line and as short a leader as possible—right down near the stream bed. Occasionally impart action to it during the drift and recovery, employing rod-tip twitches and short stripping recoveries. When fishing heavy current, it's sometimes advisable to weight this nymph with lead wire, or to wrap the leader knots with fine lead wire to promote a deep run of the fly (Fig. 182). Stoneflies are rarely found in lakes, except in rocky, fast-moving inlet or outlet streams. This pattern is an easy-to-tie prototype that can be varied in size and color to suit virtually any regional need. Originated by the late Jack B. Schneider, it's suggestive, but not imitative, of several large stonefly nymphs, including *Acroneuria nigrata*, a species found in both the East and West.

Tying and Fishing a Stonefly Adult

Pattern: Dark Stonefly (wet version)

Fig. 183. On a size 6 or 4 long-shanked hook, wrap a brown or black wet-fly thread base. Tie the tail out of a small bunch of brown-mottled turkey-wing feathers. Wrap a full, well-tapered body from tangerine-orange synthetic yarn. Rib it with gray buttonhole twist.

Fig. 184. Wrap six or eight turns with a dark, stiff-fibered furnace saddle hackle. Over this, tie in a long bucktail wing. Use natural dun-colored bucktail dyed with coffee-brown Clairol hair dye. Wrap a large black head. You may want to paint a hot orange band on top of the head adjacent to the wing butts.

Try to drift this fly within a few inches of overhanging stream banks and bushes where hatched-out adults fall or are blown into the water (Fig. 185). To locate a fish, pinch a natural between your fingers so it can't fly and drift it downstream next to the bank. Watch for the insect to disappear in a heavy swirl. In rainbow-trout waters, look for rises near the edge of fast current, in front of large boulders, at the bases of riffles and the tails of pools. Other good stonefly patterns are included in Chapter 14. This tie comes from the creative fingers of noted Oregon professional E. H. "Polly" Rosborough. It was developed for Oregon waters, but is useful wherever large, dark stoneflies abound.

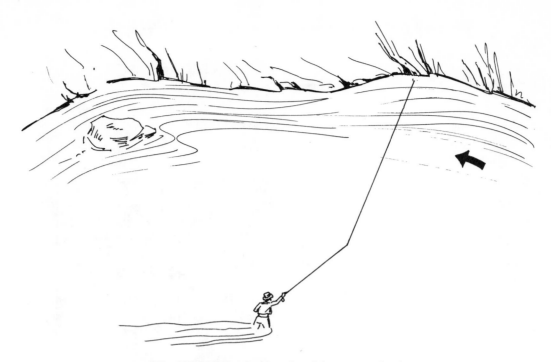

Fig. 185. Fishing the stonefly adult next to a bank.

Fig. 186. Caddisfly cased pupa and adult.

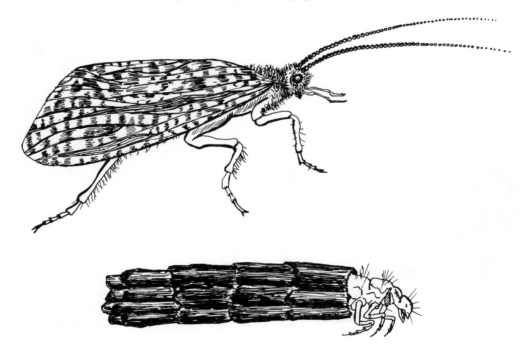

Caddis Flies (Order: Trichoptera)

Caddis flies (Fig. 186), including pupae and larvae, are eagerly sought by a wide variety of lake and stream fish. The metamorphosis from larva to pupa parallels that of the midges and mosquitoes. But unlike the dipterous insects, caddis-fly larvae build traveling "houses"—cylindrical cases—around their wormlike bodies. The cases are usually constructed of sand, sticks, pieces of plant stems and other underwater rubble. Some species weave net-like cocoons similar to those fashioned by silk worms.

The adults are nocturnal, somber-colored insects that fly erratically and hold their wings tented over their backs when at rest. Caddis-fly adults have no tails but possess long antennae that sometimes give the observer the impression of a mayfly flying backwards.

The creative fly dresser should bear in mind the high, tent-shaped wings and tailless body of the adult and the leggy, disorganized appearance of the pupa emerging from the case at hatching time. Game fish prey on all three physical forms of caddis. The famous Strawman Nymph, a standard pattern, is one of the most effective flies for suggesting certain caddis-fly larvae. It consists primarily of gray deer-body hair loosely spun on a hook and ribbed with thread (usually yellow or greenish-yellow). The hair is roughly trimmed to tubular shape.

Tying and Fishing
a Caddis-Fly Pupa (emerger)

Pattern: Big Ugly Nymph

Fig. 187. With dark brown thread, wrap a wet-fly base on a size 6, 3XL hook. The original dressing calls for a woven body of dark brown

wool on top, dark olive chenille underneath, woven with six-pound-test clear monofilament. An easier method shown here is to first tie in three strands of dark brown yarn and a piece of monofilament. Then, wrap a full body of dark olive chenille.

Fig. 188. When the chenille is wrapped, pull the three strands of yarn over the top to form an overbody and rib it with the monofilament. This body lacks the enticing segmentation of the original tie but is effective and can be fashioned by virtually any tier of limited skill. Sometimes a rusty-orange dubbed-fur tip is added before the body is wrapped. The tip suggests the transparent part of the pupal case from which the adult insect has partially withdrawn its abdomen.

Fig. 189. The trimmed hackle legs of the original dressing are omitted from this simplified version, but the original is included in Chapter 14. Now, tie in six brown hen- or pheasant-tail fibers as a long beard underneath the hook. They should be about the same length as the body.

Fig. 190. Trimmed, lacquered sections of dark gray goose primary are tied in on each side of the hook to simulate wing cases.

Fig. 191. Fish the Big Ugly Nymph on a floating line and long leader from an anchored boat when pupae are rising to hatch and the fish are taking them in just beneath the surface. A light breeze will permit use of the dead-drift technique and with the aid of Polaroid glasses, the strike can be observed as a flash just below the surface. When no hatching is evident, try a mooching troll or long, slow, stripping recoveries in lakes. For nymphs suggesting stream-bound caddis species, fish pupa imitators with either floating or sinking-tip lines, attempting to duplicate the rising movements of naturals toward the surface during periods of hatching.

The Big Ugly Nymph, originated in 1963 by Jim Kilburn of Vancouver, B.C., is in my opinion one of the more significant nymph innovations of recent years. It's an almost ideal design prototype to suggest the emergent stage. The wings, lying along the body, and the long, tufted legs are adaptable to the imitation of caddis pupae throughout North America simply by changing hook size and general coloration to match a regionally prevalent natural.

One of the fascinating aspects of studying artificial fly patterns is that, occasionally, you chance upon nearly simultaneous and identical design efforts from widely separated regions. It is interesting to note that Swisher and Richards show a similarly configured caddis pupa in their book *Selective Trout,* as well as some other caddis nymphs strikingly similar in design to that popular Western lake pattern, the Beaverpelt Nymph described in Chapter 14.

What these parallel creative developments prove, to me at least, is that, finally, more fly fishermen in this country are starting to closely observe the shapes and behavior of the aquatic insects that abound in their regions. The angler-tiers are developing rapidly into creative fly fishermen. I think that is why one sees fewer and fewer so-called standard patterns on regional lists as the years go by.

Tying and Fishing a Caddis-Fly Adult
(newly emerged)

Pattern: Tom Thumb

Fig. 192 (next column). On an extra-fine-wire dry-fly hook ranging from size 12 to 6, wrap a wet-fly thread base and cement the wraps. Starting about ⅛-inch behind the eye, tie down a matchstick-sized bunch of dark deer-body hair by the butts, allowing the tip ends to form a tail about the same length as the body.

Fig. 192.

Fig. 193. Thoroughly cement the surface of the wrapped-down hairs. Then wrap in by the butts a similar but longer bunch of deer-body hairs toward the tail. Return-wrap the thread to the head and pull the tip ends forward, tying them down at the head.

Fig. 194. Pull the hair ends upright and support them with thread wraps in front to form a single wing, tilted slightly forward. This unusual tie represents a just-hatched caddis fly that's extended its wings upward and forward after departing the casing. Normally, the pattern is most effective on lakes and streams during the earliest stages of a hatch.

**Tying and Fishing a Caddis-Fly Adult
(downing phase)**

Pattern: Salmon Candy

Fig. 195. On a size 8 dry-fly hook, wrap an olive wet-fly thread base. Wrap a moderately
large, tapered body out of medium-dark olive
wool or polypropylene yarn.

Fig. 197.

Fig. 196. After hackling with one brown and
one grizzly gamecock-neck hackle of dry-fly
quality, tie a bunch of dark gray deer-body
hair over the back of the fly for a wing.

Fig. 197 (next column). Clip the butts of the
bucktail to form a small head. Finish the tie-
down wraps with a whip-finish knot and a
couple of coats of head cement. Dry flies of
this basic configuration are used to suggest
adult caddis flies during the later stages of a
hatch—while they're scurrying around on the
surface waiting for their wings to dry. In sizes
from 16 to 6, such flies can be employed effectively on both lakes and streams. This pattern
was originated by Lloyd Frese, Bend, Oregon,
for landlocked salmon on famed Hosmer Lake.

Mayflies (Order: Ephemeroptera)

Mayflies undergo a two-stage, incomplete metamorphosis somewhat similar
to that of stoneflies, damselflies and dragonflies. The nymphs (Fig. 198) have two or
three tails and slim roundish or flatish
bodies. They're found in a wide variety of
lake and stream habitats, from rocky riffles
to mud bottoms. In the adult stage the insect has long tails jutting up from a body
that curves upward at the rear.

Adult mayflies shed their skins once between hatching and the reproductive act.
The newly hatched mayfly "dun" is usually
more somber colored and has shorter tails
than the glassy-winged "spinner" stage.
Mayfly duns are usually observed floating
with upraised wings on lakes and streams,
and flying from the water toward the
shorelines. Spinner mayflies are normally
seen flying from the shore toward the water or lying dead on the surface with wings
"spent"—flat—following mating, egg laying
and death.

Major mayfly hatches occur from late
spring through fall across North America.

There are hundreds of species of these ubiquitous insects, but less than a dozen patterns of artificials are needed for fishing in most regions.

For fly-tying purposes, significant physical features include the length of the tails; the body, leg and wing colors; the overall length; and the developmental stage to be imitated. Some mayfly adults need to be simulated on hooks as tiny as size 28; others are as large as some of the biggest caddis flies. You'll have to be guided by the hatches in a given locale. Trout fishermen should bear in mind that mayfly nymphs have gills along the sides of their abdominal surfaces which may influence the choice of materials for bodies and ribbings. (See some of the nymph dressings in Schwiebert's book *Nymphs).*

The degree of naturalistic detail exhibited by an artificial mayfly nymph varies dramatically from tier to tier. Before it emerges, a mayfly nymph is a rather nondescript creature, and some expert tiers feel that fur dubbing wrapped loosely on the hook and picked out with a needle at the thorax is more than sufficient. Others create monuments to detail and fly-tying art. This book, while avoiding both extremes, illustrates patterns that virtually any angler can dress quickly and fish effectively. One very simple and almost universally popular method of tying mayfly nymphs is described in connection with the Martinez Black in Chapter 8. Other styles, some even simpler, others more complex, are to be found in the dressings in Chapter 14.

Fig. 198. Mayfly nymph.

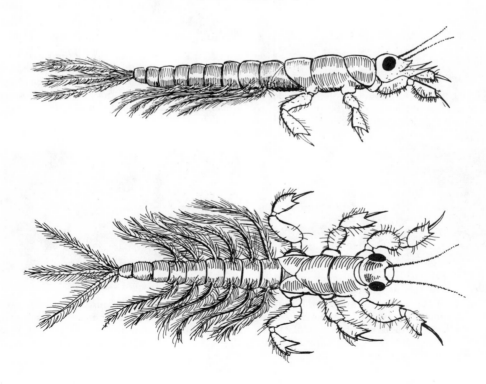

Tying and Fishing a Mayfly Nymph
(emergent phase)

Pattern: Omnibus Nymph

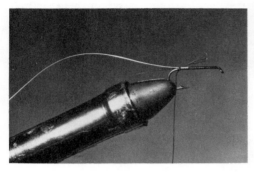

Fig. 199. On a wet-fly hook ranging in size from 20 to 8, wrap a black wet-fly thread base. Tie in three soft, natural black hackle fibers to form a tail as long as the body. Then tie in a three-inch length of primrose-yellow thread.

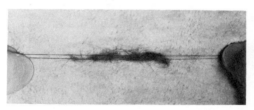

Fig. 200. With a dubbing needle, tease out a small amount of brownish beaver-belly fur on your pants leg, or a similar surface.

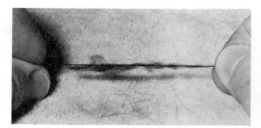

Fig. 201. Double a foot-long piece of tackily waxed yellow thread and lay the two strands on top of the fur. Twist the strands so that they grab the fur which should be apportioned on the thread so that there is a definite taper from one end to the other. This will help you taper the body, making it larger at the thorax.

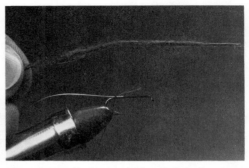

Fig. 202. Roll the spun fur lightly between your palms to form a noodle-shaped mass. Snip off the thread of the noodle at the small end.

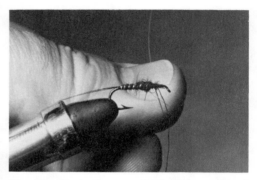

Fig. 203. Tie in the spun fur by the small end and, twisting it slightly as you wrap, form a tapered body, allowing adequate room for tying in and wrapping the thorax, legs and wings. Rib the fur body with five or six turns of yellow thread.

Fig. 204. Tie in two medium-slate or grizzly hackle tips with their concave sides down (flat), about half to three-quarters the length of the body. Tie in by the tip a natural or dyed black ostrich or emu herl.

Fig. 205. Wrap the herl to form an enlarged thorax. Then tie in a short, sparse beard of six natural black hackle fibers. Wrap and finish the head in the usual fashion. In streams, fish this nymph with the Leisenring Lift or any other technique that lets you impart a rising movement. In lakes, fish it on a floating line during the early stages of a dun hatch, imparting rising movements with quick, jerky hand-twist recoveries. This pattern, originated by the author and tested extensively since 1967, is generally effective wherever there are dark-colored mayfly nymphs in abundance. It is a varietal pattern and not designed to imitate any specific mayfly nymph. Like the Adams dry fly, it entices trout over a wide range of hatches. Another version, dressed without wings, is deadly when no hatch is in progress.

Tying and Fishing a Mayfly Adult (dun)

Pattern: Hendrickson Dun

Fig. 206. On a size 16, 1XL or 2XL dry-fly hook, wrap a tan dry-fly thread base. Tie in two dark slate-blue wings that have been trim-shaped from the webby parts of large neck hackles. To do this, hold the wings upright, one on each side of the hook with their concave sides out. Take a double-loop around the stems and cinch down slowly and carefully.

Fig. 207. Take three or four more turns around the tied-down stems, then double the butt ends of the stems back under the hook and tie them down with a few neat thread wraps, snipping off the excess stems.

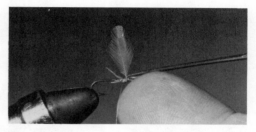

Fig. 208. Take a few criss-cross thread wraps between the wings and place a drop of cement on the windings.

Fig. 209. Between the wings, tie a superior-quality dark blue dun or honey-dun gamecock-neck hackle by the butt, concave side up. Then wrap the thread neatly back to the tail position and tie in a tail using four blue dun or rusty dun spade hackle fibers.

Fig. 210. Spin a small amount of reddish-tan or dark yellow dubbing fur on a doubled, well-waxed piece of thread of similar color. Wrap the dubbed fur as a body and thorax to one turn in front of the wings. Do not trim off the remaining fur. Allow it to hang below the hook, under tension, or take a single turn of tying thread around it.

Fig. 211. X-wrap the hackle, 1½ turns angling front to back, one full turn angling back to front, with the longest fibers at the lower rear and shortest at the lower front. Tie off the hackle and trim the excess. Complete the wrapping of the thorax with the remaining fur. Finish the head with a whip-finish knot and a couple of coats of cement. The objective of this criss-cross hackling is to raise the fly's rear end high off the water the way a natural dun mayfly rides, with abdomen and tails held high. A dun, after all, represents a live—newly hatched—insect, so it must be tied and presented in a lifelike manner. The angler also has

to consider how, merely by dressing the fly on a different hook size, he can suit the offering to his region. The dressing described here is imitative of the Eastern and Midwestern species *Ephemerella subvaria*, *E. rotunda* and *E. invaria* in smaller sizes (16 and 14). On a size 12 hook, no doubt it would do a pretty fair job of imitating the spinner of the Great Red Quill of Western waters, *E. hecuba*. It is one of numerous innovative ties for Eastern waters listed in Vincent Marinaro's masterful book, *A Modern Dry Fly Code* (Crown Publishers, N.Y., 1970).

Tying and Fishing a Mayfly Adult (spinner)

Pattern: Red Quill

Fig. 212. On a size 12 extra-fine-wire hook, wrap a brown dry-fly thread base. Tie in matched light gray sections from paired mallard primary flight feathers. Tie back butts of feathers just behind the wing wraps. Tie in two natural red-brown game-cock neck hackles, facing forward between the divided upright wings.

Fig. 213. Snip off the butts of the wings and hackle stems in a taper. Tie in a tail of natural

red-brown gamecock hackle fibers. Wrap a body from a single stripped peacock eye quill that has been dyed dull red.

Fig. 214. Wrap two or three turns with each hackle behind and in front of the wings, as shown. Then tie off hackles and finish the head with a few thread turns, a whip-finish knot and two coats of head cement.

Crustaceans

Tying and Fishing the Scud (Freshwater Shrimp)

Pattern: Trueblood's Otter Nymph

Fig. 215. On a size 8 or 10, 1X short nymph hook, wrap a tan wet-fly thread base. Tie in a short tail from a few strands of brown-speckled partridge breast. Spin or dub a fairly fat body from a mixture of undyed otter fur and a little natural cream-colored seal fur.

Fig. 216. To form a throat tie in a small bunch of brown speckled partridge-breast feather fibers. Finish the head with a few neat wraps of thread and a whip-finish knot. The pattern can be varied to any color scheme that imitates scuds in a particular body of water, from almost whitish-cream to deep olive. This nymph is frequently dressed in a weighted version. Originated by noted angling authority and writer Ted Trueblood of Nampa, Idaho, it's usually fished near the bottom with rising movements toward the surface.

Tying and Fishing the Crayfish

Pattern: Montreal Streamer (Western)

Fig. 217. On a size 6 or larger heavy-wire hook, wrap a black wet-fly thread base. As a tail, tie in a medium-sized bunch of webby scarlet hackle fibers. Wrap a fairly plump body of crimson yarn. Hackle it with a collar of long, webby medium-ginger hen-neck hackle.

Fig. 218. Tie on a flat down-wing from two reddish-wine (redder than magenta) dyed mallard-flank feathers extending back about the same length as the tail. Finish the head in the usual way.

Fig. 219. In lakes, fish this streamer on a sinking fly line near rocky shoals or cliffs, preferably after sundown when the crayfish become active. Be prepared for exceedingly heavy strikes. Slow trolling or retrieving to simulate the ambling of the naturals is usually the most productive technique. Resign yourself to losing flies on the rocks. This pattern rarely works well unless fished practically on the bottom. In streams, fish it in the shallow, rocky backwaters where crayfish are most abundant, or in slow-moving, rocky pools. This deadly creation of Terry Tyed Flies seems to depend for its killing qualities on the unique color of the wing more than on shape.

Terrestrials

Tying and Fishing the Ant

Pattern: Flying Ant

Fig. 220. On a size 10, 2XL dry-fly hook, wrap a black wet-fly thread base. Tie down a long matchstick-thick bunch of black-dyed bucktail by the butts, tips extending rearward. The butts shouldn't be trimmed off, merely wound down to about two-thirds the length of the shank.

Fig. 221. Pull the ends of the bucktail forward and tie them down to form an ant-shaped abdomen. Trim off the hair ends. Then tie in two dun or light blue-dun hackle-tip wings.

Fig. 222. Hackle the fly with a couple of turns of black-dyed gamecock-neck hackle, trimming

off the fibers on top and bottom to leave a few strands extending to the sides to suggest legs. The Flying Ant is very effective on lakes during mating flights and when fished in the flow from an inlet stream to suggest a natural insect being washed into the lake. It's very productive on streams almost anytime. Fish it close to overhanging brush and tree limbs, within a few inches of undercut banks and near partially submerged logs.

Tying and Fishing the Terrestrial Ant

Pattern: Terrestrial Ant

Fig. 223. On a size 14 to 28 dry-fly hook (TDE), wrap a wet-fly thread base. Use black thread for a black ant, tan or brown thread for a brown ant. Form an ant-shaped body out of brown or black dubbed or spun fur. Do not trim off the excess.

Fig. 224. Tie in and wrap two turns of a black or natural red gamecock-neck hackle to match the body color. Wrap a thorax smaller than the abdomen, using the remainder of the dubbed fur. Finish the head with thread wraps, a whip-finish knot and two coats of cement. Fish the ant very close to the banks of streams and lakes, where small terrestrial ants may fall or be blown into the water.

Tying and Fishing the Bee

Pattern: Western Bee Bucktail

Fig. 225. Wrap a wet-fly thread base on a size 10 or 8, 1X-fine hook. Omit the tail, or tie in a short bunch of natural brown deer-body hair or bucktail. Wrap the body with four alternating bands of black and orange chenille, or polypropylene yarn.

Fig. 226. Tie in a bunch of natural brown bucktail so the hairs lie in wing position, slightly spread and low over the body. Then tie in several wraps of a natural red-brown game-cock saddle hackle in front of the wing. East or West, this is an excellent fly to fish dry at the mouths of inlet streams on lakes, during the late fall when bees are swarming, and sometimes during caddis or stonefly hatches on streams.

Tying and Fishing the Grasshopper

Pattern: Joe's Hopper

Fig. 227. On a size 10, 2XL hook, wrap a wet-fly thread base and tie in a few scarlet hackle fibers as a tail. This is a palmered fly, and the next step is to tie in a brown saddle hackle from which the fibers have been stripped from the side to be wound down while palmering.

Fig. 228. Wrap a medium-full yellow yarn body, leaving a short, loose loop of yarn extending to the rear over the tail. Palmer-wrap four or five turns of hackle up the body and tie off, trimming away the excess.

Fig. 229. Along each side of the body, tie in wings made from long, lightly lacquer-glazed sections of mottled brown turkey-wing feathers, extending slightly beyond the body. Hackle heavily in front of the wings (four turns

each) with one brown and one grizzly saddle hackle. Complete the head with the usual thread wrappings, whip-knot and cement.

On streams, fish this fly as close as possible to overhanging bushes and undercut banks bordered by meadows or stubble fields, or wherever grasshoppers are plenti-ful (Fig. 230). On lakes, fish it with active struggling motions on a floating line near shorelines where hoppers have jumped or been blown into the water. There are almost as many grasshopper patterns as there are fly tiers. This is one of the few that have become universally popular.

Fig. 230. Fishing the grasshopper.

Tying and Fishing the Beetle

Pattern: Black Beetle

Fig. 231. On a size 6 to 22 hook, wrap a wet-fly base with black thread. Closely palmer-wrap black gamecock hackle to form a body. Then trim the hackle-body on top and bottom.

Fig. 232. Take a small, roundish, black or blue-black breast or shoulder feather and lightly glaze it with thin head cement. Trim the feather end to the shape of a beetle wing. Tie the wing feather flat on top of the fly, concave side down, and finish the head. Complete the fly by lightly brushing the wing feather with a second coat of cement. On lakes, fish it near inlet flows following strong winds. In a wide range of sizes from 22 up, this type of beetle is deadly in most streams, especially after winds or rainstorms when numerous terrestrial insects are blown or washed into the water. A sinking version can be easily fashioned by hackling with webby hen hackles instead of gamecock hackles. When fished wet, the fly is usually drifted freely or manipulated with darting movements. It's deadly on limestone streams, spring creeks and certain lakes across the country.

Tying and Fishing the Spider

Pattern: Badger Spider

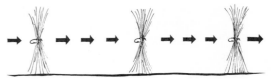

Fig. 235. Skating action of spider fly. On both Eastern and Western streams, fish spider flies by skating them lightly across the surface, following an up-and-across stream delivery. Sometimes, skating spider-type flies is also deadly on lakes.

Minnow Imitations

Tying and Fishing the Feather-Wing Streamer

Pattern: Colonel Bates Streamer

Fig. 233. Wrap a short thread base on a size 16 or 18, extra-fine-wire, TDE dry-fly hook. Tie in two very stiff gamecock-neck or spade badger hackles. Badger hackles have black centers and pale frosty-white to golden tips. The fibers should be 2 to 2½ inches in diameter when wrapped on.

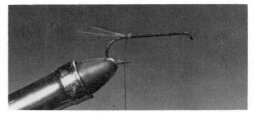

Fig. 236. On a 4XL streamer hook, wrap a black wet-fly thread base and tie in a tail—a fairly long section of scarlet goose or swan primary feather. Some anglers prefer the tail tied from scarlet saddle hackle.

Fig. 234. Wrap on the hackles, dry-fly style, at least three turns with each hackle. Finish the head in the usual way.

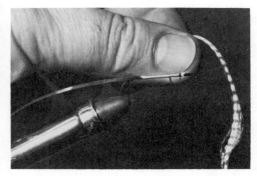

Fig. 237. Taper-trim the end of a six-inch piece of medium flat silver tinsel and tie it in slightly ahead of the tail. Wrap a smooth, untapered underbody of white floss.

Fig. 238. Wrap the tinsel over the floss base in tight, even wraps, tying it off with four thread turns and a Scotch hitch. Trim away excess floss and tinsel ends. Apply a coat of thin, clear cement to the tinsel and allow adequate drying time.

Fig. 239. Tie in a small bunch of dark brown saddle-hackle fibers as a hackle beard. Tie on an inner wing of two matched yellow saddle hackles, with the concave sides facing inward. Then, outside them, tie two white saddle hackles slightly shorter than the yellow. If the hackles are excessively curved, steam them well and press between layers of paper with a flat-iron set on the "silk" mark.

Fig. 240. Shoulder feathers of matched, barred teal breast should be tied outside the hackle wings. These shoulders should be about half the length of the wings.

Fig. 241. Tie on two jungle-cock eye-feather cheeks, if available, and finish the head with unwaxed scarlet monocord thread and red celluloid enamel. Fish this streamer on floating, sink-tip or sinking fly line, with stripping recoveries to suggest the erratic darting of a minnow. The pattern is also an excellent trolling fly for trout, bass and salmon. (See Chapter 14 for additional details.)

Tying and Fishing the Bucktail-Wing Streamer

Pattern: Little Brown Trout

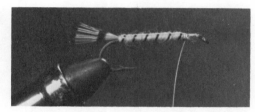

Fig. 242. On a 3XL or 4XL streamer hook, wrap a wet-fly thread base. Then tie in a bunch of golden-pheasant tippets for a tail. Form an orange wool-yarn body and rib it with gold tinsel.

Fig. 243. Tie in a throat of dyed yellow hackle fibers over red hackle fibers.

Fig. 244. Form the wing of equal-sized bunches of red squirrel tail, over red-dyed bucktail, over black bear, over yellow-dyed bucktail. Tie in each bunch of hair separately, placing a drop of cement on each winding area prior to tying down. Work a little cement into the butts of hair before tying them in. As cheeks, add small jungle-cock eye feathers (if available) and finish the head with yellow thread or enamel. Fish the fly as you would a feather-wing streamer. (See Chapter 14 for more data and variations.)

Tying and Fishing
the Marabou-Wing Streamer

Pattern: Marabou Muddler

Fig. 245. Wrap a black wet-fly thread base on a large, long-shanked streamer hook. Tie in scarlet saddle-hackle fibers for the tail. Wrap a silver tinsel-chenille body, allowing more than the usual amount of room in front for the bulky wing, hackle and long head.

Fig. 246. Add wings with the tips of two or three fluffy white marabou feathers, tied flat on top of the hook. The wings should be at least 1½ times the hook length. As topping over the wing, tie three or four peacock or black ostrich-herl fibers.

Fig. 247. Around the shank and inside a thread loop, spin a bunch of gray deer-body hairs to form a collar-hackle.

Fig. 248. Form the muddler's head by tying in small bunches of gray deer-body hair. As you

pull the thread loop down on each bunch of hair, they'll spin around the hook shank. Take a few turns of thread in front of each bunch of wound-down hair and half-hitch before tying down the next bunch. Three or four bunches should form a full dense head.

Fig. 249. Trim the head to a cylindrical tapered shape. Wrap a small thread head, forward of the hair head, and complete the fly with a whip-finish knot and a couple of coats of cement. Being highly mobile, marabou streamers are often fished best by employing a broadside drift on a sinking or sink-tip fly line. A stripping retrieve will suggest the swimming and darting movements of a minnow. Extremely fine tippets are not recommended. Game fish usually take these flies with very solid strikes. This pattern is one of professional tier Dan Bailey's creations, circa 1959. It catches fish in virtually any lake or stream where there are fairly plump, silvery bait fish.

Chapter 10

Flies for Salmon & Steelhead

The Fishes

Atlantic Salmon *(Salmo salar)*

ATLANTIC SALMON, considered by many to be North America's most spectacular freshwater battlers, range from the coastal rivers of Maine through Canada's maritimes. They're also found in northern Europe, England, Greenland, Labrador and Newfoundland.

Although there's only limited evidence that salmon feed at all on their upstream migrations into fresh water, their primary marine foods include other fishes, crustaceans and marine annelids. Salmon entering the rivers of Maine and eastern Canada usually begin their runs in the spring and travel to their spawning beds during the summer. They tend to use the same travel routes each year, just as steelhead trout do. Spawning is generally accomplished in the fall. Unlike the Pacific salmons, Atlantic salmon are constituted to survive spawning, but they do suffer a high mortality rate afterward.

A salmon rarely rests in the classic holding waters associated with trout fishing. Instead, it seems to prefer specific pools, the tails of pools, flows against a river-bend bank, sudden drop-offs, the protection of large rocks and boulders, flows over gravel bars and fairly shallow lies three to four feet deep.

There are numerous effective fly-fishing techniques for salmon, including the patent method, greased-line and riffling techniques described earlier. Flies used range in size from 18 to 5/0. Most experienced salmon fishermen agree that smaller flies are more effective in low, clear water. Wet, dry, nymph, streamer and bucktail styles all are used effectively at times.

Steelhead Trout *(Salmo gairdneri)*

Steelheads, or steelhead trout, are sea-run rainbow trout that spawn in Western coastal rivers from northern California to Alaska. They average between six and nine pounds, but are known to exceed 30 pounds.

Like Atlantic salmon, steelheads show no evidence of active feeding in freshwater; at sea their diet includes fishes, crustaceans, amphipods and squids. Also like Atlantic salmon, steelheads tend to follow traditional travel routes and prefer the same holding lies season after season, provided the river bottom isn't dramatically altered by flood or man.

There are winter and summer steelhead runs. Some of the rivers experience runs of fish only in the winter, some only in the summer, some in both seasons. Winter-run steelheads usually enter the rivers between December and February, spawning in the spring. Summer-run fish usually start trickling into their spawning streams some-time between April and September and they don't spawn until the following spring.

Angling techniques for steelheads are similar to those for Atlantic salmon, but steelheads are considerably spookier than salmon. Under clear-water conditions the approach and presentation require more care.

Steelheads, especially summer-run fish, jump and run very well, although their leaps are not usually quite as spectacular as those of Atlantic salmon. A 10-pound-plus fresh-run summer steelhead is fully capable of peeling 200 yards of backing from a fly reel in a matter of moments. And it's frequently necessary to follow a steelhead in the 15- to 30-pound class for quite some distance before beaching the fish. Very big steelheads, usually those over 15 pounds, tend to jump less when hooked than smaller steelheads. Those in the 2½- to 12-pound class may be out of the water half a dozen times within moments after feeling the barb. Very large steelies have a tendency to roll to the surface when hooked, make a short run, roll again, then head downstream in a rapidly accelerating run.

Steelhead flies range in size from 10 to 3/0. Popular colors for wet flies include black and white, all black, scarlet and hot orange, yellow and white, and combinations of fluorescent red, orange, yellow and green. Bucktail-wing and bivisible-types are the most popular dry flies.

Large, weighted bucktails are popular during periods of high off-color water. When the water is low and clear, low-water-style bucktails and Atlantic-salmon flies are apt to produce the most strikes. Steelheads will move quite a distance to a fly when the water is relatively warm during the summer and early fall. But when the water temperature drops below 45°, very thorough water coverage is often necessary.

Chinook Salmon
(Oncorhynchus tshawytscha)

Chinook salmon, known in salt water as king or tyee salmon, are the largest of the Pacific salmons. Their average size is 15 to 20 pounds and may exceed 60 pounds. They're found in rivers from California to the Aleutians. Runs of Chinook salmon occur in the spring, summer and winter, depending on the river.

These outsized, exceedingly powerful fighting fish do not feed in fresh water. At sea, their foods include shrimps, squids and fishes. Surprisingly, their travel routes in rivers closely follow the shorelines. Some of the better fly-fishing locations include long runs of even current flow, pools near river mouths that are affected by tides, and runs where the river swings against a bend.

The most successful Chinook fishermen employ lead-head and extra-fast-sinking shooting-taper fly lines, short leaders and colorful bucktail flies. Some anglers also wrap their leader knots with fine lead wire to prevent the fly from billowing up in the current, because these salmon practically hug the bottom during their upstream migrations.

Chinook salmon are so powerful and engage in such long runs when hooked that it's sometimes necessary to follow a fish in a boat. Quite a few anglers prefer to do most of their fly-fishing for Chinooks directly from a small boat or pram.

Silver Salmon
(Oncorhynchus kisutch)

The range of the lightning-fast, high-jumping silver salmon—also known as the coho—is much the same as that of the Chinook. (And in recent years, both of these Pacific salmons, as well as steelhead trout, have been successfully introduced into the Great Lakes and some other isolated inland waters.) Silver salmon average less than 10 pounds, but specimens caught in British Columbia and Alaska sometimes exceed 20 pounds.

The silver salmon is another species that feeds only in salt water, mostly on other fishes, squids and crustaceans.

In most rivers, the runs of silver salmon occur in late summer and early fall. The fish tend to follow travel routes similar to those preferred by steelheads—long runs of even flow, bedrock channels, etc.

Although most anglers fish with weighted spinners for these salmon, silvers respond to wet flies swum broadside in the current and manipulated with occasional stripping recoveries. Bright-colored steelhead flies, like the Cole's Comet and Fall Favorite are usually the most productive. Sinking lines are preferred by flyrodders who do a lot of fishing for silver salmon.

Silvers are noted for their spectacular and frequent jumps as well as for their blazing-fast runs. But because of their energetic flight and relatively small size, they play down much faster than Chinooks or large steelheads.

The Flies

Tying and Fishing
an Atlantic-Salmon Wet Fly

Pattern: Blue Charm

Fig. 250. On a turned-up, loop-eyed salmon-fly hook, wrap a black divided wet-fly thread base. Tie the tip of fine flat or oval silver tinsel and the tail from a single golden-pheasant crest feather curving upward.

Fig. 251. Wrap a black floss body, tapered slightly larger toward the head, and rib it with fine flat or oval silver tinsel. Wrap a sparse beard of light blue hackle.

Fig. 252. Wing the fly with two sections of brown mallard-flank feather, tips curved down, concave sides facing inward. Tie in narrow strips of barred teal-flank feather outside the wings. Top with a single golden-pheasant crest feather the same length as the tail, and finish the head. On streams and rivers fish the Blue Charm on floating or sinking line, employing one of the several techniques described in Chapter 4.

Tying and Fishing a Low-Water Atlantic-Salmon Wet Fly

Pattern: March Brown

Fig. 253. On a low-water, turned-up, loop-eyed, salmon hook, wrap a wet-fly thread base and tie in as a tail a few wisps of brown speckled partridge-breast feather. Proportion the entire fly two full sizes smaller than would be normal for the hook size selected (i.e., on a size 4 hook, the entire dressing should be proportioned for a size 6 or 7 fly). Wrap an orange floss tip in front of the tail.

Fig. 254. Tie in a piece of fine oval or flat gold tinsel. Wrap a tapered body of spun brown fur and rib it with the gold tinsel.

Fig. 255. Wrap two turns of brown speckled partridge-breast feather to form a sparse collar hackle. Tie in a pair of matched brown turkey-wing feather sections for the wing and finish the head in the normal fashion. Fish this pattern with the greased-line tactics described in Chapter 4.

Tying and Fishing an Atlantic-Salmon Nymph

Pattern: March Brown (Wm. J. Keane)

Fig. 256. On a size 4, 6, 8 or 10 low-water salmon hook, wrap a dark brown thread base and tie in a tail from three cock ringneck pheasant tail-feather fibers. The fibers should be separated slightly when tied in.

Fig. 257. Tie in a piece of dark brown thread. Wrap a body of spun, blended tan fox and amber-colored seal fur. Tie in a 3/16-inch width of dark brown turkey-tail feather.

Fig. 258. With the remaining spun fur, wrap a thorax slightly larger than the body. Form a wing case by pulling the turkey feather over the thorax. Tie in a slightly splayed beard from a few dark brown speckled partridge-feather fibers. Lacquer the wing case, then finish the head of the fly in the normal way. Fish this nymph deeply on a sinking fly line, or just under the surface on a floating line. A dead drift is sometimes very productive.

Tying and Fishing
an Atlantic-Salmon Dry Fly

Pattern: White Wulff

Fig. 259. On a size 8 Wilson dry-fly salmon hook, wrap a white wet-fly thread base over a coat of cement, then wrap the thread back to a forward position, a hair less than ¼-inch from the eye of the hook.

Fig. 260. Tie in a bunch of white bucktail, tips forward. Hold the tips upright and wrap thread in front of them until they stand erect. Divide the hairs and criss-cross the wrapping to form two hair wings. Cement the windings.

Fig. 261. Trim the butts of the wing hairs to a taper and wrap the thread back over them to the bend of hook. Tie in a tail from a medium-sized bunch of white bucktail. Trim off the butts and wrap down. Tie in two dry-fly-quality badger hackles between the wings, with the tips facing forward. Return the thread to the tail. Tie in a piece of cream-colored spun fur or synthetic yarn.

Fig. 262. With the spun fur or synthetic yarn, wrap a body to behind the wings. Wrap the hackles in the usual way and finish the head. Fish the White Wulff on a floating line and fairly long leader. If a salmon rolls under the fly, try several more casts. If that fails, change to a different pattern or a smaller or larger version of the White Wulff but rest the fish several minutes between pattern changes. Remember to carry a wide range of sizes in each of your dry and wet salmon-fly patterns.

Tying and Fishing
a Silver-Salmon Casting Fly

Pattern: Gold/White

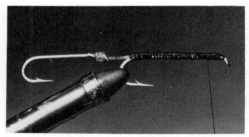

Fig. 263. Affix a size 1 or 1/0 turned-down-eye saltwater hook to a section of 40-pound-test monofilament. Any of the positive, high-strength mono knots will suffice, provided the end of the mono passes through the hook eye. Then place a size 1/0 or 2/0 saltwater hook in the vise and lash to it the first hook with wraps of size E nylon tying thread, doubling the mono back over the first thread wrappings so it can't slip loose. Cement the wrappings.

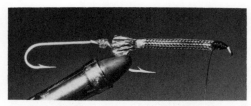

Fig. 264. Construct the body from tubular silver Mylar or wrappings of silver tinsel.

Fig. 265. Tie in a six-inch-long bunch of straight white polar-bear guard hairs. The wing should extend about an inch beyond the bend of the trailer hook. Cement the hair butt well before tying down. Wrap a smaller but similarly long bunch of golden-yellow dyed polar-bear hairs over the white hairs. Taper-trim the butts and finish the head in the usual way. Some anglers apply white eyes with crimson pupils.

floating or sinking-tip fly line are productive at times in water shallow enough for you to spot moving schools of salmon, or when they're ravaging bait fish. Interest in this type of salmon fly is limited to the West Coast.

Tying and Fishing a Steelhead Bucktail

Pattern: Skunk

Fig. 266. On a size 4 TULE salmon hook, wrap a black wet-fly thread base and tie in a scarlet hackle-fiber tail, followed by a thick black chenille body ribbed with medium oval silver tinsel.

When fishing salt-chuck for silver salmon, look for signs of small bait fish, like candlefish, leaping frantically and for salmon ravaging the bait schools immediately below the surface. Very fast stripping recoveries are sometimes productive when the fish are working bait in shallow water or near the surface. Fast trolling in the prop wash, sometimes behind a spinner, is also a killing method. Troll the fly on monofilament line fast enough so it skips out of the water every few moments.

For casting and retrieving in salt water, you can either use the double hooks or dress the fly on a size 2 to 1/0, long-shank hook. Very fast stripping retrieves on a

Fig. 267. Now wrap on three or four turns of long, mobile black hackle as a collar.

Fig. 268. In front of the hackle, wrap in a medium-sized bunch of white bucktail or polar-bear hair. If the fly is to be fished in very fast water, take a few turns of thread behind the wing so that it rides at a high angle. The wing length should not exceed that of the tail plus the body. Finish the head with black epoxy cement. Jungle-cock-eye cheeks can be added, if desired, before finishing the head. But it's questionable if jungle cock truly enhances the effectiveness of steelhead flies. Those without jungle cock seem to catch just as many fish. Use the fly on a floating, sink-tip or sinking fly line with either a dead- or broadside drift. A tippet lighter than six-pound test is rarely practical. Eight-, 10- or 12-pound-test tippets are preferred, depending on the average size of the fish in a specific river.

Tying and Fishing
a Steelhead Streamer Fly

Pattern: Chappie

Fig. 269. Wrap a wet-fly thread base on a size 4, 2X stout hook. Tie in a pair of roundish-

tipped grizzly hackles as a tail. The feathers should be tied on edge, concave sides facing inward. Wrap a full, well-tapered orange yarn body and rib it with orange thread or fine oval gold tinsel.

Fig. 270. Wing the fly with a matched pair of grizzly neck hackles, concave sides facing out. The wings should extend beyond the bend of the hook. Add a collar of grizzly hen or saddle hackle. Finish the head with thread wraps, a whip-finish knot and two coats of head cement. Steelhead streamers are at their best in the slower-moving runs. They're normally fished deeply with sinking lines and worked with gentle rod-tip twitches to activate the mobile wings. This pattern was originated by the late C. L. "Outdoor" Franklin of Klamath River fame.

Tying and Fishing a Steelhead Nymph

Pattern: Brown Burlap

Fig. 271. On a size 8 stout-wire hook, wrap a tan wet-fly thread base and tie in a small bunch of brown natural bucktail for the tail. Then wrap a full body from a strand of gunnysack burlap. Pick out the burlap fibers with a needle to give a fuzzy appearance.

Fig. 272. **Wrap two or three turns of grizzly hen-neck hackle as a collar. Fish this fly in the same ways you would a salmon or steelhead wet fly, bucktail or nymph. Somber flies of this sort are usually most effective on steelheads when the water is low, clear and fairly warm.**

Tying and Fishing Steelhead Dry Flies

Dry flies for steelhead are tied and fished in much the same way as regular trout dry flies. Bivisibles, hopper imitations, Wulff-type hair-wing dries and Montana-style hair flies are all effective at times. Steelheads come most readily to dry flies during summer and fall low-water periods but are very spooky under those conditions. Extreme caution should be exercised in both the approach and the presentation. Daybreak and dusk are usually the best times of day for summer-run fishing in low water. Rainy or overcast days are often more productive than sunny weather.

Chapter 11

Flies for Bass, Pike & Muskellunge

The Fishes

Largemouth Bass
(Micropterus salmoides)

LARGEMOUTH BASS are North American natives and are found in lakes, ponds and rivers throughout most of the contiguous states. Generally, Southern largemouths are bigger than bass caught in Northern waters. Fish weighing more than five pounds are not uncommon in the South. Bass of that size are considered exceptional in most Northern states.

Largemouth bass thrive in weedy, shallow lakes, ponds, canals, lagoons, bayous, backwaters and sloughs. The species can tolerate water temperatures in the 90's and is usually in depths of 20 feet or less. Spawning generally takes place when the water temperature ranges between 62° and 73° in water from a few inches to three feet deep.

Bass are among the wariest of North American freshwater fish. Care in approach is usually far more important than fly pattern. Popular fly styles vary from trout-type dry flies to cork-bodied surface poppers and include both conventional and unusual streamer and bucktail flies for sub-surface fishing. Some of the most effective colors are solid black, solid purple, black and white, black and yellow, and black and brown.

Largemouth bass are especially fond of dense cover like that provided by sawgrass, submerged tree trunks, brush piles and aquatic vegetation. As a result, big bass can be very difficult to control on fly-fishing tackle. They have what sometimes seems to be a studied ability to grab a bug or streamer and dive into the thickest possible entangling cover in practically the same instant. Because of this tendency, leader tippets ranging from eight- to 20-pound test are frequently essential. Powerful-action fly rods ranging upwards of nine feet long assist in providing the necessary "horsing" leverage in debris-choked waters.

As a general rule, very slow retrieves are the most effective on largemouth bass. Allow a surface bug to remain motionless on the surface for several minutes before commencing a retrieve. When fishing for largemouths with streamers or bucktails, allow your fly to sink close to the bottom, then recover it slowly with line strips or hand-twists.

Smallmouth Bass
(Micropterus dolomieu)

Natural habitats of the smallmouth bass are cool, rocky streams, lakes and backwaters throughout most of the U.S. and eastern Canada. Like its largemouth cousin, the species feeds on other fishes, aquatic insects and crustaceans, exhibiting a special preference for small crayfish.

Smallmouths usually spawn in waters ranging from 60° to 70°. Preferred spawning areas are over sand, gravel or rocks in two to 20 feet of water during the spring months. Stream-bound smallmouths often seek out the gravelly or rocky parts of sloughs and backwaters to spawn. As is the case with spawning crappies, they're sometimes extremely easy to catch while so concentrated. At other times of the year, stream smallmouths will be located in a variety of rocky areas, including the toes of riffles and rapids, near the edges of submerged gravel bars, near inlet or tributary mouths, drifting in and out of backwaters and off gravelly points of land—to name only a few of the prime spots.

Except during the spawning season, smallmouth bass in lakes frequently feed actively on crayfish beginning at sundown in the vicinity of rocky underwater cliffs, rock-falls, reefs and ledges—wherever there's a concentration of the nocturnally active crawdads. When the bass aren't hunting crayfish, they're usually feeding on minnows or aquatic insects, whether in lakes or streams. If annelids such as leeches are present, they'll gobble them up with relish. But regardless of what the smallmouths are feeding on in lakes, you'll rarely find them far away from some sort of rocky underwater cover.

Dry flies, small hair-bodied bass bugs, leech imitations and streamers are all deadly on smallmouth bass at times. Tippets ranging from four- to six-pound test are usually quite adequate. Smallmouth bass weighing more than a couple of pounds are not too common.

Once in a while a fish exceeding six pounds is caught from a large highly productive stream like the Snake River, which flows through parts of Idaho, Washington and Oregon. In fast water, a really large specimen puts on a fight rivaling that of a small steelhead. It's been my experience that outsized smallmouth bass rarely jump as much or in as spectacular a manner as largemouths. Smallmouths of moderate size are more acrobatic.

Northern Pike *(Esox lucius)*

The North American distribution of northern pike is primarily in the shallower parts of lakes and slow-moving reaches of rivers above the 40th parallel. Among the most predaceous of all freshwater fishes, northern pike—or northerns as they're often called—prefer weedy shallows, shoals, underwater obstructions, sand bars, deep weed beds and shallow bays. They usually spawn in shallow bays immediately following ice-out. River spawning commonly takes place in shoal waters or on flooded marshlands.

Very little finesse is generally required to lure northern pike to surface bugs or sunken streamer flies. The real key to successful fishing seems to be in the retrieve speed: the slower the better.

Conventional cork- or hair-bodied bass bugs are among the most effective surface flies for pike. Streamers or bucktails in combinations of red and yellow, red and white, red and orange, black and green, black and brown, and in solid yellows, whites, blacks and browns are preferred both for surface and sinking line. Six-inch-long streamers on 1/0 to 3/0 hooks usually sucker the largest pike. Since these fish have very sharp teeth shock tippets of 60- to 80-pound test hard nylon are recommended.

Muskellunge *(Esox masquinongy)*

The range of these highly predaceous members of the pike family includes Wisconsin, Michigan, Minnesota, Ohio, New York, Kentucky, Pennsylvania, Quebec and Ontario. Muskies weigh up to 60 pounds or more. Their main foods include other fishes, crustaceans, snakes, small aquatic and terrestrial animals, ducklings and other waterfowl.

Muskellunge are found in lakes and rivers, lurking among weed beds, backwaters, lily pads, submerged cover, drop-offs and channels. They spawn in the spring when the water temperature ranges between 48° and 56°, over relatively soft, detritus-covered bottoms.

Either a trolled or cast fly will provoke a muskie into striking. Generally speaking, faster retrieves than those used for pike are the most productive, but there's very little that can be stated definitively about muskie fishing with flies or any other kind of lures. Most successful muskellunge fishermen will agree that September and October are the best months, and that ideal fishing weather is stormy and rainy with northerly winds. But there's never any guarantee of success. Most old hands also agree that, even after locating one of the marauding monsters, the only time you're going to coax him into a strike is when he happens to be in the mood. If you're looking for a genuine fly-rod challenge and you're persistent enough to spend a lot of time on the water without catching many fish, then muskellunge could be your game.

Be sure to use a heavy monofilament or fine braided-wire tippet. A muskie's teeth are razor-sharp. And if you're fishing near weed beds or stump-filled areas, use a powerful bass- or steelhead-action fly rod. You'll probably have to do some heavy horsing once you've hooked a fish.

The Flies

Tying and Fishing a Simple Bass Bucktail

Pattern: Integration Bucktail

Fig. 273. On a size 2 or larger extra-long-shank hook, wrap a black wet-fly thread base and ce-

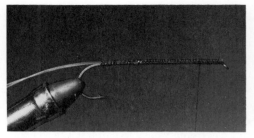

ment it. Tie in two four-inch strands of 15- to 20-pound test soft monofilament. The mono strands will be used later to form a double-loop weed guard.

Fig. 274. Affix a piece of medium oval silver tinsel at the bend of the hook and wind a neat, close-wrapped, untapered body all the way to the eye of the hook. This is to prevent the bucktail wing from flaring out when tied down.

Fig. 275. Tie in a four-inch black-dyed bucktail wing on top of the shank and an equal length of white bucktail underneath. The bucktail should be straight, without kinks.

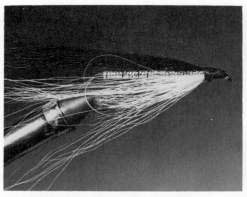

Fig. 276. Pull the strands of monofilament forward underneath the shank to form a weed guard, tie them at the head and finish in the usual way. (The weed guard may be omitted if the fly is to be used for trout in rivers or for saltwater fishing over sandy bottoms.) Originated by outdoor writer Ted Trueblood, the Integration Bucktail should be fished to simulate a minnow, with swimming action imparted during the retrieve.

Tying and Fishing a Deep-Running Bass Streamer

Pattern: Fly Rod Eel

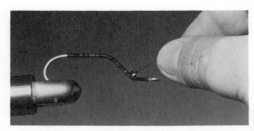

Fig. 277. Wrap a wet-fly thread base on a size 1/0 hook. Since you can easily get snagged during a deep, slow retrieve in bass waters, I used a keel hook to demonstrate this tie in the photo sequence. Tie in a pair of bead-chain eyes about ¼-inch from the hook eye with criss-cross thread wraps. Cement the wraps thoroughly.

Fig. 278 (next column). Wrap three turns of .030 lead wire behind the eyes and secure it with thread wrappings. Cement the wrappings.

Fig. 278.

Fig. 279. Tie in six black saddle hackles in two equal bunches concave sides facing in, to form a five- or six-inch-long streamer tail.

Fig. 280. Tie in six more black saddle hackles by the butts and palmer-wrap them separately to just behind the bead-chain eyes. Palmer two more black saddle hackles in front of the eyes and finish with a smoothly wrapped, cemented head.

Fig. 281. Trim the hackle body round. The Fly Rod Eel should be fished very close to the bottom in lakes and backwaters. Retrieve it with very slow stripping recoveries. Size and color can be varied to suit regional preferences.

Tying and Fishing a Deer-Hair Bug

Pattern: Gray/Yellow Stripe

Fig. 282. On a 1/0, 4XL ring-eye hook, wrap a wet-fly thread base and cement the wrappings. Sizes A to E tying thread are preferable for hair-bodied bugs of this size. In two equal bunches, tie in six four-inch-long yellow saddle hackles, concave sides facing out.

Fig. 283. Wrap two yellow saddle hackles immediately in front of the tail streamers. As described in the directions in Chapter 9 for tying the hair head on a Marabou Muddler, spin-wrap bunches of gray and yellow-dyed deer-body hair around the shank to form a gray body with a yellow center stripe.

Fig. 284. Trim the spun body hair to a tapered shape. The top of the bug should be trimmed

somewhat semi-circular in shape after the initial tapering, but the underside should be trimmed fairly close to the hook shank in a gentle curve so that the bug can be swum or rocked rather gently on the surface. Nylon weed-guard loops can be added to hair bugs for fishing in dense cover or sawgrass.

Tying and Fishing a Cork-bodied Popping Bug

Pattern: Black Popper

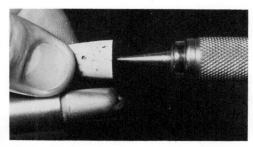

Fig. 285. Employing a drill bit slightly smaller than the head of the hook, drill a neat hole through the center of a formed cork popping head. (Cork heads can be purchased preformed in a variety of styles and sizes, or they can be hand-made from round stock.)

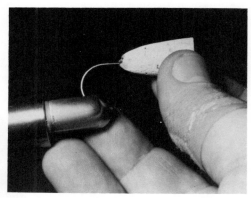

Fig. 286. Cement the hook in the hole with epoxy cement and allow it to dry overnight. Then fill any holes in the cork with wood dough or a mixture of fine cork fillings and cement. Sand the surface smooth with fine emery paper. Apply a coat of cork sealer and sand it smooth.

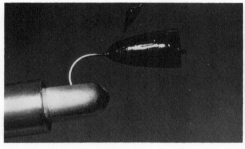

Fig. 287. Apply three or four coats of black celluloid enamel, sanding lightly between the coats, but do not sand the final coat. Although I usually omit painted eyes on this black popper used for night fishing, some anglers prefer yellow eyes with black or red pupils. The eyes are applied with round-headed finishing nails of appropriate size.

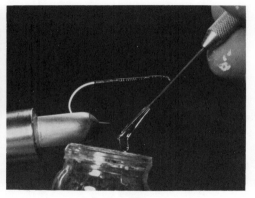

Fig. 289.

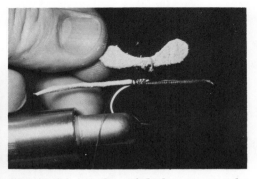

Fig. 290. Place a drop of thick cement on the shank and very firmly tie in the tail, finishing the tie-down with a Scotch-hitch knot. Allow the cement to dry before continuing. Note the chamois ears cut to size.

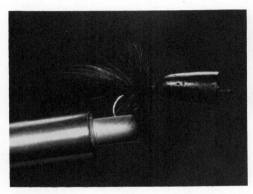

Fig. 288. Tie on six saddle hackles by the butts for tails, then wrap a dense black hackle collar immediately behind the cork head. Fish the bug on the surface with gentle rod-tip twitches to induce gurgling and popping noises.

Tying and Fishing a Hair-Bodied Mouse

Pattern: Pilkey's Mouse

Fig. 289 (next column). Wrap a gray or tan wet-fly thread base on a size 3/0 long-shank hook. Cement the thread wrap. While the thread base is drying, cut a tail and pair of joined ears from a piece of chamois skin.

Fig. 291. Using the same technique as in the previously described deer-hair bug, spin on bunches of brown antelope-body hair to within ⅜-inch of the head. Tie each bunch down so the butts spin on shorter than the tips by about ⅛-inch.

Fig. 292. Tie on the ears and complete the head by spinning on a couple of additional bunches of antelope hair.

Fig. 293. Trim the mouse's face and underside, then tie in a few long, dark whiskers on each side of the head so they extend back at about a 45-degree angle. Complete the head with a whip-finish knot and a couple of coats of clear head cement. Cast this bug very close to the bank or lily pads, allowing it to remain motionless for a few minutes before commencing a swimming, slow retrieve. For debris-choked or grassy waters, a looped nylon weed guard should be added. The pattern is shown as tied by Pete Pilkey of Seattle, Washington. It's useful anywhere there's a largemouth bass—and mice, of course.

Tying and Fishing a Pike Streamer

Pattern: McNally's Magnum

Fig. 294 (next column). Wrap a wet-fly thread base on a size 3/0 stainless saltwater hook. Then wrap a body out of medium-size yellow chenille.

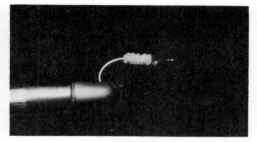

Fig. 294.

Fig. 295. Tie in half a dozen six-inch-long yellow saddle or neck hackles, three on each side with their concave sides facing inward.

Fig. 296. Wrap on a dense collar of scarlet saddle hackles in front of the wings and finish the head in the normal fashion. Fish this streamer with a very slow retrieve on either a floating or sinking fly line. Make certain to incorporate a 60- or 80-pound-test nylon shock tippet into your regular tippet, because pike and muskies have very sharp teeth. Originated by outdoor writer Tom McNally, this long streamer is very attractive to fish of the *Esox* clan.

CHAPTER 12

Flies for Panfish & Shad

The Fishes

Crappie *(Pomoxis nigromaculatus; P. annularis)*

CRAPPIES ARE found in most of the United States. Black crappies are most common to the North, white crappies more prevalent in warmer Southern waters. These flaky-fleshed panfish commonly weigh about half a pound or less, but in some areas they run up to about four pounds.

The best time of year to catch crappies on flies is during their spawning season, which occurs in the spring when water temperatures approach 64° to 68°. But crappies begin schooling in tremendous numbers for a month or two preceding the spawning, and the fishing can also be very fast then if a school is located.

Spawning crappies prefer water two to eight feet deep over sand or gravel bottoms. Some of the better places to seek them are around partially submerged brush, stumps or underwater debris, along shore lined with partially submerged willows, near inlet streams and lily-pad areas.

After spawning, the schools break up and move to deep water where they're of-ten located in weed beds, near submerged trees and in the vicinity of deep sand bars. They're frequently found surface-feeding at night during the heat of summer.

When the lakes cool in the fall, crappies are scattered at various depths and feeding very actively. Very slow, deep trolling with fast-sinking fly lines is usually quite productive at this time. Once the water temperature drops under 60° the fish stay down in deep-water hangouts.

When crappies are spawning or in deep water, cast or trolled bucktail flies fished on sinking lines are normally the most productive. Extremely slow stripping or hand-twist retrieves seem to elicit the largest number of strikes. The take of a crappie on a deeply submerged fly is usually very light. The hook should be set at the slightest suggestion of a tug or tightening of the fly line. Crappies have soft, fragile mouth parts, so play them gently. Those of average size are excellent table fish but weak fighters. Much of the fun comes from catching a fish on virtually every cast.

When they're surface-feeding, cork-bodied or hair-bodied bugs dressed on size 10, 8 or 6 hooks provide some fine sport. A wide range of fly styles and colors isn't necessary for successful crappie fishing. The simplest of bucktails in combinations of yellow, white, red, or black are usually sufficient. The same holds true for panfish-sized cork or hair-bodied bugs.

The Sunfishes

Sunfish of one species or another range throughout most of the U.S. The species most commonly sought by flyrodders include bluegill *(Lepomis machrochirus)*, pumpkinseed *(L. gibbosus)*, green sunfish *(L. cyanellus)*, redear sunfish *(L. microlophus)*, spotted sunfish *(L. punctatus)*, longear sunfish *(L. megalotis)* and yellowbelly sunfish *(L. auritus)*. Depending on the species and location, they vary in size from a few inches to about four pounds, probably averaging about 10 inches.

In the North they spawn in the spring when the water temperature ranges between 60° and 70°. Some species spawn more than once a season in the Deep South. They spawn in areas similar to those favored by crappies, in water from one to four feet deep.

The summer habitat of sunfish is deeper water, up to about 15 feet. Schools usually lie near drop-offs, submerged trees, weed beds, rocky areas and sand bars. They're often observed surface feeding on warm summer evenings near the shorelines and in shallow bays. Stream-bound sunnies are found in shallow areas during spawning season. They move to pools and shady, brushy, stumpy areas when the weather warms. The winter habitat of lake-inhabiting sunfish is near the bottom in deeper water.

Angling techniques that bring sunfish to the fly are the same as those employed by lake and stream trout fishermen. Sunfish respond to small nymphs, wet flies, miniature streamers and bucktails as well as to tiny dry flies and ultra-small cork-bodied bugs. Ounce for ounce, sunfish are among the scrappiest freshwater game fish. Very-light-action fly rods provide the best sport.

Yellow Perch *(Perca flavescens)*

Yellow perch are found throughout most of the United States in ponds, lakes, backwaters, sloughs and slow-moving streams and rivers. They run in size from a few inches to about two pounds. Spawning usually begins right after ice-out and lasts until the water temperature ranges from 45° to 52°. Most of the spawning takes place in weedy shallows and up inlet streams.

During the summer, perch prefer water ranging from 20 to 35 feet deep. The largest ones are usually located at the deepest levels within that range. During the winter they can be found in water 15 to 50 feet deep.

Flyrodding for perch is most productive with small nymphs, wet flies and bucktails fished very close to the bottom on sinking lines. Slow, jerky recoveries usually provoke the most strikes. Perch feed exclusively during the daylight hours, and they school in age groups. If you find one large perch, you'll probably locate others nearby. For their size, perch are reasonably scrappy on light tackle.

Walleye *Stizostedion vitreum*

Although isolated walleye populations are found in the West, they mostly inhabit clear lakes and rivers of the Northeastern states, plus the Tennessee and Mississippi River drainages and provinces of Saskatchewan, Manitoba, Ontario and Quebec. The record walleye weighed over 25 pounds, but these fish usually average between two and three pounds. Their main diet is other fishes, which makes them prime targets for proficiently worked streamer flies.

Walleyes spawn in shallow water during

the early spring. They prefer lake and river bottoms of sand, gravel and rock. On bright summer days they retire to deep water, usually too deep to reach with even the fastest-sinking fly lines. At night they move into shallows to feed on small fish.

If walleyes fought as well as they eat they'd probably be the most sought-after species. When hooked on a fly, a walleye is apt to swim up to the boat, sound a couple of times and give up ingloriously.

Very slow stripping retrieves and dead-slow trolling provide the most action. Simple bucktail or feather-wing streamer flies are the most productive, especially when fished behind some sort of spinner. Once in a while a school of walleyes can be observed feeding near the surface on bait fish that have been attracted there by hatching aquatic insects. When this happens, casting and retrieving a bucktail through the school can bring results in short order.

Some of the more deadly color combinations for walleye flies include red and yellow, red and orange, red and white, black and green and solid shades of the above colors.

American Shad (*Alosa sapidissima*)

In terms of its life cycle and habitat, the shad properly belongs in the section on anadromous fishes since, like the steelheads and salmons, it attains its growth in the ocean and spawns in freshwater rivers. But it is included here because of the parallel styles used to dress wet flies for most panfish and for shad.

American shad are found in coastal rivers along both coasts of the U.S. and Canada. Spawning runs begin as early as January in some rivers at the southern end of the range. In the Maritime Provinces and in Washington, June is the usual month for shad runs.

Shad are excellent fighters on fly tackle. Their runs are long and determined and they jump frequently. Males average about three pounds. The female "roe shad" run six pounds or better, occasionally reaching almost twice that weight in some watersheds.

Standard wet-fly and streamer techniques apply well to shad fishing. The most popular flies are simple, colorful bucktails and bead-chain optics ranging in size from 10 to 4, with sizes 8 and 6 most common.

Migrating shad tend to move along very close to the stream bank, pausing periodically to rest in the backwaters near inlet mouths. Sinking fly lines and artificials fished very close to the rocky bottoms provide the fastest action. A shad's hit is not usually strong. The line should be kept as straight as possible during the run of the fly so that bumps or a gentle tightening can be readily detected.

The Flies

As stated previously, effective panfish and shad flies are dressed and fished similarly to trout flies and cork-bodied bass poppers. Numerous effective shad and panfish flies are listed in Chapter 14. All the tying techniques required to make them have been covered in preceding chapters.

A few of the more deadly panfish and shad flies are also illustrated in the color plates.

Chapter 13

Saltwater Flies

The Fishes

Atlantic Horse-Eye Jack
(*Caranx latus; C. sex faciatus*)

Opinions vary but most marine-fisheries authorities seem to agree that the range of the jack runs along the Atlantic Seaboard from New Jersey all the way to Brazil and extends possibly into the Indo-Pacific regions.

Normally, jacks run up to about two feet long, but there are reports of 30-pound specimens caught by anglers. Crabs and shrimps are their main foods. Saltwater fly-rodders usually seek them along sand beaches, islands, channels, drop-offs and in coastal streams and rivers.

Jacks respond well to both surface poppers and streamer flies in sizes 1/0 to 3/0, fished with an accelerating slow-to-fast stripping retrieve. As table fare they're mediocre but as sporting game on light tackle they're fine. They have a well-earned reputation as strong fighters.

Atlantic Permit
(*Trachinotus falcatus*)

The Atlantic permit is a powerful, tenacious fighter that makes long runs, and some specimens weigh upward of 50 pounds. Like other members of the Family Carangidae, the permit is an excellent table fish. However, the species is often difficult to lure to the fly. It's found along the Eastern Seaboard from Massachusetts to Florida.

Subsisting primarily on a diet of crabs, small fish, shrimps and mollusks, the permit is usually hooked over sandy flats, channels, holes and inlet passages. It normally enters the tidal flats on the tide flood (somewhat later than bonefish) and feeds into early ebb tides over sand bottoms, rocky areas and pebbles.

Atlantic permit show a preference for brown flies ranging in size from 4 to 1/0. Considerable experimentation in the retrieve is usually required to arouse a permit's interest in an artificial.

Barracuda (*Sphyraena barracuda*)

The barracuda, or great barracuda, is a rather spooky saltwater predator inhabiting both inshore and blue-water regions of the Atlantic from South Carolina to Brazil. Though an average barracuda weighs about nine pounds, 100-pound monsters have been caught.

Fly fishermen usually hook 'cuda near reefs, on tidal flats during flood tides, along lagoons and mangrove-lined shores and in harbors. Because the species is extremely sharp-toothed, a 12-inch wire leader is recommended at the tippet end of the mono-filament leader.

Barracuda respond to both surface poppers and brightly colored streamer flies dressed in white, yellow and red, yellow, red or white and red shades and combinations. Very fast strip-in recoveries with streamers and continuous popping with surface bugs are generally the most productive fishing techniques.

Bluefish *(Pomatomus saltatrix)*

Bluefish—or blues, as they're commonly called—range the relatively warm oceans the world over. In the Atlantic waters of this continent they're found from Massachusetts south through Argentina. Most of them weigh less than 10 pounds, but 40-pounders aren't unknown. They feed chiefly on small fishes, crustaceans and mollusks. Some of the best American fly fishing for blues can be had in Rhode Island's Narragansett Bay, when hordes of bluefish corral menhaden against the reed beds and rocky shorelines.

These exceptionally strong fish respond very well to simple bucktails and streamers in yellow, white, green and white or pink and white. And as Kukonen noted, cork-bodied popping bugs with long bucktail tails are also effective, and preferred hook sizes range from 1 to 3/0.

According to Paul Kukonen, noted fly-rodder and producer of some fine films on fishing and hunting, the points and shallow bays at the north end of Prudence Island—mostly rocky shores with reeds that are flooded at high tide—provide one of the very few areas where large bluefish can be taken by casting flies from the shore. Of his experience there, Paul said:

"Very often the blues herded bait fish (menhaden two to 3½ inches long) against the shoreline or at the edge of the reed beds, making for very short casts—15 to 20 feet. There was no need for the monster fly rods usually associated with saltwater fly fishing." He added that his angling party used rods under nine feet long, handling 7 and 8 weight fly lines plus 150 yards of 20-pound-test backing line. The flies were simple bucktails tied on Wright & McGill #SS 90 hooks, usually sizes 1 or 1/0. These thin hooks afford the better penetration needed with light fly rods.

"I occasionally used surface cork-bodied bugs," Paul told me, "with a concave face and a long bucktail tail, on a size 3/0 hump-shanked hook. They didn't last long—sometimes one blue would mash the cork. But it's exciting to see a seven- or eight-pound blue take a bug on the surface. The leader was about eight feet long, 30-pound-test level mono, with six or eight inches of very thin stainless-steel wire to the fly. At times I used a tiny barrel swivel for a connector, or simply tied the mono to a very small eye formed of the wire itself. The wire is a must. Regardless of the mono's strength—even 40- or 50-pound test—an 11- or 12-pound blue could cut through. We had to play some of them for 20 minutes, or longer.

"In that shallow water they made long runs, which of course never happens in deep water, where they sound. At times I'd be playing a blue 200 feet away and between me and the fish two or three schools of blues would be smashing into the countless thousands of menhaden.

"A few times they chopped through the tight Dacron backing, resulting in a loss of fish, fly line, backing and fly. That adds up to about $20, but the fishing was worth it. This is very exciting sport.

"Once in a while a fish would engulf the fly and keep on feeding for a few seconds, not realizing it was hooked. This usually allowed time to get slack line back onto the reel before the panic started. The initial run of a large bluefish in shallow water is very fast. It's powerful and spectacular. The small, single fly hook lets the fish close its mouth, as opposed to the handicap presented by most lures and plugs. That makes quite a difference.

"The larger, faster boats in our area chased the breaking schools all over the bay. Jim Reid and I used my old 14-foot Aerocraft and a good 10-hp. Mercury. We stuck to the shorelines and shallow coves where the larger boats couldn't operate. We were almost always alone and we preferred to cast from shore. In 10 days, while making a film, we released about 85 blues uninjured. This is the greatest argument for fly fishing. It's next to impossible and dangerous, to try to release a blue with three sets of trebles in its jaws.

"We had a perfect opportunity to compare the fighting qualities of striped bass and bluefish, since we often caught both on the same tackle at the same place. A six- or eight-pound striped bass was good for about four or five minutes of fight. A blue of the same size fought 15 minutes or more. Bear in mind that we were using rods meant for 14-inch trout and those rods took tremendous punishment because we didn't baby the fish.

"There are, of course, a great many other very fine fly-fishing areas in the bay—it covers about 100 square miles of water. But we prefer the sheltered coves and passes of Prudence."

(See Chapter 14 for the dressing of the Kukonen Bluefish Bucktail.)

Bonefish *(Albula vulpes)*

The fast-running, sporty bonefish is found in virtually all of the world's tropical oceans. Most bonefish weigh anywhere from a couple of pounds to 10, but they can grow to more than 15 pounds.

Bonefish are bottom feeders that favor crustaceans and mollusks. They frequent the deeper inshore waters on ebb tide and roam the flats during flood tides. Sometimes they're also found around reefs, coral islands and beaches.

Bonefish are spooky game. To take them on the tidal flats anglers look for tailing, feeding bonefish, then wade cautiously to within casting distance. The technique is to cast well ahead of the fish and let the fly sink close to the bottom before commencing a slow, stripping retrieve. Small shrimplike flies and bucktails from size 6 to 1/0 are preferred by most flyrodders. Brown seems to be one of the more effective colors for bonefish flies, and pink, yellow and white are popular. Though the bones don't amount to much as table fare, they put up a fine running battle, and they present quite a stalking challenge when a mudding, tailing school is spotted on the shallow flats.

Dolphin *(Coryphaena hippurus)*

The dolphin is an offshore species found in warm tropical and subtropical seas. Ranging from five pounds to more than 70, this handsome and colorful fish is usually found around the debris and flotsam associated with tidal rips and currents. In some regions the dolphin is called a dorado, and this can cause misunderstandings since an entirely different species—*Salminus maxillosus*, an outstanding South American freshwater game fish—is also named dorado. To avoid confusion, it might be better to call a dolphin a dolphin and a South American dorado a dorado.

To catch dolphin on a cast fly, anglers usually begin by trolling until a first dolphin is caught and a school is thus located. The hooked fish is tethered on a line aft of the transom to keep the rest of the school in the vicinity.

Brightly colored bucktails in sizes 1/0 to 3/0 are then cast and retrieved with fast, short, stripping recoveries. The main foods of the dolphin are crustaceans, squids and various fishes.

Crevalle *(Caranx hippos)*

Crevalle—also known as crevally, common jacks or jack crevalle—are found in both the Atlantic and Pacific. The unusual habitat includes deeper flats, drop-offs from bonefish flats and some deep-water areas. A five- to seven-pound crevalle is about average. It's considered worthless for the table but is a strong, tenacious fighter on a fly rod.

Both surface poppers and streamer flies will trigger a crevalle's appetite. Color doesn't seem to make much difference if the fly is worked with a slow-to-fast accelerating retrieve. Jacks feed mostly on other fishes and crustaceans.

Red Drum *(Sciaenops ocellata)*

Red drum—alias redfish, channel bass and puppy drum—range the Atlantic Seaboard and the Gulf Coast, from Delaware to Mexico. They're bottom feeders that frequent areas favored by permit and bonefish, but red drum also forage in deeper waters for shrimps, other fishes, crabs and mollusks. They weigh up to 40 pounds or more. Though a red drum doesn't jump when hooked, the species is noted for its tough, sustained fighting ability.

When a drum is spotted in fairly shallow water, the usual technique is to get its attention by slapping the fly hard on the water, within a foot or two of the fish. If a streamer fly is being used, it's normally recovered with fast stripping of the line, but drum will also take poppers fished with a slow, steady popping retrieve.

Brightly colored red and yellow or red and orange flies, dressed on 1/0, 2/0 or 3/0 hooks, are usually the most effective.

Sharks

Sharks are found most everywhere in the world's tidal waters, and there are a great many different species. These ubiquitous fishes are omnivorous. They're usually quite easy to fool with streamer flies fished in shallow water, but sharks are so nearsighted that they must rely heavily on the sense of smell to locate much of their food. Because of their poor eyesight, rather slow retrieves of size 5/0 or 6/0 tarpon-type streamer flies are necessary. Once hooked, sharks make strong runs and fight well, especially the big ones.

Great caution should be exercised in handling sharks once they've been played down. Their teeth can inflict horrid wounds. A 12-inch wire leader is recommended to any flyrodder who goes after sharks.

Snook *(Centropomus undecimalis)*

The snook is a fine fly-rod fish inhabiting the mangrove shores, grassy flats and warm brackish waters of the lower Pacific and Atlantic coasts. An active jumper and runner, the snook has an unnerving ability to streak under mangrove roots when hooked. Although 50-pounders have been recorded, a snook is normally comparable in size to a Southern largemouth bass. It's likely to weigh from four to five pounds to about 10.

Brightly colored poppers, streamers and bucktails in sizes 1/0 to 3/0 are favored. Both streamers and poppers are usually fished on a monofilament shock-tippet. As a rule, popping bugs are worked quite slowly. Streamer flies and bucktails should be recovered with a stripping retrieve, experimenting with the speed until some fish respond.

Spotted Weakfish
(*Cynoscion nebulosus*)

Spotted weakfish are also known in various regions as sea trout, spotted sea trout, weakfish, speckles and squeteague. They range Atlantic inshore waters from New York to Florida and are also plentiful on the Gulf Coast. They generally weigh less than four pounds.

Preying on fish and crustaceans, spotted weakfish inhabit shallow waters. They like grassy flats, sand beaches, bays, river mouths and brackish creeks, and they feed most actively from dusk through dawn. Fly fishermen catch them most often on brightly colored streamers and poppers in sizes 2 to 3/0. Accelerating stripping retrieves are usually the most productive with streamer flies. Popping bugs are normally worked quite slowly for weakfish. Their gill plates are sharp, so take care when you're handling them. They're called weakfish only in reference to their very delicate mouth parts—nothing else about them is weak, and they put up a good fight, dashing this way and that or making long, hard runs. Sometimes a fish hits the fly hard and hooks itself. Otherwise, care has to be taken not to set the hook too quickly, too forcefully or with too long a pull or it may simply tear out of the fish's mouth. For the same reason, there has to be a certain degree of finesse in playing a weakfish once it's hooked; it's scrappy, but with that weak mouth it can't be horsed in.

Striped Bass *(Morone saxatilis)*

Striped bass, or stripers as they're usually called, are anadromous battlers found in both the Pacific and Atlantic waters of North America. Their habitat is usually in bays, estuaries and deltas, except when they're on their river spawning runs. They usually prefer rocky or sandy shores. Like steelheads and the Pacific salmons, striped bass have been successfully transplanted to landlocked lakes and impoundments. South Carolina's Santee-Cooper Reservoir is the most notable example of striper introduction to freshwater with no access to the sea. The stripers there spawn in streams that empty into the reservoir. It's worth noting that Pacific striper fishing has also been a product of successful transplanting. Originally confined to the Atlantic, striped bass were introduced to West Coast bays beginning in 1879.

Also known as greenheads or rockfish, striped bass can grow to 70 pounds or more. But most of them range from three or four pounds to about 40. Their main foods are other fishes, squids, annelids, clams, eels and crustaceans.

Brightly colored streamer flies and surface bugs are popular with fly fishermen seeking striped bass. Preferred hook sizes run from 2/0 to 5/0. But since stripers are notorious for hitting a fly short, knowledgeable anglers usually dress their flies on very long-shanked hooks or, preferably, tie a smaller trailer hook to the shank or bend of the fly hook.

Depending on the water depth, streamers and bucktails are fished on floating or sinking fly lines. Slow, long pull-ins are among the best methods of retrieving the streamers. Surface bugs are twitched or popped slowly as in surface fishing for largemouth bass. Incidentally, stripers are very wary fish. If you see a school of feeding stripers, either let the tide carry your boat toward the fish or, better yet, wait for the fish to feed to within casting distance. If the water can be waded, approach the feeding school very quietly in your chest waders, and don't go too close.

Big stripers can put up a terrific fight, but they're not as strong as bluefish of comparable size. They're first-rate table fish.

Tarpon *(Megalops atlantica)*

Flyrodders can have tremendous sport with tarpon of all sizes—from little schooling fish that weigh a few pounds to "dock tarpon" that seldom go more than 30 to full-grown monsters that weigh more than 100. For that matter, tarpon sometimes attain a weight of more than 200 pounds, and specimens weighing well over 100 have been taken on a fly rod. These "silver kings" are found in tropical and sub-tropical Atlantic waters. They're normally hooked by flyrodders in shallow waters—brackish coastal estuaries, lagoons, lakes in mangrove flats and coastal streams.

The normal technique used to coax tarpon into striking a fly is to cast well ahead of the fish and retrieve your bucktail or streamer with slow pulls on the line. Tarpon have hard mouth parts and it's necessary to plant the 2/0 to 5/0 streamer hook with a very hard strike. A stiff, powerful fly rod is recommended. You also need a quality saltwater fly reel that can withstand the punishment of handling very heavy fish. Tarpon are inordinately strong, spectacular jumping fish, though they're not capable of the blazing-fast runs of some saltwater species. The main tactic in handling an outsized tarpon is to exert maximum pressure—all that the tackle will bear—if you don't want to spend an inordinate amount of time wearing the fish down before you can gaff or release it.

Large tarpon have been known to inflict serious injury to anglers who attempted to handle them while "green"—that is, while they were still full of fight. So it pays to play a big tarpon down thoroughly before attempting to bring it aboard.

Saltwater Big Game: The Billfishes

Fly casting for the several species of billfish indigenous to waters off the coasts of North and South America, Australia and New Zealand has become popular enough in recent years to warrant more than passing mention in this book.

A man who pioneered many of the important techniques of flyrodding for sailfish and marlin was the late Dr. Webster Robinson of Key West, Florida, who fished not only in that area but also off Baja, California, and Panama. He passed away several years ago, but he left a legacy of proven methods that have tremendously aided other big-game fishing enthusiasts to enjoy the incredible thrills associated with hooking and playing these spectacular battlers on fly-fishing tackle.

In preparing this section I consulted closely with William W. "Billy" Pate, Jr., of Islamorada, Florida, who is considered to be one of the world's foremost authorities on the subject, and with Robert D. Stearns of Miami, Florida, a fellow outdoor writer and avid saltwater fly-fishing expert.

At this writing, Mr. Pate holds the world fly-fishing record for Atlantic sailfish with 15-pound-test leader; world fly records for black marlin on 15-, 12- and 6-pound-test leaders; and the world fly record for striped marlin on 15-pound-test leader.

Anglers unfamiliar with big-game fishing should note that there's a tremendous size differential between certain of the billfish species. Atlantic sailfish *(Istiophorus americanus)* are the smaller of the two sailfish species sought by North American anglers. They average about 40 pounds. Their cousins the Pacific sailfish *(Istio-*

phorus greyi) normally run about twice as heavy and, according to Bob Stearns, are the easier of the two species to tease up and hold at the surface for reasonably extended periods of time. However, the Atlantic sailfish generally fight harder than the Pacifics.

For North American anglers at least, the white marlin *(Makaira albida)* is probably the most numerous, but it is also the smaller of the two species of marlin found in Atlantic waters, the other being the blue marlin *(Makaira nigricans ampla)*. Fish in the 50-pound class are the most common size of white marlin taken.

The unquestioned granddaddy of the marlins is the black marlin *(Makaira nigricans marlina)*. It ranges Pacific waters all the way from the Mexican coastline and Chile to New Zealand, Australia and Mozambique. It is known to attain weights in excess of 1,500 pounds and is considered second in importance only to the broadbill swordfish by the world's non-fly-fishing big-game anglers.

Blue marlin are the larger of the two species caught in the Atlantic, and they range warm seas of both North and South America. Some of the best fishing areas for blue marlin are off Florida and the Bahamas. This fish is known to exceed a half-ton in weight, but one over 200 pounds can be considered a worthy trophy.

Incidentally, a hefty marlin might seem a highly desirable trophy until one considers the space such a fish will take up on a wall. A 700-pound blue marlin, for example, would probably run a bit over 13 feet long—not exactly the sort of thing a fellow's wife would probably care to have hanging permanently over the fireplace, unless of course one's home is blessed with a 15-foot-long mantelpiece. A 7- or 8-foot-long Atlantic or Pacific sailfish, on the other hand, makes an incredibly beautiful and practical wall mount for a basement recreation room—provided one can figure out how to get it into the basement. And, although these comments are made with tongue partially in cheek, they do bear consideration from a practical point of view.

For example, a friend of mine once went to the expense of having a magnificent mount made from an 8-foot-long Pacific sailfish he'd caught off Cabo San Lucas. The mounted sailfish was too wide to fit through the basement windows and too long to angle through the rear entrance to the basement or down through the stairwell.

So he decided to hang the fish-mount on the wall of his fourth-floor office. After two frustratingly unsuccessful attempts to jockey the fish up the office-building stairwell, which was an exceptionally narrow one, he finally resorted to hiring a "cherry picker" crane (at no small cost, I might add) and bringing it in through his office window. That was on a Saturday. And the crane operator naturally charged him an overtime rate.

Unable to obtain the aid of a carpenter in hanging the fish that day, he laid it out with care on the carpet in front of his desk, which soon proved to be a mistake.

And so help me, this is a true story. The following Monday morning his secretary, not having been forewarned of the fish's presence, waltzed into the office, tripped over the mount and broke the sail-like dorsal fin! If my friend's disposition had not benefited from his financial affluence the mistake could have resulted in the secretary's immediate economic demise. But fortunately, he was well heeled and took this temporary setback in good humor. However, the expense of removing the damaged mount by means of the "cherry picker" technique, and returning it to the taxidermist for repairs, was nonetheless staggering!

So, if you truly want a big-game-fish trophy mount, do yourself a favor and first determine if you have room for one. Otherwise, you could end up in the same predicament as the poor chap who built a 65-inch-wide boat in a basement with a 30-inch-wide exit door—only in reverse.

The final marlin species of interest to North American flyrodders is the striped marlin *(Makaira mitsukurii)*. This beautiful sea-giant ranges from California to Japan, and south along this hemisphere's coastline to the waters off Chile. It is also plentiful off Equador.

Although not in the same size class as the black marlin, the striped marlin is a hefty battler and is known to top 600 pounds, although the average fish caught is probably about half that size.

Fly-Fishing Techniques for Billfishes

Fortunately for the angler seeking his first billfish on a fly rod, there are some definite elements of commonality between the methods used to attract the various species to the surface and tease them into striking artificial flies.

Rendered down to bare-bone essentials, the basic method involves teasing the fish as close to the boat as possible with a hookless bait, then jerking the teaser-bait from the water and immediately replacing it with a streamer fly which, hopefully, the billfish will spot and strike.

This all sounds easy enough, but actually the technique requires close teamwork and no small amount of attention to detail.

Almost any kind of bait may be employed as a teaser—live, dead or artificial. But Billy Pate's personal preference is strip-bait, because it's tough and doesn't tear off the line when swallowed by the fish or struck by its bill. The strip-bait also has the advantage of having a taste, which an artificial teaser does not have. Be that as it may, some anglers do prefer artificial teasers, and one of the most popular is a plastic, 10-inch-long squid weighted with a one-ounce sinker.

Once the fish is teased close to the boat, the hookless teaser-bait is snatched from the water and the angler makes his cast to the fish.

"While this can be done with only two people, three or four makes it a whole lot easier," according to Pate.

The participants in this carefully timed series of maneuvers usually include not only the fly caster, but also the boat captain (or operator) and a chap who operates the teaser-bait. Normally, if the caster is right-handed, he stands on the port side of the boat (left side facing forward) so the craft's superstructure doesn't interfere with his backcast.

The teaser-bait is trolled from the starboard side of the boat, in this case, and watched closely by the person who will ultimately do the actual teasing.

Billy Pate says, "I have found it best to troll only one line, and usually no other teaser. Extra lines or teasers require another hand on board to get them out of the way in a hurry, and this usually results in more confusion than they are worth. One might raise fewer fish with only one line out, but he can do a lot more effective job with the ones that do come up."

The preference seems to be to troll the teaser-line flat, rather than on an outrigger. Once the fish comes up to inspect the bait, the mate rapidly reels it in to within easy casting range of the angler. Then, he usually allows the fish to take the teaser into its mouth, although this practice isn't followed 100 percent of the time. The teaser-bait handler then jerks the bait from the fish's mouth. The purpose of this maneuver is to excite the fish, and when it does he "lights up," color-wise, rather like a phosphorescent Christmas tree.

With the billfish now at the surface, teased and excited into a frenzy, the man at the teaser-bait then tries to yank it into the boat. At this precise moment, the angler makes his cast toward the tail of the fish.

"At this point the captain should put the boat into neutral also," says Billy, "so that the fly is not trolled, but is cast and worked by the angler. The angler has cast at a 45-degree angle toward the tail of the fish so that the fish must turn sideways somewhat to take the fly. He (the fish) believes the bait is coming back into the water after escaping from his mouth and jumping free of the water for a moment. His taking the fly sideways gives a better chance of hooking the fish in the corner of the mouth, which is the best spot. If he takes it coming straight on, the hook point must penetrate the hard beak on the top or a tough, wide rim on the lower jaw."

Billy Pate has experimented with laying the starboard outrigger straight aft and at about a 30-degree angle from the water, and running the line to the teaser through a ring on the end of the outrigger. This gets the bait out of the water faster and much easier than working it on a flat line, but he points out that it can sometimes get in the way of the fly line under the influences of adverse winds from the port quarter.

"The best wind, by the way, is one from the starboard side, and the next best is one from the bow," according to Pate. "The worst wind is from the port side, as it can blow the back cast into the side of the boat. A wind from the stern of under 15 m.p.h. can be cast into, as the casts are generally not too long—under 60 feet. A flat line to the teaser-bait is better, I think, because you can get it back into action faster if the fish loses interest in the fly. On

heavy spinning tackle, the teaser can be cast at the fish to revive his interest."

Although there's undoubtedly going to be a difference of opinion between various saltwater flyrodders regarding the choice of tackle for billfishing, Pate's stated preference includes a 9- to 9½-foot heavy-duty glass fly rod weighing between six and eight ounces. He recommends that the reel should be capable of at least three pounds of drag. Several makes of suitable reels are available, but they're expensive. His personal choices are a World Wide Sportsman fly rod and a Seamaster fly reel. Some other preferred fly rods include models made by Fenwick and Scientific Anglers, as well as other makes. Other popular (and expensive) saltwater reels capable of handling really outsized fish are the Fin-Nor, Bogdan and Orvis saltwater fly reels. The better saltwater reels run in the $60 to $170 price range.

According to the experts, most people use floating fly lines for billfishing, but Pate's personal preference is a shooting-head of about 26 feet of fast-sinking (AFTMA Class II) fly line.

"Next I use about 50 feet of 40- or 50-pound very supple limp monofilament. This provides much less drag than 100 feet of floating fly line. The monofilament is coiled in a bucket of water on deck ready for action. Then comes 500 yards of 27-pound Dacron backing. This much can be used with a shooting-head, but probably only 250 or 300 yards with a floating 100-foot fly line. I have needed over 400 yards on some fish," he says.

"On the end of the fly line comes about 6 feet of 30-pound mono leader attached with a double nail knot, then the lightest section of the leader, be it 15-pound, 12-pound, 10-pound or 6-pound test. This should have a Bimini twist (also known as a '20-times around' knot), in each end, with at least 12 inches of single line untwisted in the center. This is attached to the 30-pound leader with a blood knot. Attached to the other end of the lightest leader is less than 12 inches of shock tippet. This is either 100-pound mono or something like Steelon, wire covered with plastic. These will be attached to the leader with either an Albright Special knot or a double nail knot, and the fly is attached to the shock tippet."

According to Pate, most people tie their billfish flies on hooks ranging in size from 5/0 to 7/0. The fly he recommends should be dressed with the longest white saddle hackles available and should be at least 6 inches long. A few strips of Mylar should be tied on each side of the fly, and the hook should be honed or filed very sharp, and in the triangular configuration preferred by a majority of saltwater flyrodders. (Filing a hook point into a triangular shape provides the angler with not only a very sharp, penetrating point, but also three additional cutting edges that assist penetration of hard mouth parts.)

Interestingly enough, Bob Stearns notes a recent trend among some billfishing enthusiasts toward the use of smaller flies not exceeding 3 inches in length.

Once the billfish is teased to the surface and whipped into an enthusiastic frenzy, the flycaster himself has an opportunity to display his mettle.

"I usually cast to the tail of the fish at a 45-degree angle more or less, and when the fly hits the water I give it two strips and let it lie dead in the water. If the fish are going to take, they will usually do it now, and they like a fly lying dead in the water better than a moving fly. Just hooking the fish at this point is one of the most difficult parts of the whole procedure," says Billy.

"Once you feel him, hit him a couple of times, and then clear your fly line as he starts to run. Once he's on the reel, hit him a couple of more times against the drag of the reel, which should be no more than a third of the breaking strength of the leader. If he jumps, of course, bow to him." ("Bowing" to a fish means to lower the rod tip far enough so that a bit of slack is let into the line, which may prevent a tear-out or broken line in case the fish lands on it in returning to the water after a jump.)

Pate strongly recommends the angler moving to the bow of the boat for the main part of the battle and having the captain chase the fish, rather than back down on it. A rod belt is a handy thing to have on at this point. And remember, if you're after a fly-rod record, no one can touch the line or leader at any time, even in gaffing the fish. Incidentally, no flying gaffs are permitted for a fly-rod record either. A straight gaff should be used, or the fish's bill should be grasped by the mate or your companion.

The Flies

By far the vast majority of the most popular and effective saltwater flies are the simplest of bucktails and streamers. Tying methods for such flies have been amply illustrated in earlier chapters, and Chapter 14 includes many patterns for these and other consistently productive saltwater flies.

Whitney Flies

Perhaps somewhat arbitrarily, I am including in this chapter a description of the trolling and shooting flies designed by A. A. "Tony" Whitney of Stockton, California. Whitney flies are made in a freshwater series as well as a saltwater series—one of the freshwater patterns, the Crane Prarie, is listed in Chapter 14 and is great for big rainbows, browns, and brook trout in reservoirs, lakes and big rivers. But saltwater fly fishing is a relatively new sport, necessarily innovative, and Whitney flies seem to fit right in.

Whitney flies employ tandem hooks, both riding up. They are weighted, and are tied with monofilament rather than thread; they are extremely durable. Whitney bases his patterns on the "spectrum theory" of refracted light. He uses special instruments to determine the spectrum of a particular food organism in water of specific depth, clarity and mineral content. Then he finds a combination of materials that will produce the same spectrum, and he puts them together to resemble the food organism—a bait fish or whatever it happens to be. He doesn't consider existing patterns but relies on the findings of his instruments to develop the proper hues. Here's how Whitney describes their development:

"The original flies were designed with one hook riding down and the stinger hook riding up. This was a serious mistake. I found that when a fish broke free but kept the hooks, the fish would be killed because one hook was caught in the lower jaw and the other in the upper jaw, thus eliminating feeding or breathing.

"Tying the hooks in a down position wasn't practical, as they caught all underwater snags and grasses. The next answer was to give enough weight to the underside of the shank so the hooks would ride with their shanks down and their bends up. Then it was possible to cover the hook with the body of the fly. This is a true mark of a Whitney fly."

Whitney points out that he developed his incredibly beautiful and durable flies to imitate specific bait fish, and with consideration of the mineral content of the water to be fished, the amount of sunlight and the angle of sunlight. In spite of this attention to highly particular conditions, he says his Mylar trolling flies have been proved to work on all species of saltwater game fish found in the Pacific from Alaska to Pan-

ama, and there is no reason to think they wouldn't be equally effective in both salt and fresh water throughout the world.

Because of the flies being dressed with monofilament in place of tying thread, Fig. 297 lists the proper mono for various hook sizes.

Fig. 297. Whitney trolling & shooting flies—tying-monofilament sizes.

Hook sizes	Test weight of tying mono (lbs.)	Test weight of hair finishing mono (lbs.)
10/12	1	1
8/10	2	1
6/8	2	1
4/6	4	2
2/4	4	4
1/0-2	6	4
2/0-1/0	6	4
4/0-2/0	6	4
6/0-2/0	6	4
8/0	6	4

Fig. 298. Whitney trolling & shooting flies—monofilament sizes for joining trailer hook.

Hook sizes	Test weight of monofilament for joining (lbs.)
10/12	25
8/10	30
6/8	40
4/6	50
2/4	60
1/0-2	80
2/0-1/0	80
4/0-2/0	80
6/0-2/0	100
8/0	100

Trailer hooks on the Whitney trolling flies are always turned-down-eye models, 2XL. All trailer hooks are at least one size smaller than the front hooks. Fig. 298 lists the proper sizes of monofilament for joining the hooks. Whitney uses bronzed hooks for freshwater flies and either stainless steel or cadmium hooks for saltwater flies.

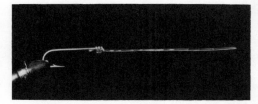

Fig. 299. This is the typical procedure for tying all Whitney flies. Tie the connecting leader to the rear hook with a whip-finish knot of four or more loops. Pull it tight.

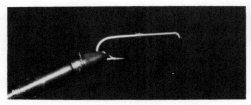

Fig. 300. Using monofilament of the proper size, start the basic tie on the front hook, beginning the wraps in the middle of the hook, wrapping forward to the eye, back to the bend, and finally returning to the starting point. Knot securely and cement the wraps.

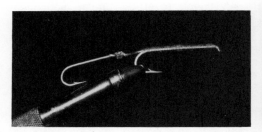

Fig. 301. Wrap the connecting leader firmly to the shank of the front hook, wrapping back to the bend, forward to the eye, and returning to the starting point. Knot the mono securely and cement the wrapping with clear acrylic.

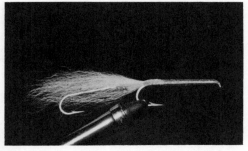

Fig. 302. Wrap on the tail and return the tying monofilament to the starting point. On feather tails, wrap on each pair of feathers separately. Cement the wraps.

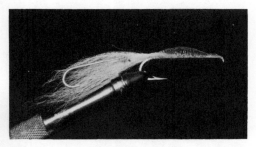

Fig. 303. Cut a keel-shaped piece from a sheet of lead no thicker than the width of the hook shank. The height of the lead keel should correspond to the size of Mylar tubing to be used so that the tubing can be slipped over it. Beginning at the center, wrap on the keel, first forward, then back to the rear, then forward to the eye. End with a whip-finish knot and cement the wrappings around the keel.

Fig. 304. Slip a piece of Mylar or metallic tubing over the shank and keel. Wrap it down at both ends with fine monofilament.

Fig. 305. Attach a piece of oval tinsel at the bend and wrap it forward over the wound-down tubing end. Tie it off with mono and trim off the excess after it's securely knotted. Coat the entire body with clear acrylic—several coats.

Fig. 308. Paint the head with several coats of red celluloid enamel and finish with two coats of red radiant lacquer.

Fig. 306. Tie in the bucktail portion of the wing and tie in Mylar strips if specified for the pattern.

Fig. 307. Wrap on the feather wings and top with Mylar strips if specified.

On some of the patterns for big game, both the front and rear hooks are dressed. The two hooks are sometimes joined by means of a snap swivel affixed to the rear of the front hook on a piece of stout nylon monofilament.

Trolling with the Tony Whitney Trolling & Shooting Flies is normally done with a spinning rod and a trolling or spinning reel loaded with monofilament line. For freshwater trolling, several techniques are suggested by Whitney. Surface trolling is accomplished by hooking two #7 barrel snap-swivels together. The monofilament fishing line is affixed to one of the swivels. To the other is tied a six or eight foot leader. The fly is knotted securely to the leader. In areas with a lot of underwater obstructions, 20 to 50 feet of line is let out. Troll through and around passable obstructions no faster than four miles an hour. In an alternate method with the same rigging, rod jerks are imparted at the rate of 30 to 40 per minute.

At times a faster surface troll is effective. Let out 50 to 75 feet of line and increase the speed, trolling at six to 10 miles an hour. Use this technique only in open water. (You might damage a boat running among obstructions at the higher speed.)

To probe waters from a foot to five feet deep, Whitney fastens the solid end of a sinker release to the end of the fishing line. Then he attaches a 12-inch leader to the trip end of the sinker release. A salmon-type sinker release weighs approximately ¾-ounce. The trolling fly is tied to the end of the foot-long leader and trolled at a speed of three to four miles an hour while imparting 30 to 40 rod-tip jerks per minute.

For fishing from five feet down to the bottom you can fasten a 12- to 14-inch leader to the sinker desired for the depth to be trolled. Attach the loop end of the sinker leader in the trigger end of the sinker release. This allows the sinker to ride below the level of the line and trolled fly. The sinker should be heavy enough to take the line down as straight as possible. If fish fail to respond at a trolling speed of three to four miles an hour, lift the line up and down in a slow rhythm—20 to 30 times a minute.

During extremely hot weather, bottom-bouncing is often the most productive method. Rig up with a sinker release as described above. Stop the boat and let the sinker down to the bottom. Start the boat and troll at three to four miles an hour. Let out the line as required to keep the sinker bouncing on the bottom every few feet. Do not drag the sinker over the bottom as that would stir up silt. When a fish strikes, the sinker is released automatically and the battle is on.

The suggested rig for trolling for sailfish and marlin off Mexico and south to Panama consists of an eight- or nine-foot heavy saltwater spinning rod equipped with a Penn Senator reel that's filled with 80-pound-test limp mono knotted to two heavy snap-swivels attached to the line. The flies are trolled fast enough to make them skip through the top of swells. They should be 100 to 150 feet behind the boat.

If you see a marlin or sailfish at the surface, let out enough line so you can circle the fish and drag the fly across its line of vision. In this case 200 to 300 feet of line may be needed, because the fish is likely to sound if you run the boat too close. The flies themselves are very important when fished by this method. They're used in a two-fly combination as follows.

First Fly for Whitney Billfish Rig

This fly is dressed on a size 8/0 stainless-steel ring-eye hook. A #3 or #5 snap-swivel attached to 80-pound-test mono is tied onto the first fly close to the hook bend. The body of the fly contains the lead keel previously described.

Here's the dressing.

BODY: silver tubing over lead keel.
WINGS: long white bucktail—long enough to cover swivel—topped with silver Mylar strands as long as the bucktail, topped with blue or green long saddle hackles, topped with blue or green Mylar strands.
HEAD: red, with eyes.

Second Fly for Whitney Billfish Rig

The second fly is dressed on a 6/0 stainless ring-eye hook with a 2/0 or 4/0 steel down-eyed 3XL tail-hook attached by 80-pound-test mono.

TAIL: long yellow impala or polar-bear hair—long enough to cover the tail-hook.
BUTT: red.
BODY: lead keel, covered with silver Mylar tubing.
WING: long white bucktail, topped with silver Mylar strands, topped with long green or blue saddle hackle,

topped with blue or green Mylar strands. All must be long enough to cover the tail hook.

HEAD: red, with eyes.

Weighted trolling flies can also be cast or shot. In shooting with spinning tackle, whether from shore or from a boat, add a casting sinker to a swivel at the end of your spinning line. Then attach a leader no more than two feet longer than your rod. Attach the fly to the end of the leader and cast it in the normal plug- or spin-casting fashion.

In casting the lighter (though weighted) shooting flies with a fly rod, use a weight-forward fast-sinking fly line. The line weight is determined by the depth to be fished and the distance to be cast.

CHAPTER 14

Fly Patterns

T HIS CHAPTER contains detailed dressings for, and pertinent notes concerning, 175 flies presently in use on North
American waters. The compilation is based
on my own experience plus extensive research and consultation with highly es-
teemed tiers. Each regional contributor to
this section and to the following appendix
of regional pattern lists was asked to provide detailed dressings of the most productive patterns in his geographical region, and to list the six most killing
patterns in each of four fly types. They
were also asked to send sample flies in the
case of patterns employing hard-to-de-
scribe techniques.

Most of the non-standard ties listed here
have been in use long enough and by
enough anglers so that there is no doubt
whatever about their usefulness. You might
say they're on the verge of becoming
standard, at least regionally. The few exceptions are simply newer flies and they,
too, have proved themselves.

Dressings are described in the standard,
abbreviated language commonly employed
in fly-tying literature except in a few cases
requiring lengthier wording to describe
some innovative technique.

Unless an exception is noted, all flies
listed have the standard proportions shown
in Fig. 68 at the end of Chapter 7. The
"Notes" section on each fly includes a reference to any illustrations from earlier in

the book that depict the tying of a more or
less similar fly.

The tying materials are listed in the order of tying. However, it should be noted
that in dressing certain dry flies and
nymphs, the hackles, legs, overbodies and
wing cases are wrapped or tied down after
the wrapping of the body or thorax. (See
Chapters 8, 9 and 10 for illustrations of
methods employed for many of these flies.)

Colors listed are the standard dye shades
used by American material suppliers, except where otherwise noted.

Primary regional use of each pattern is
indicated by one or more of the following
symbols, listed with the name of the fly: (E)
Eastern, (EC) Eastern Canada, (W) Western, (WC) Western Canada, (MW) Midwestern, (G) General—that is, useful
throughout North America for the appropriate type of fishing.

Nymphs & Wet Flies

Artesan Green (MW)
HOOK: 12-4, 3XL, 2X-stout.
THREAD: yellow except for the head.
TAIL: small bunch of yellow-dyed rabbit
  hair.
BODY: tapered and wrapped with em-
  bossed gold tinsel.
WING: mixed yellow, green and blue ring

tail hairs, topped with natural brown bucktail.

HEAD: large and well-tapered, wrapped with yellow and black variegated thread.

NOTES: Normally dressed weighted, this bucktail-style nymph is tied to imitate a large stonefly that emerges about the first of June on the Wolf River, Wis. Created by professional tier Edward Haaga of White Lake, Wis., it's said to work well all season long on down-and-across-stream casts. TYING TECHNIQUE: See Figs. 83-101 and 242-244.

Atherton Medium Nymph (G)

HOOKS: 12-8, 2XL.

TAILS: three short fibers from cock-pheasant center tail feather.

ABDOMEN: roughly dubbed hare's-ear fur ribbed with narrow oval gold tinsel.

THORAX: same as abdomen, wrapped over padding or weighting wire.

WING CASE & PADS: bright blue silk floss or Lurex tinsel, or lacquered section of dyed-blue goose primary.

LEGS: speckled-brown partridge.

NOTES: Generally considered to be one of the deadliest of Atherton's excellent mayfly nymphs. TYING TECHNIQUE: See Figs. 112-116 and 199-202.

Beaverpelt Nymph (G)

HOOKS: 8-2, 2XL.

THREAD: black.

BODY: thickly dubbed dark brownish-gray beaver fur with guard hairs left in.

HACKLE: wrapped out of soft black hen neck hackle or, more often, out of single greenish-gray Chinese pheasant rump feather tied in by tip and wrapped as collar.

NOTES: Originated by Don E. Earnest, retired fisheries biologist with Washington State Department of Game, to suggest large dragonfly nymphs. It's usually fished on a sinking fly line with a stripping retrieve. A deadly lake fly! TYING TECHNIQUE: See Figs. 175-176, 199-202.

Bicolor Walker (G)

HOOKS: 8 & 10, 3XL Sproat.

TAIL: a few short dyed-brown cock-pheasant breast-feather fibers.

BODY: fuzzy yarn, dyed brownish-wine.

RIBBING: corn-yellow buttonhole twist.

WING CASE: tuft of fluff from hackle butt dyed purplish-brown.

NOTES: Originated by E. H. "Polly" Rosborough, of Chiloquin, Ore., one of the West's top professional tiers, it's dressed to suggest a mayfly nymph found from Oregon to New York state (but not south of those states). It should be fished in the top inch of water from late June through July. TYING TECHNIQUE: See Figs. 112-116, 165-168.

Big Hole Demon (W)

HOOKS: 10-4, 2XL.

THREAD: white Nymo.

TAIL: grizzly or badger hackle tips, divided.

BODY: rear half, flat silver tinsel ribbed with oval silver tinsel; front half, black chenille, palmered with grizzly or badger hackle.

NOTES: Tier Dan Bailey of Livingston, Mont., named this 1964's "fly of the year" for Montana. A darker version is dressed with a gold-tinsel body and furnace or dark brown hackles and tails. TYING TECHNIQUE: See Figs. 83-101, 129-133.

Big Ugly Nymph (W, WC)

HOOK: 6, 3XL.

THREAD: dark brown.

BODY: dark brown wool yarn around shank; woven olive chenille underbody picked up on top with six-pound-test monofilament.

WING CASE: sections of dark gray goose primary, lacquered, trimmed to shape and tied on either side of body.

LEGS (OPTIONAL): formed by spreading fibers at tips of two brown hackles trimming 3/16-inch-long tip section to 1/16-inch width. Strip away remaining fibers and tie in with hackle (Fig. 309).

HACKLE: sparse, fairly long beard of brown hen- or pheasant-tail fibers.

NOTES: Originated by Jim Kilburn of Richmond, B.C., to represent the pupa of the traveling sedge (a large caddis), which emerges in late June or early July on Knouff and Badger Lakes, near Kamloops. Sometimes a rusty-orange wool tip is tied in before the body is wrapped to suggest the transparent pupal case from which the emerging adult has partially withdrawn its body. The fly is usually fished with a dead-drift on a floating line. TYING TECHNIQUE: See Figs. 175-176, 187-190 (simplified version, 134-136).

Fig. 309. Big Ugly Nymph.

Bird's Stonefly Nymph (W)

HOOKS: 10-4, extra-long shank.

THREAD: orange.

TAIL: two sections of turkey pointer quill, dyed brown and divided.

BODY: dark brown fox fur dubbed on and ribbed with orange floss.

THORAX: peacock herl overlaid with strip of clear plastic, tied down fore and aft.

HACKLE: brown, trimmed to extend out at sides only.

HEAD: orange tying thread.

NOTES: Calvert T. Bird of San Francisco designed this nymph to simulate large stoneflies *(Pteronarcys californica)* of Montana streams and rivers. TYING TECHNIQUE: See Figs. 199-202 (dubbing), 179-181 (body configuration), 134-136 (overbody).

Bitch Creek Nymph (W)

HOOKS: 8-4, Mustad 9671 (size 6 preferred).

THREAD: black.

TAIL: two white rubber hackle fibers.

BODY: black chenille.

THORAX: black chenille, built up larger than body and underlaid with strand of orange chenille.

HACKLE: brown, palmered over thorax.

FEELERS: same as tail.

NOTES: There are several popular dressings for this standby Montana favorite; this version is probably the easiest to tie. TYING TECHNIQUE: See Figs. 179-181.

Black Gnat (G)

HOOKS: 14 & 15.

THREAD: crimson or claret.

BODY: black silk, or two or three crow-wing secondary fibers.

HACKLE: purplish-black, taken from cock starling's shoulder.

WINGS (OPTIONAL): dark starling.

NOTES: Here's an excellent example of how a famous and popular wet fly was modified into even deadlier form by a creative fly fisherman—in this case by the late James E. Leisenring. It's very deadly fished as a flymph, and is very good on limestone streams and spring creeks during hatches of duns. TYING TECHNIQUE: See Figs. 83-101.

Black Hackle, Peacock Body (G)

HOOKS: 18-6, regular, or extra-long shank.

THREAD: black.

TAIL: black hackle fibers or hackle tips.

BODY: peacock herl, dressed full.

HACKLE: black hen-neck hackle wrapped sparsely.

NOTES: One of the deadliest standard patterns for trout and panfish in both lakes and streams. TYING TECHNIQUE: See Figs. 83-101.

Black Midge Nymph (G)

HOOKS: 20-16, 1XS.

THREAD: black.

TAIL: a few black hackle fibers.

BODY: a moose-mane hair, wrapped in tight turns, or brown thread.

THORAX: black hackle wound on thickly, then clipped to shape about same diameter as a herl wrap.

FEELERS: a few black hackle fibers, sticking out on each side of thorax, unclipped.

NOTES: This excellent nymph was created by Dan Bailey and Gary Howells about 1958. It suggests a midge pupa prior to hatching. TYING TECHNIQUE: See Figs. 154, 231-232.

Blue Winged Olive (G, E)

HOOKS: 24-14.

THREAD: black or dark olive.

TAIL: medium-blue dun hackle fibers.

BODY: dressed slim out of medium olive floss.

WINGS: two dark dun hackle tips, about same length as body, tied flat over the back.

NOTES: This important Eastern wet fly, as dressed by the Orvis Company, suggests the ubiquitous *Baetis* mayflies, whose big hatches provide moments of sensational fly fishing across the nation; and in size 18 or 16 it would probably serve well fished as an emerger during the early stages of a hatch of *Ephemerella attenuata* (Slatewing Olive)—strictly an Eastern mayfly that hatches between early June and early July. TYING TECHNIQUE: See Figs. 83-101, 237 (floss), 221 (wings).

Bread Crumb (E)

HOOKS: 14 & 12.

THREAD: primrose yellow.

BODY: white fur dubbed on primrose-yellow thread.

HACKLE: two or three turns of ginger hen hackle.

NOTES: The Bread Crumb is an especially useful trout nymph in the East. Tying technique: See Figs. 83-101, 199-202.

Breadcrust (G)

HOOK: wet-fly type, regular-length shank.

THREAD: black.

BODY: center stem of dark brown saddle hackle with fibers stripped off. Stem is soaked thoroughly, flattened and wound on in tight turns.

HACKLE: a few turns of webby grizzly hackle.

NOTES: One of the most important nymphs for trout in Northeastern streams, and useful in other regions as well. TYING TECHNIQUE: See Figs. 154, 83-101.

Brown Bomber (G)

HOOKS: 14-10.

BODY: gray wool or dubbed muskrat fur.

RIBBING: fine flat or oval gold tinsel.

HACKLE: brown-speckled partridge, wrapped as sparse collar.

NOTES: Listed by Bill Cairns of The

Orvis Company as one of the six best Eastern nymphs. Undoubtedly it will catch fish consistently from nymph-rich trout waters across the continent. There's hardly a knowledgeable trout fisherman who doesn't carry at least a dozen muskrat-bodied nymphs of this basic design, with minor variations, in his box at all times. TYING TECHNIQUE: See Figs. 83-101, 199-202.

Caddis Worm (E)
HOOKS: 14 & 12.
THREAD: black.
BODY: dirty-white fur dubbed with hard twist.
HEAD: dubbed black-bear underfur.
NOTES: An especially useful nymph in the central and mountainous parts of Maryland. This dressing supplied by Simion V. Yaruta of Owings Mills, Md. TYING TECHNIQUE: See Figs. 147-148.

Cahill, Dark (G)
HOOKS: 12 & 10.
THREAD: tan or brown.
TAIL: a few brown hackle fibers.
BODY: spun or dubbed muskrat fur, well-tapered.
HACKLE: a few brown hackle fibers tied to form a beard.
WING: section of lemon-colored wood-duck flank feather, rolled between palms or fingers, then tied in down-wing style on top of shank.
NOTES: This is one of the standards, providing the angler with a reasonably good imitation of a drowned March Brown mayfly dun. Good on both lakes and streams, East and West. TYING TECHNIQUE: See Figs. 199-202, 103-104, 83-101.

Carey Special (W, WC)
HOOKS: 12-2, regular or long-shank (6 & 8 preferred).
THREAD: black.

TAIL: choice of groundhog hairs, pheasant-rump feather fibers, scarlet hackle fibers or a few black-bear hairs.
BODY: choice of yarn, chenille, floss or spun or dubbed fur. Most effective colors are black, brown, magenta, olive green and yellow. Peacock herl is also excellent.
RIBBING (OPTIONAL): gold or silver tinsel.
HACKLE: three brownish or brownish-green cock-pheasant rump feathers wound on as dense, collar-type hackle so body scarcely shows.
NOTES: Designed by Dr. Lloyd A. Day, Quesnel, B.C., and first dressed by one Col. Carey, circa 1925. The fly suggests a caddis pupa rising to the surface prior to emerging. The Carey is either trolled or cast and retrieved on a sinking fly line. Deadly in any waters where there are large caddis. TYING TECHNIQUE: See Figs. 175-176.

Colorado Caddis (W)
HOOK: Mustad 9671 (size 8 recommended, but 12 is standard).
THREAD: black.
WEIGHTING: lead wire wrapped inside body.
SHELLBACK (OVERBODY): a section of the darkest natural gray duck or goose primary. Cut it from 3/16- to ¼-inch wide, depending on hook size.
BODY: tapered out of pale-yellow yarn (Sayelle Buttercup is recommended shade).
HACKLE: black, cut or pulled aside for shellback, which covers entire body.
HEAD: black and large.

NOTES: Developed by Bob Good of Denver, Colo., for Western streams. Tying technique: See Figs. 134-136, 83-101.

Cow Dung: (G)

HOOKS: 14-8, regular-length shank.

THREAD: black or olive.

BODY: spun or dubbed mustardy-olive fur.

HACKLE: brown hen-neck hackle.

WINGS: matched sections of dark gray duck primary feathers.

NOTES: Also dressed with a dark deer-body-hair bucktail wing, this is a famous standard pattern. The late Joe Brooks, one of this era's most knowledgeable fly fishermen, listed the Cow Dung as one of his basic wet-fly selections for Western waters as recently as 1972. The fly also enjoys considerable popularity in Northeastern trout areas. Anglers frequently snip the wings to about a third of their normal length and fish the Cow Dung as an emerger. TYING TECHNIQUE: See Figs. 83-101, 199-202.

Damselfly Nymph (G)

HOOK: 12, regular or light wire, depending on riding qualities desired.

TAIL: See abdomen instructions.

ABDOMEN: Select six ostrich flues dyed golden-olive or medium brown-olive. Flues should have unbroken tips. Align tips and, with fine thread of similar color, secure with a couple of wraps and knot ⅜-

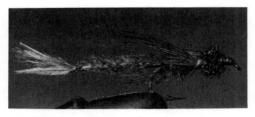

Fig. 310. Damselfly nymph.

inch from tip ends. Cement knot and place tips in vise with jaws just covering knot. Braid flues together (two flues to each strand) to make braid at least two inches long. (Braiding is easier if the flues are wet first.) Secure braid with another knot to prevent unravelling, then remove from vise. Place hook in vise and attach braided flues at normal tail position, leaving about ¾-inch of braid as an extended body.

THORAX, HACKLE

& HEAD: Move remainder of braid out of the way and tie in one small gray partridge feather, dyed medium brownish-olive, by its tip at thorax position. Take one turn of the hackle around shank and tie off. Wet hackle fibers, distribute half to each side of shank and secure with figure-eight wraps. Wind remainder of braided herl up shank to just past hackle and tie off. Wrap tying thread back down shank to midway between hackle and body tie-in points. Select dyed-brown Chinese pheasant green-phase rump feather, wet and smooth into long, thin shape and clip off extreme tip ends. Tie in, leaving short portion of tips extending as wing pads over abdomen. Twist remaining rump feather into "noodle" and carry forward, backward and forward again to produce shell-back type of wing case overlaying thorax and hackle. Form head with a few turns of peacock herl.

NOTES: This fly is still in the experimental stage of development, but is listed because of the highly imaginative method of dressing the abdomen. The technique could be applied very effectively to mayfly nymphs as well. Fig. 310 illustrates the silhouette. Originator of the nymph is Jack "Hutch" Hutchinson of Everett, Wash., one of the West Coast's most creative fly-tying anglers.

Darbee's Stonefly Nymph (E)

HOOKS: 14-6, 3XL.

THREAD: brown.

TAILS: two fibers from center tail feather of cock pheasant.

BODY: dubbed, amber-colored seal fur.

RIBBING: stripped center-stem from brown hackle, well soaked before wrapping.

WING CASES: two pairs of jungle-cock eye feathers; first pair tied in at juncture of body and thorax and extending about half of body length, second pair tied in behind head to lie over thorax.

THORAX: amber-dyed seal-fur dubbing, over which forward pair of wing cases is tied.

HEAD: amber-dyed seal-fur dubbing, followed by a few wisps of partridge hackle, followed by brown thread.

NOTES: Originated by the noted Eastern tier Harry Darbee, this pattern imitates the *Perla capitata* stonefly nymph. TYING TECHNIQUE: See Figs. 112-116, 199-202.

Dark Caddis Pupa (W)

HOOKS: 10 & 8, regular length and weight.

THREAD: orange Nymo.

BODY: tapered pinkish-orange mohair.

LEGS: dyed dull-orange grizzly hackle, dressed as a beard.

WING CASES: two hackle tips, same shade as legs.

NOTES: This is one of the fine patterns originated by E. H. "Polly" Rosborough, mentioned in an earlier chapter. TYING TECHNIQUE: See Figs. 199-205.

Dirty Olive Nymph (G)

HOOK: Mustad 3906 Sproat, various sizes.

THREAD: black.

TAIL: pheasant-tail fibers.

BODY: olive-brown yarn.

RIBBING: gold tinsel.

WING PAD: slate-colored duck.

HACKLE: brown-speckled partridge.

NOTES: A particularly effective nymph in the Yellowstone region, but also useful elsewhere. This dressing was provided by Mrs. Merton J. Parks of Parks' Fly Shop, Gardiner, Mont. TYING TECHNIQUE: See Figs. 112-116.

Doc Spratley (WC)

HOOKS: 10-4, regular weight and length.

TAIL: a few grizzly hackle fibers.

BODY: black wool yarn.

RIBBING: narrow oval or flat silver tinsel.

THROAT: a few grizzly hackle fibers.

WINGS: bunch of Chinese pheasant tail-feather fibers, rolled and tied down-wing style.

HEAD: peacock herl.

NOTES: Originated by the late Richard Prankard of Mt. Vernon, Wash., about 1949. It's one of the most effective wet patterns for British Columbia lakes containing caddis flies. TYING TECHNIQUE: See Figs. 83-101.

Duck Lake Wooly Worm (W)

HOOKS: 8-2, 4XL.

THREAD: olive or black.

BODY: dark olive chenille.

HACKLE: grizzly, palmered entire length of body.

NOTES: An unknown angler created this design for luring the outsized rainbows at famous Duck Lake in Montana. Wooly Worm patterns are popular and effective throughout the West, on both lakes and streams. Some of the best body colors are black, brown, olive and yellow. Most are dressed with palmered grizzly hackle. Some tiers add contrasting chenille over-bodies before wrapping on the hackle. TYING TECHNIQUE: See Figs. 129-132.

Early Brown Stone (G)

HOOK: 14.
THREAD: olive.
TAIL: none.
BODY: center stem of natural red game-cock hackle, soaked in water and wrapped on in tight turns.
WINGS: small dun hackle points tied flat.
HACKLE: blue dun hen-neck hackle.
NOTES: An Art Flick original, the Early Brown Stone is effective virtually any-where small stoneflies of this coloration are abundant. TYING TECHNIQUE: See Figs. 154, 204, 112-116.

Forked-Tail Nymph (G)

HOOKS: up to size 4.
TAIL: two fibers from short side of dyed-brown goose primary, dressed forked.
BODY: peacock herl.
RIBBING: flat gold tinsel, or reverse-wrapped with fine gold wire.
HACKLE: two turns of furnace hackle.
WINGS: two fibers from white goose primary.
NOTES: A useful fly in many parts of the country, this nymph is said to have been originated by Don and Dick Olson, of Bi-miji, Minn., and developed later by D. R. Prince of Monterey, Calif.

Fuzzyesco (G)

HOOKS: 12-4 (8 & 6 recommended as all-around sizes).
AFT-HACKLE: black.
BODY: peacock herl tapered toward both ends over lead wire.
FORE-HACKLE: black.
NOTES: Originated by Elmer C. Maynard

of Chicago, about 1935, for Midwestern stream fishing, it performs nicely in other regions as well. Work it right on the bot-tom with a stripping retrieve. TYING TECH-NIQUE: See Figs. 83-101 for basic method, though the appearance of the Fuzzyesco is unique.

G. B.'s Brown Stone Nymph (W)

HOOKS: Mustad 9672, Mustad 36680, or 2X-stout 3XL steelhead hook in sizes 10-4 (8 or 4 recommended).
THREAD: dark brown.
TAIL: brown-variant hackle fibers or dyed dark brown mallard-flank fi-bers, tied cocked-up and spread.
RIBBING: fine oval gold tinsel, over body only.
BODY: dubbed from mixture of medium-brown hare's-mask fur and brown beaver or opposum fur.
THORAX: lead wire underwrapping of brown yarn, cemented and flat-tened with pliers, then over-wrapped with body dubbing.
WING CASE: dark brown section from white-tipped turkey-tail feather, tied down over tho-rax only, cemented with vi-nyl cement for durability.
LEGS: same as tail, slightly longer than thorax and slanting down at sides.
HEAD: dark brown, fairly large.
NOTES: A dressing supplied by George M. Bodmer of Bodmer's Fly Shop, Colo-rado Springs. George ties this killing nymph in four colors—brown, gray, tan and near-black—with the same pattern, varying the tail, legs, wing-case and body colors. He recommends the fly for fishing deep in heavy water. TYING TECHNIQUE: See Figs. 112-116, 100-202, 204, 134-1359

Ginger Quill (G)

HOOKS: 14-10.
THREAD: tan.
TAIL: ginger hackle fibers.

BODY: stripped peacock-eye-feather quill. Some tiers (author included) prefer natural cream-colored raffia.

HACKLE: sparse collar of ginger hen-neck hackle, or bearded.

WINGS: matched sections of gray mallard primary or barred lemon-colored wood duck, dressed rolled, down-wing style.

NOTES: Some Western tiers prefer a sparse bucktail wing made from natural gray deer-body hair. This is one of the truly basic mayfly patterns for both Eastern and Western waters. It's fished both wet and dry. TYING TECHNIQUE: See Figs. 154, 103-104, 83-101.

Gold-Ribbed Hare's-Ear Nymph (G)

HOOKS: Mustad 9671, sizes 8-20 (12 & 14 recommended for Colorado region).

THREAD: medium or dark brown.

UNDERBODY: forepart (two-thirds of body) weighted with lead wire, wrapped with brown yarn to shape taper and cemented well to fill air pockets.

TAIL: brown partridge fibers, about six for size 14 fly.

BODY: very shaggily spun of dubbed dark fur from ears or poll of European hare.

RIBBING: fine gold wire wrapped in 3/16- to 1/8-inch turns.

LEGS: brown partridge, tied underneath and divided to lie along underbody on each side, extending just short of hook point.

NOTES: Known as one of the very best flies in the Colorado region, it catches fish virtually anywhere. This dressing was suppliee by George M. Bodmer, mentioned earlier. TYING TECHNIQUE:See Figs. 112-116, 199-202, 256-258.

Grant's Black Creeper (W)

HOOK: 7, Mustad 9492.

THREAD: black Nymo.

OUTER BODY: black Sunset Unifilament #707, 25-pound test.

INNER CORE: black yarn.

BRASS PINS: ½-inch, dressmaker's type.

BELLY STRIPE: orange floss.

WOVEN HACKLE: black Tynex, .005-inch.

NOTES: Originated circa 1931 by George F. Grant, Butte, Mont. Because of the unique tying techniques employed in weaving the hackle, it is recommended that the tier study Grant's 1971 book, *The Art of Weaving Hair Hackles for Trout Flies.* This particular nymph is one of the deadliest flies for Montana's Big Hole River and other blue-ribbon trout streams of that region.

Gray Hackle (G)

HOOKS: 14, 13, 12.

THREAD: primrose.

BODY: bronze-colored peacock herl.

RIBBING: narrow gold tinsel.

HACKLE: yellowish or creamy-white furnace hen hackle.

NOTES: A killing variation of the universally popular old standard, from the vise of the late James E. Leisenring. TYING TECHNIQUE: See Figs. 83-101.

Gray Hackle, Peacock Body (G)

HOOKS: 16-4, regular length and weight or 2XL, 1X-stout.

TAIL (OPTIONAL): scarlet hackle fibers or golden pheasant tippets.

BODY: peacock herl, tapered fullest toward eye.

HACKLE: two or three turns of webby grizzly hen-neck hackle.

NOTES: This one is useful for trout and panfish virtually everywhere in the U.S. and Canada. When a tail is omitted, a gold tinsel tip is frequently added. In streams, fish it as a mayfly nymph. In lakes, irregular hand-twist recoveries usually produce the most strikes. TYING TECHNIQUE: See Figs. 83-101.

Gray Nymph (G)

HOOKS: 16-2, 2XL.

THREAD: black or brown.

TAIL (OPTIONAL): muskrat guard hairs, badger guard hairs or grizzly hackle fibers.

BODY: usually dressed weighted from dubbed or spun muskrat fur with guard hairs teased out.

HACKLE: sparse collar of grizzly hen-neck hackle.

NOTES: Virtually every trout and panfish flyrodder has a gray-fur nymph as one of his staple patterns. Like the Adams dry fly, the Gray Nymph seems to have great appeal for fish of all regions. This is one of the more effective ties, but I've fished with at least a dozen variations that work nearly as well. TYING TECHNIQUE: See Figs. 199-202, 83-101.

Green Drake Nymph (E)

HOOKS: 8 & 10, 2XL.

TAILS: two small honey-dun neck-hackle tips.

BODY: dubbed white fur, teased out in thorax area.

WING CASES: two small jungle-cock eye feathers.

HACKLE: pale honey-dun.

NOTES: Originated by C. M. Wetzel, this tie is especially useful on some of the Northeastern trout streams. TYING TECHNIQUE: See Figs. 199-202, 204, 115.

Grizzly King (G)

HOOKS: 14-4, regular length and weight.

TAIL: scarlet hackle fibers.

BODY: green yarn or floss.

RIBBING: fine flat or oval gold tinsel.

HACKLE: grizzly, dressed bearded or as sparse collar.

WING: section of barred gray mallard-flank feather, dressed in rolled, down-wing style, or natural gray deer-body hair tied in standard bucktail fashion.

NOTES: The Grizzly King is one of the most deadly standard patterns throughout the U.S. and Canada. Seems to suggest the general colors of certain caddis species. It's sometimes dressed and fished as a dry fly in the size-14-to-10 range. TYING TECHNIQUE: See Figs. 83-101, 103-104, 115.

Heather Nymph (W)

HOOKS: 12 & 10, 2XL or 3XL.

TAIL: scarlet hackle fibers.

BODY: insect-green spun fur, ribbed with fine oval gold tinsel.

THORAX: peacock herl.

HACKLE: sparse collar of grizzly hen-neck hackle.

HEAD: black.

NOTES: Designed in 1960 by Fenton Roskelley of Spokane, the Heather Nymph suggests damselfly and large mayfly nymphs. It's fished either subsurface or deep, primarily in Western lakes. A deadly fly on rainbow trout during damselfly hatches. TYING TECHNIQUE: See Figs. 112-116, 199-202.

Hendrickson Nymph (E)

HOOK: 10.

THREAD: olive.

TAIL: section of mandarin-duck flank feather.

BODY: dubbed from blend of gray-fox belly, beaver and claret-dyed seal fur, giving body overall gray-brown caste.

RIBBING: fine gold wire or tying silk.

LEGS: partridge.

WING CASE: blue heron-wing feather section.

NOTES: Another of Art Flick's dandy nymphs. In dressing this fly, make a yarn hump on the shank near the eye. Tie in the tail, then start winding the body, spinning the fur loosely over the hump. Tie in the heron section, wind the hackle, wind the gold wire to hump, and tie off. Tie in the other end of the wing case and lacquer the wing case. TYING TECHNIQUE: See Figs. 256-258, 199-202, 112-116.

Henry's Lake Nymph (W)
HOOK: 8 weighted.
THREAD: black.
TAIL: small bunch of gray-squirrel tail hairs about same length as body.
BODY: yellow chenille or choice of gray, hot orange, red, insect-green, brown, olive or black.
OVERBODY & WHISKERS: gray-squirrel tail hairs. After tying in tail, tie in match-stick-thick bunch of squirrel by the butts. Wrap the body, then pull the hairs forward to head, dividing tips with criss-cross wraps into two bunches cocked forward, almost parallel to hook shank.
NOTES: Fish this nymph with an erratic stripping retrieve on a fast-sinking fly line. It catches fish in any lake with an abundance of freshwater shrimps. TYING TECHNIQUE: See Figs. 134-135 for overbody.

Iron Blue Nymph (E)
HOOKS: 14 & 15.
THREAD: crimson or claret.
TAIL: two or three very short, soft white hackle fibers.
BODY: dark mole fur spun on crimson or claret thread with two or three turns of thread exposed at rear.
HACKLE: two turns very short jackdaw-throat hackle.
NOTES: One of Leisenring's killing wet flies. This pattern is most useful in the East. TYING TECHNIQUE: See Figs. 83-101, 199-202.

Kemp Bug (G)
HOOKS: 14-8, regular length and weight or 2XL, 1X-stout.
THREAD: black.
TAILS: tips of three or four peacock herls, tied about same length as body.
BODY: peacock herl, dressed fullest toward thorax.
HACKLE: sparse beard of furnace hackle.
WING CASES: two short grizzly hackle tips tied in flat and slightly divided on top of body.
NOTES: The Kemp Bug is an excellent lake and stream nymph that's easy to tie and lethal when mayfly nymphs are emerging. This pattern, also known as the Davis Special, may have sired another great trout nymph called the Zug Bug. TYING TECHNIQUE: See Figs. 199-205.

Lowe's Gray Nymph (W)
HOOKS: 16-8.
TAIL: six to eight partridge fibers.
BODY: weighted, dubbed with mink, muskrat or otter fur.
RIBBING: fine gold wire.
BEARD: six or eight partridge hackle fibers.
NOTES: This is a very useful nymph for waters in the southern Sierra-Nevada range, including the Kings, Kern, Kaweah, San Joaquin and Merced Rivers. Originated by Allen Lowe, the dressing was submitted by the Inglewood Fly Fishermen. TYING TECHNIQUE: See Figs. 83-101, 199-202, 115.

Michigan Nymph (MW)

HOOK: 2XL.

TAIL: speckled mallard fibers.

ABDOMEN: stripped center stem of grizzly hackle.

THORAX: blue-gray rabbit dubbing, flattened slightly.

WING PADS: orange floss.

LEGS: natural red-brown hackle.

NOTES: The Michigan is considered a
standard pattern for the upper Midwest.

Nyerges Nymph (W)

HOOK: 10, 4XL.

THREAD: black or dark olive.

BODY: dark olive chenille.

LEGS: brown saddle hackle palmered
over full length of body, then
trimmed off on top and sides to
suggest shrimp's leg-like gills.

NOTES: Body color and size can be varied to suit regional needs. (This version is a
staple in eastern Washington.) Fish it
deeply in lakes on a sinking fly line with
short, erratic hand-twists or strip-ins. TYING
TECHNIQUE: See Figs. 129-132.

Orange Asher (W)

HOOKS: Mustad 94840, 14 & 12.

THREAD: orange or black.

BODY: choice of burnt-orange floss, fluorescent-orange floss or orange
wool.

HACKLE: palmered grizzly or badger.

NOTES: Popular on Colorado lakes for
use with a spinning rod and plastic bubble.
The fly is also used by that region's stream
flyrodders. Essentially, the Orange Asher is
one of the endless variations of the wooly
worm. TYING TECHNIQUE: See Figs. 129-
132.

Otter Shrimp (G)

HOOKS: 14-6.

THREAD: cream-colored Nymo.

BODY: dubbed from pale otter-belly fur
mixed with a little (natural cream-
white) seal fur.

NOTES: Variations include bodies dressed
with pine squirrel, eastern red squirrel and
tan cat furs. Also known as Trueblood's Otter Nymph, this great artificial was originated by outdoor writer Ted Trueblood of
Nampa, Idaho, about 1950 to simulate
freshwater shrimps and insect nymphs. It's
usually fished on a sinking fly line and is
useful in rich limestone and spring creeks
as well as in lakes. TYING TECHNIQUE: See
Figs. 199-203.

Pal's Wire Body (E)

TAIL: Coachman-brown hackle fibers.

BODY: copper wire.

HACKLE: Coachman-brown beard.

WINGS: white rabbit hair.

NOTES: An interesting and effective variation on the Coachman theme, dressed by
A. I. "Pal" Alexander, Andover, Mass. It
was designed for Eastern angling but
would probably catch trout anywhere.
TYING TECHNIQUE: See Figs. 83-101, 115.

Perla Capitata Stonefly Nymph (E)

HOOK: 8, 3XL.

THREAD: brown.

TAILS: pheasant-tail fibers divided into
two sections.

BODY: mixed, spun, tan fox and amber-
colored seal fur.

OVERBODY & WING CASE: section of medium mottled
brown turkey
feather.

RIBBING: brown thread, over abdomen
only.

LEGS: light partridge or light grayish-
brown hen hackle fibers in two
whisker-like bunches, one on each
side of thorax.

NOTES: This design, by professional fly
dresser William J. Keane of Bronxville,
N.Y., simulates the *Perla Capitata* stonefly
nymph found in some of the medium and
large rocky trout streams of the East. An

effective nymph that's fairly easy to tie. TYING TECHNIQUE: See Figs. 256-258.

Professor (G)

HOOKS: 14-2, regular length and weight.

TAIL: a few scarlet hackle fibers.

BODY: yellow floss or mohair.

RIBBING: gold tinsel, choice of type and width.

HACKLE: brown, collar or beard.

WING: choice of barred gray mallard-flank feather section, rolled and tied down-wing style, or bucktail of natural gray deer-body hair.

NOTES: The Professor is useful as a trout, panfish and bass fly throughout the U.S. and Canada. Like the Royal Coachman, it's one of the oldest, still-popular, standard patterns. It catches fish consistently in lakes and streams. TYING TECHNIQUE: See Figs. 83-101, 103-104.

Pumpkin Pupa (E)

HOOKS: 14 & 12.

THREAD: black.

BODY: tan dubbing.

HEAD: brown dubbing.

NOTES: The Pumpkin was originally designed by a Mr. Helm for fishing the small Maryland trout streams. It ought to work on similar streams throughout much of the East. TYING TECHNIQUE: See Figs. 147-148.

Royal Coachman (G)

HOOKS: 16-2, regular or extra-long shank, regular or stout wire.

THREAD: black.

TIP: gold tinsel.

TAIL: a few golden pheasant tippets or scarlet hackle wisps.

BODY: peacock herl joints, divided by slim band of scarlet floss or yarn.

HACKLE: natural red-brown hen or game-cock hackle, dressed as collar or beard.

WINGS: matched sections of white duck primary or white bucktail.

NOTES: The Royal Coachman has probably hooked more fish than any other single pattern. It's great for trout, panfish, largemouth and smallmouth bass, steelheads and shad, and it's dressed in wet, streamer, bucktail and dry styles. The Royal Trude and Royal Wulff are two of the most popular variations. TYING TECHNIQUE: See Figs. 83-101.

Savage Special (E)

HOOK: 14.

THREAD: black.

TAIL: dark, natural blue dun hackle fibers.

BODY: mixed beaver- and fox-fur dubbing.

HACKLE: two or three turns of dark, natural blue dun hackle with top clipped off.

NOTES: This is another fine Eastern fly by S. V. Yaruta of Owings Mills, Md. TYING TECHNIQUE: See Figs. 83-101, 199-202.

Slate/Brown Emerger (G)

HOOKS: 22-10.

TAILS: brown-speckled partridge or wood-duck fibers.

BODY: brown spun fur.

HACKLE: partridge or wood-duck fibers.

WINGS: dark gray hackle tips dressed emerger-style.

NOTES: Here's one of the very important and deadly flies originated by Doug Swisher and Carl Richards. This one is an excellent all-purpose nymph in streams and lakes during early stages of mayfly hatches. TYING TECHNIQUE: See Figs. 199-205.

South Platte Brassie (W)

HOOKS: 14-20, Mustad 3906 or 3399a.

THREAD: black.

BODY: tying thread, built up to taper, then tightly wound with copper wire.

THORAX (OPTIONAL): dubbed with very short mole or other

dark fur (omitted by most amateurs and some commercial tiers).

NOTES: Originated by Gene Lynch of Colorado Springs, this is one of the most productive flies on the Colorado River and it produces well elsewhere, too. Dressing submitted by George Bodmer. TYING TECHNIQUE: See Figs. 112-116. The wire is handled like most other body materials, tied in tightly and wrapped close.

Tellico Nymph (G)

HOOKS: 12 & 10.
TAIL: a few guinea hen fibers.
BODY: yellow yarn, wrapped rather fat.
RIBBING: peacock herl in spiral wraps.
OVERBODY: cock-pheasant tail fibers.
HACKLE: dark red-brown hen hackle.
NOTES: Originated by the Rev. Edwin T. Dalstrom for fishing the famed Tellico River in Tennessee. A Western version is dressed with a tail of scarlet hackle fibers, a yellow chenille body with the pheasant overlay and a wing and hackle of bronze pheasant-neck feathers. Both versions are excellent stream flies and deadly on beaver-pond brook trout. TYING TECHNIQUE: See Figs. 83-101, 134-135.

Water Boatman (G)

HOOK: 10, regular length and weight.
THREAD: black.
BODY: weighted with lead wire, then wrapped with reddish-tan dubbing.
OVERBODY: section of metallic blue-black drake-mallard flight feather. (Tie in tip before wrapping body, then—when body is wrapped—pull feather section over and tie down at head.)
PADDLE-LEGS: two fibers taken from leading edge of gray Canada goose-wing feather, tied to flare out slightly to sides.
NOTES: The Water Boatman is the creation of fly-tying instructor Everett Caryl, Sr. of Spokane. It's fished on a sinking line in lakes where natural water boatmen are present. The water boatman, or boat bug, resembles a water-strider in shape. Trout are especially fond of this fast-moving insect. TYING TECHNIQUES: See Figs. 134-135, 199-202, though appearance differs from these somewhat.

Werner Shrimp (W)

HOOK: 10, regular length and weight.
TAIL: natural gray deer-body hair.
BODY: dyed-olive spun or dubbed seal fur, palmered sparsely with natural brown hackle.
OVERBODY: natural gray deer-body hair tied in after tail by the tips, then pulled over in shellback style after body and hackle are wound.
NOTES: Originated by Mary Stewart and popularized by Werner Schmid, both of Vancouver. This is a deadly lake fly wherever there are freshwater shrimps. A similarly dressed fly, called the Tied-Down Caddis, differs from the Werner Shrimp only in body color, which is orange. TYING TECHNIQUE: See Figs. 134-135, 199-202.

Yellow Dun (E)

HOOK: 6, low-water salmon.
THREAD: tan.
TAIL: narrow section of black and white barred wood-duck flank feather.
BODY: mixed pink wool and cream-colored fox fur dubbed on underbody of silver tinsel. (Tinsel keeps body color from darkening when wet.)
HACKLE: medium brown, bearded.
WING: dressed in classic Eastern wet-fly

style, with matched sections of lemon-colored wood-duck flank.

NOTES: This dun was created by Bronxville, N.Y., tier William Keane for night trout fishing on the Delaware River. TYING TECHNIQUE: See Figs. 83-101, 199-202.

Zug Bug (G)

HOOKS: 14-6, 2XL or 3XL.

THREAD: black.

TAILS: three strands of green peacock-sword herl.

BODY: peacock herl, dressed very fully.

RIBBING: fine oval silver tinsel (or, if desired, fine lead wire to produce weighted nymph).

WING CASE: mallard-flank feather, trimmed to extend over forward quarter of body. (In some regions, wood duck or mandarin is substituted for mallard.)

HACKLE: long, soft brown hackle. (In some regions, tiers beard hackle under shank wrap sparse collar.)

NOTES: The Zug Bug is one of the more universally effective trout nymphs that have evolved in the past 30 years. Bill Cairns of the Orvis Company lists it as one of the six important nymphs that fish well in most Eastern waters, and its popularity doesn't end west of the Mississippi. It's a killer on countless American lakes and streams—including the legendary Firehole River in Yellowstone National Park where it is a most important early-season pattern. The original design is attributed to Eastern tier, J. Cliff Zug. Kemp's Bug (also known as the Kemp Bug or the Davis Special) is said to have been the forerunner of the Zug Bug. The wing cases on the Kemp are dressed from a pair of grizzly hackle tips and the body lacks the tinsel ribbing. TYING TECHNIQUE: See Figs. 83-101, 134-135, 115.

Dry Flies

Adams (G)

HOOKS: 20-10, extra-fine wire.

THREAD: tan.

WINGS: grizzly hackle tips, tied upright or spent.

TAIL: mixed natural red-brown and grizzly gamecock-neck hackles.

HACKLE: same as tail.

BODY: dubbed or spun muskrat fur.

NOTES: The Adams is a "must" on practically every dry-fly list. There's little variation in the basic pattern and tying method from region to region, but some Eastern tiers use white instead of tan thread. TYING TECHNIQUE: See Figs. 102-111, 199-202, 206-207.

Autumn Ant (W)

HOOK: 16, Mustad 94840.

THREAD: black.

TAIL: black hackle fibers.

BODY: black fur dubbed and wrapped on in ant-body shape.

WINGS: cree hackle tips tied flat over body behind hackle.

HACKLE: black gamecock-neck hackle.

NOTES: Originated by Oregon tier Lloyd Byerly to suggest a small flying ant that appears on some Western streams in the fall. This is a perfect example of a dry fly dressed to meet specific regional needs by an observant angler. TYING TECHNIQUE: See Fig. 102-111, 206-207, 199-202.

Bird's Stone Fly (W)

HOOKS: 8-4, 2XL or 3XL.

THREAD: orange.

TAIL: two hairs from brown bear's paw.

BODY: burnt- or hot-orange floss alternating with bands of furnace saddle hackle, trimmed on top and bottom, and shorter at ends than the hackle.

WING: dressed behind hackle with brown

bucktail fanned out flat over body and extending slightly past hook bend.

HACKLE: dense brushes, fashioned by wrapping on furnace saddle hackles, then clipping the wound hackle top and bottom and lacquering lightly.

HEAD: orange.

NOTES: Originated by Calvert T. Bird, this fly imitates the large *Pteronarcys* stoneflies. TYING TECHNIQUE: See Figs. 102-111, 183-184, although these do not exactly match this unique and rather advanced tie.

Black Ant (G)

HOOKS: 18-16, extra-fine wire.

THREAD: black.

BODY: four black crow-feather fibers tied in by the butts. (Fibers are twisted as abdomen is wrapped, leaving ¼-inch tip ends as legs extending out to sides. Four more fibers are tied in by the tips, leaving tips extending out as additional legs. Thorax is wrapped, then a turn or two of thread is taken between each pair of legs to spread them naturally at sides.)

NOTES: This is a natural-looking ant dressed by S. V. Yaruta of Owings Mills, Md. Other effective ants are dressed with spun fur, polypropylene or nylon bodies. TYING TECHNIQUE: See Figs. 223-224 for somewhat similar ant imitation.

Black Beetle (G)

HOOK: 16, fine wire.

THREAD: black.

BODY: dubbed black-bear underfur.

WINGS: two sections of black crow primary, tied down flat so tips curve slightly outward to sides.

HACKLE: two turns of black gamecock-neck hackle.

NOTES: Another of Mr. Yaruta's innovative ties, designed for Maryland waters, but obviously a pattern applicable in other regions. Anglers utilizing imitations of small terrestrial insects can gain considerable insight into their development and use by reading Vincent C. Marinaro's fine book *A Modern Dry Fly Code*. TYING TECHNIQUE: See Figs. 231-232, 199-202.

Blue Dun Midge (E)

HOOK: 18, extra-fine wire.

TAIL: a few medium-blue dun hackle fibers.

BODY: spun muskrat fur, dressed thinly.

HACKLE: turn or two of medium-blue dun gamecock hackle.

NOTES: This is another of the six dry flies listed by Bill Cairns as most generally effective on Eastern trout waters. Other good colors for chironomid imitators are black, gray, cream-white, grizzly, tan and pale insect-green. Midges range in size from 28 to about 12, depending on the species. A large Western midge known as the Snow Fly is larger than some mosquitoes. TYING TECHNIQUE: See Figs. 102-111, 199-202.

Brown & Gray Parachute (G, W)

HOOKS: 18-12, extra-fine wire.

THREAD: black or brown.

TAIL: natural red-brown gamecock hackle fibers.

BODY: spun muskrat fur.

POST: hackle stems tied to shank, raised upright and held erect by thread wrappings and cement.

HACKLE: two natural red-brown gamecock-neck hackles, wound around a post constructed from their butt-end stems.

NOTES: This fine stream fly was originated in 1959 by Western tier Lloyd Byerly. It is listed in this chapter not only because of its general usefulness, but also because of the way it employs hackle stems to form the post. TYING TECHNIQUE: See Figs. 137-141, 199-202.

Cahill, Light (G)

HOOKS: 14 & 12, extra-fine wire.

THREAD: tan, cream or primrose yellow.

WINGS: light lemon wood duck, tied rolled, upright and divided.

HACKLE: cream-ginger gamecock spade or neck hackle.

BODY: spun cream-colored red-fox-belly fur.

NOTES: Imitative of the *Stenonema ithaca* mayfly, the Light Cahill is generally considered one of the essential mayfly imitators throughout the nation. Thread, tail, body and hackle hues are varied considerably to match the hatches in diverse regions. TYING TECHNIQUE: See Figs. 102-111, 199-202.

Colorado King (G, W)

HOOKS: 18-10 (sizes 18 and 16 recommended).

THREAD: black.

TAIL: two stiff moose-body hairs, ¼ inch long on a size 14, tied in widespread. Little ball of body material is dubbed at hook bend before tying tails, which are crimped into fur to insure their spread.

BODY: dubbed dark muskrat for dark version; dubbed pale yellow-dyed rabbit fur for light version. (Dye white rabbit for 1½ minutes in 1½ teaspoons yellow Rit to three quarts boiling water.) Dress body full with slight taper.

HACKLE: grizzly, palmered 7 or 8 turns. Hackle fibers should not extend past the hook point more than 1/16 inch for best results.

WING: natural tan-gray deer-body hair, tied bucktail-style to flare back just beyond bend of hook.

NOTES: This is an excellent caddis imitation originated by George Bodmer. TYING TECHNIQUE: See Figs. 195-197, 210, 199-202.

Fig. 311. Cooper Bug.

Cooper Bug (E)

HOOKS: 12 & 10 for brook trout; 14 and smaller for browns.

BODY: choice of red, green, black, orange or scarlet yarn or chenille.

OVERBODY: bunch of natural gray deer hair laid over top of the body and tied off at both ends. Ends of hair should be clipped off to leave short, bristly bunch of hairs as tail and shorter bunch as a head (Fig. 311).

NOTES: This fly may have been created by John Cooper of Salem, N.H. for brown trout in Maine's Sandy River, but there are disagreements about its origin. It's used with some success for Atlantic salmon in sizes 4 and larger. The Cooper Bug is most often fished dry, but takes brookies on a sinking fly line. It's also been used to entice landlocked salmon late in the evenings. TYING TECHNIQUE: See Figs. 134-135.

Cream Variant (E)

HOOK: 12, extra-short shank.

THREAD: yellow.

TAIL: cream gamecock spade or neck hackle fibers.

BODY: cream or white stripped hackle quill thoroughly soaked in water to prevent cracking.

HACKLE: large-radius cream gamecock spade or neck hackle with very stiff fibers.

NOTES: This Art Flick tie is high on the list of the most important dressings for Northeastern streams. It imitates the *Potamanthus distinctus* mayfly, which is often called the Pale Evening Dun. TYING TECHNIQUE: See Figs. 154, 102-111.

Dark Olive Dun (E, MW)

HOOK: 22.

THREAD: olive.

WINGS: shaped blue dun hackle points.

HACKLE: honey-colored gamecock-neck hackle, wrapped in Marinaro's criss-cross style.

TAILS: two pale blue dun hackle fibers, spread.

BODY & THORAX: greenish-olive fur dubbing, dressed thinly.

NOTES: See Chapter 9 (Hendrickson Dun) for instructions on how to X-wrap (criss-cross) the hackle. This dressing is an excellent imitator of the dun stage of the darker little blue-wing Olives (like *Baetis vagans* and *B. levitans*) found on Eastern and Midwestern trout streams. Chances are, it also would fool any Western trout interested in a hatch of *B. parvis*.

Dun/Brown Hen Spinner (G)

HOOKS: 18-12, extra-fine wire.

THREAD: brown.

WINGS: light gray hen hackle tips, tied in spent-wing fashion.

TAILS: gray hackle fibers (three fibers to imitate *Ephemerella subvaria*, the Hendrickson; or *E. dorothea*, the Sulphur Dun spinner).

BODY: brown fur dubbing.

NOTES: A Swisher-Richards pattern that's effective throughout the nation, the Dun/Brown Hen Spinner can be used to imitate Midwestern spinner flights of *E. subvaria, E. dorothea, Pseudocloeon anoka* and *E. lata* as well as the Western *E. flavi-linea* and the tiny pale morning duns of *E. inermis*.

Dun/Cream Hen Spinner (E, W)

HOOKS: 16-8.

THREAD: pale tan or cream.

WINGS: tips of light gray hen hackle, dressed spent.

TAILS: three gray hackle fibers, well-spread, to imitate Eastern green drake spinner (*E. guttulata*); two tail fibers to suggest smaller Western *Callibaetis* species.

BODY: dubbing of cream-colored German fitch fur.

NOTES: Although not as universally adaptable as the Dun/Brown Hen Spinner, this Swisher-Richards creation can be a very important fly in the box when the green drakes are flying on Eastern streams. Western flyrodders will also find the Dun/Cream Hen Spinner useful periodically throughout the season, dressed in sizes 18 and 16. At least four species of *Callibaetis* have been noted on Western trout streams.

Dun Variant (E, MW)

HOOK: 12, fine wire, short shank.

THREAD: olive.

TAIL: dun spade or barb hackle fibers, quite long.

BODY: stripped and soaked center stem of natural red gamecock hackle.

HACKLE: natural dark dun, spade or saddle hackle.

NOTES: Another of Art Flick's easy-to-tie and lethal dry flies, this one imitates the *Isonychia bicolor* mayfly found in the East and Midwest. This mayfly hatches periodically from May through late September, mostly in the afternoon and evening. Other useful patterns suggesting *I. bicolor* are the Red Quill dressed with black hackle-tip wings, the Slate/Brown Paradun, Slate/Brown No-Hackle and Dun/Brown Hen

Spinner. TYING TECHNIQUE: See Figs. 102-111, 154.

FFF Mayfly (G, W)

HOOKS: 18-12, extra-fine wire.

THREAD: black or tan.

WINGS: grizzly or white hackle tips, tied upright and divided.

HACKLE: mixed natural red-brown and black gamecock-neck hackles.

TAIL: mixed natural red-brown and black gamecock hackle fibers.

BODY: dark brown fur dubbing.

RIBBING: beige thread.

NOTES: A deadly varietal fly created by fishing-writer Fenton Roskelley in 1966 to suggest the broad range of dark brownish mayflies. Named in honor of the Federation of Fly Fishermen, it's excellent in the early part of the season. TYING TECHNIQUE: See Figs. 102-111, 199-202, 206-207.

Flot-n-Fool (G)

HOOKS: 12 & 10, extra-fine wire.

TAIL: medium-small bunch of white calf-tail hairs, wrapped down forward to the post position instead of having butts trimmed off.

POST: white calf-tail butts wrapped and cemented erect.

HACKLE: choice of mixed dark ginger and grizzly, mixed brown and black, or mixed furnace and blue dun gamecock-neck hackles, dressed parachute-style around post.

BODY: peacock herl.

RIBBING: fine flat gold tinsel.

NOTES: It's a deadly varietal fly, attributed to the late Wayne "Buz" Buszek of Visalia, Calif., which falls into the same category of broad general interest as the Adams—perhaps more so because of the variations of color. The white wing post makes it extremely visible on the water. I use this fly in sizes from 16 to 10. TYING TECHNIQUE: See Figs. 137-141.

Gray Fox (E)

HOOKS: 12 & 14, extra-fine wire.

THREAD: olive.

WINGS: gray mallard-flank feather, dressed rolled, upright and divided.

HACKLE: light ginger and light grizzly gamecock-neck hackles, mixed.

TAIL: light ginger hackle fibers.

BODY: spun or dubbed light-fawn-colored red-fox-belly fur.

NOTES: This staple Eastern stream fly is imitative of the *Stenonema fuscum* mayfly. It was originated by Preston Jennings. TYING TECHNIQUE: See Figs. 102-111, 199-202.

Gray Fox Variant (E)

HOOKS: 12 & 10, extra-fine wire.

THREAD: primrose yellow.

TAIL: ginger gamecock-neck or spade hackle fibers.

BODY: center stem stripped from light ginger or cream hackle, soaked well in water before winding.

HACKLE: mixed from one light ginger, one dark ginger and one grizzly gamecock-neck hackle.

NOTES: Art Flick's design, this killing Eastern dry fly suggests the Green Drake, *Ephemera guttulata*. TYING TECHNIQUE: See Figs. 102-111, 154.

Gray/Olive No Hackle (G)

HOOKS: 24-16.

WINGS: matched gray duck-wing (shoulder) feathers. (See *Selective Trout*, by Swisher and Richards, Crown Publishers, N.Y., 1971, for alternative winging styles and tying instructions.)

TAIL: two gray gamecock hackle fibers, divided to stabilize fly on water.

BODY: dubbed olive fur or polypropylene yarn. Dub small ball of fur on shank before tying in tails to assist in spreading tail fibers. (Also see Colorado King above.)

NOTES: One of the hackleless ties of Doug Swisher and Carl Richards, this floater imitates the *Baetis* species of mayflies found in most of the nation's major trouting regions.

Green Drake Spinner, female (E)

HOOK: 14, short-shank, wide-gape.

SETAE: three brown gamecock hackle fibers tied to end of small white porcupine quill.

BODY: white porcupine quill, tied to extend ½- to ⅝-inch beyond hook bend.

WINGS: pale bronze-blue gamecock hackle, palmered, then shaped by trimming to semi-spent position, with tip-to-tip span of approximately 1½ inches.

NOTES: This innovative spinner by Vincent C. Marinaro is an easy-to-dress killer. It's included here, following the Swisher-Richards Gray/Olive tie, to show a different approach to no-hackle winging. This one mimics the mayfly *Ephemera guttulata*. TYING TECHNIQUE: See Figs. 206-211, though body technique is unique.

Grizzly Wulff (G)

HOOKS: 14-8, fine wire.

WINGS: brown whitetail-deer hair taken from near base of tail, tied upright and divided.

HACKLE: mixed natural red-brown and grizzly gamecock-neck hackles, dressed quite bushily.

TAIL: dense bunch of brown-gray deer-body hair.

BODY: pale yellow floss, lacquered. (Some tiers prefer non-absorbent synthetic yarn such as polypropylene.)

NOTES: This pattern was first dressed in the Lee Wulff style in 1936 by the well-known professional tier Dan Bailey, of Livingston, Mont. It suggests a mayfly or stonefly fluttering on the surface and is quite useful throughout the U.S. and Canada as a trout and salmon pattern. TYING TECHNIQUE: See Figs. 259-262, 199-202.

Hatch Matcher (G, W)

HOOKS: 18-12, short-shank.

TAIL, BODY & WINGS: fashioned from single duck-breast or -flank feather, color to match the hatch. Pull fibers from near feather's tip toward the butt. Trim out tip section to leave two or three protruding fibers (Fig. 312). Trim off butt stem, leaving enough fibers to form extended body and wings. Stroke feather fibers back from the tip and tie down at winging position. Pull feather tips

Fig. 312. Hatch Matcher.

erect and wind criss-cross to divide as wings.

HACKLE: color to match the hatch, tied on in standard fashion fore and aft of wings. A unique dry fly, probably first tied by Eastern professional tier Harry Darbee, it was popularized in the West by Dick Alf of Sun Valley, Idaho. It looks very easy to tie, but isn't. Great care must be taken to select precisely the right size and shape of feather for the wings, body and tails. (See Chapter 16 of *Fly-tying Problems and Their Answers*, by John Veniard and Donald Downs, Crown, N.Y., 1972.)

Hendrickson (E, MW)

HOOK: 12, extra-fine wire.

Dressing techniques are illustrated in Chapter 9.

NOTES: The Hendrickson dry fly, representing the female of the mayfly *Ephemerella subvaria*, is one of the most important patterns for the eastern U.S. Normally hatching from the last week of April to mid-June, it follows in sequence the Quill Gordon *(Epeorus pleuralis)* with coincidental hatching taking place. Hatches usually occur in mid-afternoon. Spinner flights follow an hour or so after the end of the hatch. *E. subvaria* is one of the few mayflies for which sexual differentiation is important. The Hendrickson is attributed to Roy Steenrod of Liberty, N.Y. According to Art Flick, Steenrod's original tie called for a body dubbed from fawn-colored fox-belly fur. Flick's version employs a pinkish, urine-stained fur from the belly of a vixen.

TYING TECHNIQUE: See Figs. 102-111, 206-211.

Hornberg (G)

HOOKS: 14-8, fine wire.

Fig. 313. Hornberg (Eastern).

Fig. 314. Hornberg (Western), underside.

THREAD: black.

BODY: silver tinsel.

WING: pair of yellow hackle tips tied on edge, extending about 3/16- to 1/4-inch beyond hook bend, outside of which are tied two brown-phase mallard-flank feathers, concave sides facing inwards. Junglecock cheeks are sometimes tied outside the mallard feathers.

HACKLE: very full collar of grizzly game-cock hackle in front of wings.

NOTES: The dressing described (Fig. 313), a preferred Eastern method of tying this very important fly, was supplied by A. I. "Pal" Alexander of Andover, Mass. A Western version (Fig. 314), as dressed by George Bodmer, is used more in lakes than in streams. It's winged with a single mallard-flank feather cupped over yellow calf hair. The wing is shaped to a point with a touch of vinyl or head cement. In still another version, called the Hornberg Special Streamer, the suggested size is 6, and teal is sometimes substituted for the mallard wing. In his fine book *Streamer Fly Tying & Fishing*, Stackpole Books, Harrisburg, Pa., 1966), Joe Bates points out that the Hornberg is frequently fished dry until it sinks, then fished streamer-fashion. George Bodmer tells me the Hornberg accounted for a 21-pound two-ounce brown trout in the North Platte river during the fall of 1972.

Jassid (G)

HOOKS: 22 & 20.

THREAD: any color to match hackle.

BODY: tying thread, to match hackle.

HACKLE: choice of color, palmer-wrapped, trimmed flat on top and bottom.

WING: single small jungle-cock eye feather tied down to ride flat over body and hackle.

NOTES: Black is a popular color for this little leaf hopper, a good trout fly in most regions. TYING TECHNIQUE: See Figs. 231-232.

Kahl's Gray Sedge (W)

HOOKS: 22-16, extra-fine wire.

THREAD: black.

TAIL: grizzly hackle fibers.

BODY: stripped peacock eye quill.

WING: mallard, teal or turkey feather tied down along top of body with ends trimmed to shape of caddis wings.

HACKLE: grizzly gamecock-neck hackle, dressed sparsely.

NOTES: A staple dry fly on Sierra-Nevada streams, including the famous Hot Creek. The fly is described as dressed by Stuart Kaplan of Beverly Hills. It was originated by Milt Kahl, Los Angeles. TYING TECHNIQUE: See Figs. 102-111; but note that wing tie is different.

March Brown, American (G)

HOOKS: 14 & 12, fine wire.

THREAD: orange.

WINGS: darkish lemon-colored wood-duck flank, dressed upright and divided, as in the Light Cahill.

HACKLE: mixed dark brown and grizzly gamecock-neck hackles.

TAIL: dark brown gamecock-neck or spade hackle fibers.

BODY: reddish-tan fox-fur dubbing.

RIBBING: light-brown cotton thread.

NOTES: Preston Jennings' version of this ubiquitous mayfly (*Stenonema vicarium*) is a standard for Eastern trout and should also be included as an important fly on Midwestern and Western waters. TYING TECHNIQUE: See Figs. 102-111, 199-202.

Meadow Grasshopper (W)

HOOKS: 10 & 8, 3XL.

BODY: pale cream-colored synthetic yarn.

PALMER HACKLE: long, pale ginger saddle hackle, trimmed.

UNDERWING: small bunch of dyed yellow bucktail.

WINGS: sections of dyed pale yellow-spotted oak-brown turkey wing feather, tied on separately on sides of hook.

HACKLE: mixed cream, darkish ginger and light grizzly hackles wrapped collar-fashion in front of wings.

HEAD: fairly long and large, cream-colored thread.

NOTES: Designed by E. H. "Polly" Rosborough and especially popular on Oregon's Wood River during the fall months. TYING TECHNIQUE: See Figs. 227-229, though technique is not precisely the same.

Muckledun (W)

HOOKS: 12-6.

THREAD: black.

BODY: black or medium-gray wool yarn.

WINGS: sections of gray Canada-goose flight feathers, dressed with concave sides out, behind hackle.

HACKLE: badger saddle, one or two turns in front of wings.

NOTES: Bob Terrell, of Basalt, Colo., originated this very simple, direct pattern which catches a lot of big trout. TYING TECHNIQUE is completely standard.

Quill Gordon (E)

HOOKS: 14 & 12, extra-fine wire.

Dressing techniques are illustrated in Chapter 8.

NOTES: The Quill Gordon (*Epeorus pleuralis*) is unquestionably the most important early-season mayfly hatch in the East. Its emergence frequently occurs under adverse climatic conditions and coincides with hatches of *E. subvaria*, the Hendrickson. When Quill Gordon mayflies hatch into extremely cold air, they're frequently unable to take off. The duns float on the surface in almost unbelievable numbers, occasioning phenomenal surface feeding by trout. The Quill Gordon was originated by the late Theodore Gordon around the turn of the century. Gordon's entomological studies and innovative dry-fly designs set guidelines that dominated American dry-fly tying for 50 years. TYING TECHNIQUE: See Figs. 102-111.

Renegade (W)

HOOKS: 16-8, fine wire.

THREAD: black.

AFT-HACKLE: brown gamecock.

BODY: peacock herl, sometimes with gold tip added before winding herl body and aft-hackle.

FORE-HACKLE: white gamecock.

NOTES: Especially good on cutthroat trout, this fly is virtually a must for Western stream and lake fishing. Tying technique is standard.

Sofa Pillow (W)

HOOKS: 6 & 4, 2XL.

TAIL: section of scarlet-dyed duck- or goose-wing feather.

BODY: scarlet wool or raffia (I use dubbed Kapok underbody to improve fly's bouyancy, then cover it completely with the body material.)

WING: fair-sized bunch of red-squirrel tail flared back over body behind hackle.

HACKLE: three or four brown saddle hackles wrapped on as dense collar in front of wing.

NOTES: The Sofa Pillow is a standard tie to suggest large Western stoneflies. TYING TECHNIQUE: See Figs. 183-184.

Tom Thumb (W)

HOOKS: 8 & 6, fine-wire or regular.

TAIL: fairly short, tied from matchstick-thick bunch of natural gray deer-body hair.

BODY: bunch of natural deer-body hairs, two matchsticks thick, tied in by the butts, tip ends pulled forward, tied off at head and pulled up to form single, slightly spread wing, supported by thread wrappings.

HACKLE (OPTIONAL): grizzly.

NOTES: Originally a Canadian tie, it simulates newly hatched sedge (caddis) flies as they extend their wings up and forward for a moment after emerging from the pupa. It's also good tied in smaller sizes (down to 16) in various shades of deer and antelope hair. TYING TECHNIQUE: See Figs. 134-135.

White/Black Hen Spinner (G)

HOOKS: 28-24, extra-fine wire.

THREAD: black.

WINGS: tips of light gray hen hackle, tied in spent-wing fashion.

TAILS: three gray hackle fibers, well-spread.

BODY: dark mole fur dubbing.

NOTES: Until Doug Swisher and Carl Richards devised this tiny gem of a dry fly, anglers throughout the United States were hard put to match the amazingly copious flights of the *Tricorythodes* genus of mayflies. Despite the artificial's minuscule size, it's reasonably easy to spot on the water because of its light-colored wings. Between the 10th of July and the end of September—the hatching period—this fly provides great action on quite a large number of America's better trout streams.

Yellow-Bodied Grayback (W)

HOOKS: 12-6.

TAIL: dark natural deer hair.

BODY: yellow chenille.

OVERBODY: same as tail.

RIBBING: black thread, counter-wound over body and overbody.

HACKLE: collar of grizzly gamecock-neck or saddle hackles.

NOTES: A great fly when large grasshoppers are being blown into the water. The origin of this fly is in doubt, but it probably comes from Montana. According to George Grant it (or something very similar) was being tied by Dan Bailey as early as 1940. It also goes under the name of Crazy Goof. In silhouette, the Horner Deer Hair, Goofus Bug, Humpy, Crazy Goof and Yellow-Bodied Grayback all resemble one another to a degree. All are excellent floaters in very fast water. TYING TECHNIQUE: See Figs. 134-135, 110.

STREAMER FLIES

Allagash Al (E)

HOOK: tandem 4/6.

THREAD: black.

BODY: flat silver tinsel (oval silver rib optional).

THROAT: red feather from golden pheasant's shin or red marabou, not too long.

WINGS: red bucktail with four thin, well-marked badger hackles over.

CHEEKS: jungle-cock eye feathers.

NOTES: This fly, named for the famous Allagash, is very popular in the Rangeley region of Maine. It's listed here as dressed by the Percy Tackle Company, Portland, Me. TYING TECHNIQUE: See Figs. 117-121.

Bandit, Gray (W)

HOOKS: 6 & 4, nickel, extra-long-shank Eagle Claw.

BODY: double row of #10 silver oval tinsel, slightly tapered.

WING: grayish-brown marabou from cock pheasant over bunch of badger guard hairs.

HEAD: painted orange.

EYES: painted white with black pupils.

NOTES: Originated by Stan Engle for big Western browns and rainbows in reservoirs and rivers. TYING TECHNIQUE: See Figs. 242-244.

Bear Hair Leech (W)

HOOKS: 8 & 6, extra-long shank.

THREAD: black.

BODY: medium oval gold tinsel, no taper.

WING: sparse bunch of black-bear or skunk guard hairs.

HEAD: black, fairly large and longer than usual.

NOTES: First introduced at Peterhope Lake, B.C., this is an extremely deadly lake fly for large rainbow and brook trout. TYING TECHNIQUE: See Figs. 242-244.

Black Knight Streamer (E)

HOOKS: 8-2, 2XL to 4XL, TDE.

BODY: flat silver tinsel.

WING: white bucktail overlayed with generous amount of black marabou.

THROAT: bunch of orange marabou extending a hair past middle of body.

HEAD: black.

NOTES: Created by Don Shiner of Nescopek, Pa., this variation of the Black Marabou is very good on smallmouth bass and rainbow trout. TYING TECHNIQUE: See Figs. 245-249.

Black-Nosed Dace (G)

HOOKS: 12-4, extra-long shank, usually 4XL.

THREAD: black.

TAIL: short tuft of red yarn.

BODY: flat silver tinsel.

WING: equal amounts of brown bucktail, over black bear, over white bucktail rather sparsely dressed.

CHEEKS (OPTIONAL): jungle-cock eye feathers.

NOTES: This dace is an Art Flick pattern, described as dressed by the Orvis Company, Inc., Manchester, Vt. It imitates the common dace minnow and is effective in numerous streams throughout the U.S. and Canada. TYING TECHNIQUE: See Figs. 117-121.

Brown Bear (W)

HOOKS: various sizes, 3XL to 6XL.

THREAD: brown.

TAIL: bunch of fox-squirrel tail hairs as long as gape of hook.

BODY: brown chenille, dressed heavy.

HACKLE: medium-brown, palmered.

WING: good-sized bunch of fox-squirrel tail hairs slightly longer than tail.

HACKLE COLLAR: brown, same as palmer, dressed in front of wing.

NOTES: The Brown Bear, offered here as dressed by George Bodmer, is a big-river fly that's used with much success in Colorado's Blue Mesa river. TYING TECHNIQUE: See Figs. 242-244.

Colonel Bates (G)

HOOK: 4XL.

THREAD: black.

TAIL: scarlet goose or swan primary feathers tied fairly long.

BODY: medium flat silver tinsel.

UNDERBODY: white floss, wrapped smooth, untapered.

HACKLE BEARD: small bunch of dark brown saddle-hackle fibers.

NOTES: Originated by Mrs. Carrie G. Stevens of Madison, Maine, and named in honor of Joseph D. Bates, Jr., this is a killing streamer in both the East and West on landlocked salmon, bass, pike, panfish and trout. It's also effective in saltwater versions. (I'm especially partial to it for brook trout in lakes and rivers.) TYING TECHNIQUE: See Figs. 236-241.

Crane Prairie (W)

HOOKS: 2/4 to 10/12 (see basic tying instructions for Whitney flies in Chapter 13).

TAIL: golden-olive calf tail.

BUTT: oval gold tinsel.

UNDERBODY: lead keel.

BODY: peacock herl.

WINGS: dark part of dyed-yellow bucktail, topped with grizzly saddle hackles.

HEAD: red.

NOTES: Here's one of A. A. "Tony" Whitney's deadly and innovative trolling and shooting flies. Particularly effective at Crane Prairie Reservoir in Oregon, it's a superior trolling fly for large rainbows, browns and brookies in stumped-filled reservoirs and lakes. TYING TECHNIQUE: See Figs. 299-308.

Dobson (E)

HOOK: 8.

THREAD: black.

BODY: none.

TAIL: none.

WING: small bunch of black skunk guard hairs, with sections of guinea-hen feather tied over each side, about two-thirds as long as hairs.

HEAD: large, black.

EYES: large, white with black pupils.

NOTES: This tie suggests a "hellgrammite"—a dobson fly nymph. It's used in trout streams in Pennsylvania, Maryland and West Virginia with great success. It was designed by Jess Harden, professional fly dresser of Owings Mills, Md., and is popular with members of the Maryland Fly Anglers Club. TYING TECHNIQUE: See Figs. 313, 242-244, though tie is atypical.

Gerlach's Leech (W, G)

HOOKS: 12-4, 3XL or 4XL.

THREAD: black or dark dun-gray.

TAIL: bunch of brown-olive marabou, half as long as hook.

BODY: choice of dark blue dun, gray dubbing or spun fur.

RIBBING: fine oval silver tinsel, spiraled on body and overbody.

OVERBODY: same as tail material.

COLLAR: small bunches of brown-olive marabou tied in at head to form short collar around shank.

NOTES: I concocted this fly in 1968 to simulate leeches in Kamloops trout lakes near Kamloops, B.C. It's effective on rainbows, brookies and smallmouth bass throughout the Northwest. A black version, sporting a wine-colored body, is also tied. The leech should be fished on a sinking line with a rather slow, easy, undulating hand-twist recovery. It also produces when slowly mooch-trolled. TYING TECHNIQUE: See Figs. 134-135, though marabou collar is unique.

Gray Ghost (G)

HOOKS: 10-2, 5XL.

THREAD: black.

TIP: narrow flat silver tinsel.

BODY: orange floss dressed quite thin.

RIBBING: narrow flat silver tinsel.

THROAT: four to five strands of peacock herl, with small bunch of white bucktail tied underneath—both extending beyond hook barb. Herl should be same length as wing, the bucktail slightly shorter. Complete by tying in golden-pheasant crest feather same length as shoulder, curved upward.

WING: one golden-pheasant crest feather curved down, same length as throat, with four olive-gray saddle hackles tied over it, concave sides facing inward.

SHOULDERS: one body feather of Ripon's silver pheasant on each side. Feathers should be wide and dressed about one-third as long as wing.

CHEEKS: jungle-cock eye feathers.

HEAD: black with red band.

NOTES: Mrs. Carrie G. Stevens first tied the Gray Ghost in about 1924 to suggest a smelt. It ranks at or near the top of the popularity list for landlocked salmon in Maine, New Hampshire and Vermont. It's also popular in some parts of the West as a trout and bass fly. TYING TECHNIQUE: See Figs. 236-244, 250-252.

Herb Johnson Special (E)

HOOKS: 4 & 2, streamer hooks.

BODY: black wool yarn, fairly full.

RIBBING: embossed flat silver tinsel, reverse-wound.

THROAT: white bucktail, same length as wing.

WING: small bunch of yellow bucktail slightly longer than hook bend;

then one strand each of red and blue fluorescent floss tied on each side of bucktail; then one strand of peacock herl tied on each side above floss; then a sparse bunch of dyed-yellow brown bucktail over herl. (All wing components are same length. Overall length of a size 2 fly is 2¾ inches.)

HEAD: silver with yellow eye and black pupil.

NOTES: According to Joseph D. Bates, Jr., this is a hot fly throughout the East. Joe's fine books on streamer and salmon flies and how to fish them are invaluable aids to the serious fly-tying angler. TYING TECHNIQUE: See Figs. 242-244.

Hussy (W)

HOOK: 2, nickel, long-shank Wright & McGill.

BODY: silver tinsel chenille.

RIBBING: #10 oval silver tinsel.

WING: white bucktail, with yellow bucktail tied over it, topped by fluorescent-orange bucktail, topped by brown bucktail dyed fluorescent orange.

HEAD: black, with bottom two-thirds painted yellow.

EYES: painted orange with black pupils.

NOTES: The Hussy is a Stan Engle original used to take big browns when they're following spawning kokanee salmon in large Western reservoirs. TYING TECHNIQUE: See Figs. 242-244.

Integration Bucktail (G)

HOOK: 2, long shank.

THREAD: black.

BODY: medium oval silver tinsel, wrapped to eye to prevent wing from flaring.

THROAT (UNDERWING): straight, unkinked white bucktail, four inches long.

WING: straight, unkinked black bucktail same length as throat.

NOTES: The well-known outdoor writer Ted Trueblood, who originated this famous fly, says it has produced from God's River to the Snake as well as in salt water on both coasts. The saltwater version can be dressed even longer. For bass fishing, a double-loop monofilament weed guard is usually included. TYING TECHNIQUE: See Figs. 273-276.

Labrador Special (E, EC)

HOOKS: 4/6 tandem.

BODY: silver tinsel, ribbing optional.

TOPPING: six or eight peacock herls.

CHEEKS: jungle-cock eye feathers.

EYES: painted yellow with black pupils on black head.

NOTES: As dressed by Percy Tackle Company, this tandem-hook trolling fly is said to be effective in the upper Northeast, and in Canada. TYING TECHNIQUE: See Figs. 263-265, though fly is atypical.

Little Brown Trout (G)

HOOKS: 3XL or 4XL.

TAIL: golden-pheasant tippets.

BODY: orange wool yarn, ribbed with gold tinsel.

WING: equal-sized bunches of red squirrel tail, over red-dyed bucktail, over black bear, over yellow-dyed bucktail.

CHEEKS: small jungle-cock eye feathers.

NOTES: A streamer developed by Samuel R. Slaymaker II, of Gap, Pa., the Little Brown Trout is popular in two versions. The one presented on p. 135 is the dressing by the Weber Tackle Company. It features a tail made from a very small ringneck-pheasant breast feather with the dark center removed; a body of spun white wool with copper-wire ribbing (gold tinsel is an alternative); a wing made from very small, equal bunches of yellow bucktail under medium-dark squirrel tail under dark brown squirrel tail; no throat; jungle-cock cheeks; and a black head. The other version is by Orvis—a tail of golden-pheasant tippets; an orange wool body; a wing of dyed yellow bucktail under black bear under dyed red bucktail under red squirrel; a throat of dyed red hackle fibers under dyed yellow; and a lacquered yellow head. Though appearances differ, both versions are quite deadly when big browns, bass or rainbows are feeding on small brown-trout fry. TYING TECHNIQUE: See Figs. 242-244.

Maynard's Marvel (E, EC)

HOOKS: 8-2, 5XL or 6XL.

THREAD: black.

TAIL: red hackle fibers or section of red swan flight feather.

BODY: silver Mylar tubing with rear tie-down wrapping painted red.

WING: golden-pheasant crest feathers. (Two flies take almost an entire crest.)

HEAD: black.

EYES: yellow with black pupils.

NOTES: As described to me by "Pal" Alexander, this relatively new pattern is highly effective on landlocked salmon. Pal points out that there's some disagreement on the dressing of the fly. The tail is sometimes dressed from a section of barred wood duck and both silver and gold tinsel bodies are sometimes used. TYING TECHNIQUE: Figs. 299-308, 250-252 contain adaptable techniques.

Mickey Finn (G)

HOOKS: 12-2/0.

THREAD: black.

BODY: flat silver tinsel.

RIBBING: oval silver tinsel.

WING: small bunch of yellow-dyed bucktail under equal bunch of red-dyed bucktail under bunch of yellow bucktail equal to first two bunches combined.

NOTES: John Alden Knight popularized

this pattern which was brought to his attention in 1932 and was originally called the Assassin. It's definitely one of the six most popular bucktail and streamer patterns now used in the U.S. and Canada—very effective on landlocked salmon, largemouth bass, trout and panfish. TYING TECHNIQUE: See Figs. 242-244.

Muddler Minnow (G)

HOOKS: 10-1/0, 3XL.

THREAD: black or brown.

TAIL: two sections of mottled brown turkey-wing feather, fairly wide and about half or two-thirds as long as body.

BODY: flat gold tinsel, well-lacquered.

HACKLE: white deer-body hair spun around shank, butts trimmed off.

WING: brown impala over white impala, same length as hook, with matched sections of brown-mottled turkey-wing feather tied on each side, concave surfaces facing in, same length as the impala.

HEAD: spun natural-gray deer-body hair, full, rounded and clipped.

NOTES: This is the Muddler as dressed by Dan Bailey, Livingston, Mont. The original was tied by Don Gapen, of Nipigon, Ontario, about 1950. That version incorporated wolf hair instead of impala and a smaller, sparser clipped deer-hair head. TYING TECHNIQUE: Figs. 245-249 show adaptable techniques.

Shuswap Silver Mallard (WC)

HOOK: 4, long-shank.

TAIL: single golden-pheasant crest feather curved upward.

BODY: thin, flat silver tinsel.

RIBBING: oval silver tinsel.

WING: medium-small bunch of white bucktail or polar-bear hairs, under three medium-blue hackles tied flat with concave sides down, topped by two gray-speckled mallard-flank feathers tied flat.

NOTES: It's given here as dressed by Lt. Col. Lee Gomes, USAF (ret.), Spokane, Wash. This is one of several streamers that have been designed to fish British Columbia's Shuswap Lake in April, when young salmon alevins are being ravaged by hefty Kamloops rainbow trout. Mooch-troll the fly on about 60 to 80 feet of sinking or sink-tip line until a fish is observed feeding on the immature salmon. Then stop and cast directly into the area of the working fish, using a stripping retrieve. TYING TECHNIQUE: See Figs. 236-241, except for atypical wing.

Snollygoster (W)

HOOKS: 6 & 4, nickel, long-shank Eagle Claw.

BODY: heavy, dark-gray wool yarn.

WINGS: four gray-brown marabou feathers from cock pheasant's rump, tied on edge vertically.

HACKLE: mixed, large-radius grizzly and Coachman-brown, dressed as collar in front of wings.

CHEEKS: cock-pheasant "church-window" feathers on which have been painted yellow eyes with black pupils.

NOTES: It's an innovative Stan Engle tie that, when wet, suggests a fat-bodied minnow such as a small chub. A highly mobile fly, ideally suited to lake fishing. TYING TECHNIQUE: See Figs. 245-249.

Spuddler (W)

HOOKS: 6-1/0, 3XL.

THREAD: black or brown.

TAIL: generous bunch of brown calf-tail hairs.

BODY: generally heavily weighted with lead wire, over which is wrapped cream-colored Angora yarn, followed by a few turns of scarlet mohair, yarn or chenille.

WING: bunch of brown calf-tail hairs, outside of which are tied four dyed-brown grizzly neck hackles extending slightly past end of tail.

HACKLE: red fox-squirrel hairs tied in semi-circular, flared shape on top and at sides, extending back about half of body length.

HEAD: brown antelope-body hair spun on in bunches to form dense, fairly long head, then trimmed to flattish-oval shape.

NOTES: Dan Bailey devised the Spuddler to suggest a sculpin minnow. The fly was conceived and named to reflect the two earlier patterns from which it evolved—the Spruce Fly and the Muddler Minnow. It's very effective on large rainbow and brown trout when fished close to the bottom on a sinking line with occasional stripping recoveries. TYING TECHNIQUE: See Figs. 245-249, 236-241.

White Marabou (G)

HOOKS: 10, 4XL or 6XL.

TAIL: small golden-pheasant crest feather, curved upward.

BODY: silver tinsel.

RIBBING: oval silver tinsel.

HACKLE: short beard of scarlet hackle fibers.

WING: white marabou feathers, with golden-pheasant crest feather, curvature downward, tied on each side and same length as marabou or slightly shorter.

CHEEKS: jungle-cock eye feathers.

NOTES: The tie described is used mostly in the Northeast. White, black, yellow, orange and gray marabou-winged streamers are productive throughout the country on a tremendous range of game species and in both fresh and salt water. TYING TECHNIQUE: See Figs. 245-249.

White Winnie (E)

HOOK: 8, tinned, ring-eye.

TAIL: none.

BODY: none.

THROAT: red capris, dressed about two-thirds of shank length.

WING: white capris, extending well beyond hook bend.

HEAD: large, white, painted with yellow eye and black pupil.

NOTES: One of Jess Harden's killing originals, it's good for early-season trout and excellent for smallmouth bass. TYING TECHNIQUE: See Figs. 242-244.

Winn. Smelt (E, EC)

HOOKS: tandem 4/6.

BODY: silver tinsel; red beads on wire between hooks.

TOPPING: six black ostrich herls extending slightly beyond trailer-hook.

EYES: white on black.

NOTES: As dressed by Percy Tackle Company, this fly is popular on New Hampshire's Lake Winnipesaukee. It should be effective wherever smelts or similar small fishes serve as prey. TYING TECHNIQUE: See Figs. 263-265, 242-244 for adaptable techniques.

Wooly Worm Streamer (G)

HOOKS: 8-4, Mustad 9672.

THREAD: black.

TAIL: none.

BODY: black chenille.

HACKLE: grizzly saddle hackle, palmered up body.

WINGS: pair of badger saddle hackles.

NOTES: As tied by Parks' Fly Shop, Gardiner, Mont., this is one version of the previously mentioned Wooly Worms—widely popular because they're effective wherever terrestrials fall into the water. TYING TECHNIQUE: See Figs. 129-133, 242-244.

Yellow & White Crappie Bucktail (G)

HOOK: 6, 2XL.

BODY: flat silver tinsel ribbed with oval tinsel as an option.

UNDERWING: small bunch of white bucktail.

OVERWING: smaller bunch of dyed yellow bucktail.

HEAD: black or yellow.

NOTES: Here's one of the simplest and best of all crappie flies and it's also effective on trout and bass in lakes and streams, both in the small versions and in sizes up to 2. Other good color combinations include red and white, red and yellow, and solid white or yellow. TYING TECHNIQUE: See Figs. 242-244.

SALMON, STEELHEAD & SEA-RUN CUTTHROAT FLIES

Badger Yellow (W)

HOOK: 6, long shank.

THREAD: black.

TAIL: scarlet hackle fibers.

BODY: yellow fluorescent chenille, dressed quite fat.

HACKLE: badger, palmered from middle of body to head.

NOTES: An effective sea-run cutthroat fly originated by Bill Nelson, of Eugene, Ore., in 1960. TYING TECHNIQUE: See Figs. 129-132.

Black Nymph (E)

HOOKS: TULE salmon, various sizes.

TIP: fine flat gold tinsel, with a few turns of orange floss in front.

TAIL: three or four brown-speckled mallard fibers extending to hook bend.

BUTT: peacock herl.

BODY: dubbed black seal fur.

RIBBING: gold tinsel.

THROAT: a few brown mallard fibers extending to hook point.

WING: jungle-cock hackle tip tied flat, extending to butt.

NOTES: Atlantic salmon go for this nymph, tied in the style pioneered by Charles De Feo. This dressing is attributed to him. TYING TECHNIQUE: See Figs. 122-128, 250-258.

Bob's Secret Fly (WC)

HOOKS: 12-6, low-water TULE.

TAIL: sparse bunch of golden-pheasant tippets.

BODY: brassy-gold or silver Mylar, wrapped thin.

HACKLE: beard of a few strands of golden-pheasant tippet mixed with several badger hackle fibers.

WING: matched, facing sections of light mallard-flank feather dressed in conventional wet-fly style.

NOTES: Bob Hurst, of Vancouver, developed this pattern. It's effective on sea-run cutthroats in salt-chuck and on coho salmon in coastal rivers. TYING TECHNIQUE: See Figs. 253-255.

Boss (W)

HOOK: 4, Sproat, 2X-stout.

THREAD: white.

TAIL: good-sized bunch of black ringtail-cat hair about same length as hook shank.

BODY: large-size black chenille.

RIBBING: medium flat silver tinsel.

HACKLE: fluorescent orange, slightly undersized for hook.

EYES: pair of silver bead-chain beads tied in front of hackle with criss-cross thread wrappings.

NOTES: This killing steelhead fly is said to have been originated by Howard Norton of Comet fame. TYING TECHNIQUE: See Figs. 266-267.

Clear Creek Special (W)

HOOKS: 8-2, stout-wire.

TAIL: yellow hackle fibers.

BODY: half yellow floss, quarter black floss, quarter red floss.

RIBBING: flat gold tinsel.

HACKLE: grizzly hen or saddle hackle.

WING: gray squirrel topped with yellow polar bear or yellow hackle fibers.

NOTES: This one is a good light-colored steelhead fly. TYING TECHNIQUE: See Figs. 266-268.

Comet (W)

HOOKS: 6-2, 2XL, 2X-stout, nickel.

TAIL: long, dense bunch of true- or hot-orange bucktail, longer than the hook shank. (Use fine, mobile bucktail for this one.)

BODY: wide oval gold tinsel over yellow floss underbody, well-lacquered for durability. (Silver tinsel is an alternative.)

HACKLE: collar of mixed yellow and hot-orange hackle, quite long-fibered and mobile.

EYES: pair of brass or silver bead-chain beads wrapped in front of hackle.

HEAD: hot-orange thread.

NOTES: One of the most killing of the bright-colored steelhead flies, it's also an excellent pattern for coho salmon in rivers when fished with a stripping retrieve. TYING TECHNIQUE: See Figs. 266-267 for adaptable techniques.

Explorer (W)

HOOK: 4, stout-wire.

THREAD: black.

TAIL: long black bucktail or hackle fibers.

BODY: flat silver tinsel with strip of fluorescent chenille laid over top. (Run fine line of thick cement under chenille for durability.)

HACKLE: orange.

NOTES: This effective fly for Chinook salmon in rivers should be fished on a lead-head or extra-fast sinking fly line. TYING TECHNIQUE: See Figs. 266-267 for adaptable techniques.

Fall Favorite (W)

HOOKS: 8-2, extra-stout, preferably nickel finish.

BODY: oval silver tinsel, with slight forward taper.

HACKLE: collar of scarlet saddle or hen-neck hackle.

WING: true- or hot-orange bucktail or polar-bear hair.

HEAD: black or red thread.

NOTES: One of the deadliest of the steelhead bucktails, popular from British Columbia's Kispiox River to the steelhead streams of California. TYING TECHNIQUE: See Figs. 266-268.

Frammus (W)

HOOK: 1, TULE salmon.

BODY: pink fluorescent Gantron.

WING: green fluorescent Gantron.

NOTES: Originated in 1967 by Vic Stevens, this is a winter-run steelhead fly for Northwestern waters. The dressing above is for the Pink Frammus. Reverse the colors and you have a Green Frammus. Incredibly easy to tie and effective. TYING TECHNIQUE: See Figs. 242-244 for adaptable techniques, though Frammus materials are very unusual.

Gill's Girl Nymph (E)

HOOKS: 10-4, TULE salmon hook.

TIP: fine flat gold tinsel, with a few turns of orange floss wrapped in front.

TAIL: three or four lemon-colored wood-duck fibers.

BODY: peacock herl.

RIBBING: gold tinsel.

HACKLE: moderately wide black hackle, palmered adjacent to the ribbing.

HEAD: red.

NOTES: Another of the fine De Feo nymphs for the Atlantic salmon. TYING TECHNIQUE: See Figs. 122-128, 129-132, 253-255.

Green Highlander (E, EC)

HOOKS: 12-3/0, TULE Atlantic-salmon hook, regular or low-water.

TIP: silver tinsel.

TAIL: golden-pheasant crest feather, curving up.

TAG: yellow floss.

BUTT: black ostrich herl.

BODY: rear half, yellow floss, ribbed with round silver tinsel; fore half, dubbed green fur ribbed with oval silver tinsel.

HACKLE: green palmered on fore body; yellow at shoulder.

INNER WING: golden pheasant tippets. (Use pair of whole, matched feathers.)

SIDE-STRIPS: narrow sections of green-dyed goose flight feather almost as long as wing.

OUTER WING: sections of brown mallard-flank feathers.

CHEEKS: jungle-cock eye feathers.

TOPPING: golden-pheasant crest feather, same length as wing.

HORNS: yellow and blue macaw.

NOTES: This is one of the more important standard flies for Atlantic salmon. TYING TECHNIQUE: See Figs. 122-128, 250-255.

Grizzly Bivisible (G)

HOOKS: 10-4, Wilson dry-fly salmon hook.

TAILS (OPTIONAL): tips of two grizzly gamecock-neck hackles.

HACKLE: densely palmered grizzly gamecock-neck or saddle hackles to eye, faced with one or two turns of white hackle.

HEAD: gray or black.

NOTES: Edward R. Hewitt's classic trout bivisibles are equally effective on both Atlantic salmon and steelheads in low-water conditions. This is one of the best shades; others include blue dun/white, black/white, natural red-brown/white and mixed brown and grizzly/white. It's dressed as a floater. TYING TECHNIQUE: See Figs. 129-132.

Hairwing Rat-Faced McDougall (E, EC)

HOOKS: 8 & 6, Wilson dry-fly salmon hook.
THREAD: black.
TAIL: bunch of stiff white bucktail.
BODY: spun, trimmed cream-gray deer-body hair.
WINGS: white bucktail, dressed upright and divided, and ¼- to ½-inch longer than radius of hackle.
HACKLE: ginger saddle hackle wound dense in dry-fly style behind and in front of wings.
NOTES: One of the most popular Atlantic-salmon dry flies. TYING TECHNIQUE: See Figs. 259-262.

Horner's Silver Shrimp (W)

HOOKS: 8-2, 2X-stout, 1X-long.
THREAD: black.
TAIL: bunch of gray or brown deer-body hairs.
BODY: wide oval tinsel, wrapped over tapered floss core, with tinsel wraps slightly spaced and grizzly saddle hackle, tied in by butt, palmered in spaces.
OVERBODY: bunch of gray deer-body hairs, tied in after tail, then pulled forward over body and hackle and tied down at head. Overbody is lacquered heavily after tying down.
HEAD: large and black.
EYES: painted white with black pupils.
NOTES: Here's an effective, different-looking steelhead fly, similar in shape and color to the Phillips Shrimp listed in the chapter on saltwater flies. TYING TECHNIQUE: See Figs. 129-136 for adaptable techniques.

Jock Scott (E, EC)

HOOKS: 12-3/0, Atlantic-salmon hook, regular or low-water weights.
THREAD: black.
TIP: flat silver, with a few turns of yellow floss wrapped in front. Some tiers use the terms "tag" and "tip," in that order, to refer to these parts. But we'll attempt to remain consistent with definitions stated in earlier chapters.
TAIL: fairly long golden-pheasant crest feather.
TAIL-TAG: short silver-pheasant crest feather.
BUTT: black ostrich herl.
BODY: rear half, yellow floss; fore half, black floss.
RIBBING: silver tinsel; flat, round or oval.
CENTER JOINT: black herl, wrapped between two halves of body.
TRAILERS (OPTIONAL): golden-pheasant crest feathers, over and under.
HACKLE: guinea hen, collared, then pulled down and bearded.
INNER WING: white-tipped turkey-tail feather sections.
OUTER WING: married strips of golden-pheasant tail, blue, red and yellow swan or goose. Married sections of brown mallard, teal and yellow, tied on above center strips.
SHOULDERS: jungle-cock eye feathers.
CHEEKS: blue chatter feathers.
TOPPING: peacock-sword fibers same length as wing, topped by golden-pheasant crest feather of same length, curving downward.

NOTES: This is probably the most famous of the standard Atlantic-salmon wet flies used in American waters. TYING TECHNIQUE: See Figs. 122-128, 250-255. There are many alternative dressings, some simpler to tie. One of the most effective is the steelhead Jock Scott, a hairwing version dressed as follows (see also Figs. 266-268 for tying technique):

Steelhead Jock Scott (W)

TAIL: a few golden-pheasant tipped strands, topped with short golden-pheasant crest feather.

BODY: rear half, yellow yarn; fore half, black yarn.

RIBBING: gold tinsel, oval or flat.

HACKLE: guinea-hen collar.

WING: small bunch of gray fox-squirrel tail hairs, topped with smaller bunches of scarlet, yellow and blue hairs.

HEAD: black.

Kispiox Sunset (W)

HOOKS: 4-3/0, stout-wire.

TIP: flat silver tinsel, dressed wide.

TAIL: mixed hot-orange and yellow hackle fibers.

BODY: large-size hot-orange chenille.

RIBBING: wide, flat silver tinsel.

HACKLE: large-radius and mobile, mixed hot-orange and yellow.

WING: dyed scarlet bucktail.

HEAD: black.

NOTES: A colorful, mobile steelhead wet-fly, designed for the Kispiox River in British Columbia. TYING TECHNIQUE: See Figs. 266-268.

Lady Caroline (G)

HOOKS: 6-2, low-water Atlantic-salmon hooks.

THREAD: black or olive.

TAIL: brick-red golden-pheasant breast-feather fibers.

BODY: spun mixture of olive and dark brown seal fur.

RIBBING: medium flat silver tinsel.

HACKLE: sparse collar of brick-red golden-pheasant breast feather.

WING: matched sections of brown mallard or widgeon-flank feather.

NOTES: This is the scaled-down version of the famous Atlantic-salmon fly, usually dressed low-water style—i.e., fly size two sizes smaller than normal for the hook. TYING TECHNIQUE: See Figs. 253-255.

Lead-Wing Coachman (E, EC)

HOOKS: Atlantic-salmon type, various sizes.

THREAD: dark brown or black.

TAIL: three small, dark gray hackle tips, tied as for March Brown Nymph described in Figs. 256-258.

BODY: dubbed blend of black-bear, dark gray-fox and fiery-brown seal furs.

RIBBING: dark brown cotton thread.

LEGS: section of dark gray hen hackle, splayed slightly to sides.

WING CASE: section of dark gray duck or goose flight feather, tied down and lacquered.

NOTES: Originated by William Keane, this is a nymph designed for Atlantic salmon. TYING TECHNIQUE: See Figs. 256-258.

Minnow Fly (W)

HOOK: 8, long-shank, usually 2XL.

TAIL: see overbody.

BODY: oval silver tinsel.

OVERBODY: about 10 strands of stripped peacock-herl quill, lashed down at butt-end, pulled over body and tied off at head. Butt ends of herl quills are clipped to form short tail about ¼- to ⅜-inch long.

HEAD: wrapped with peacock herl, completed with red tying thread.

NOTES: A sea-run cutthroat fly originated by Ken McLeod, of Seattle, in 1939. Used when the fish are feeding on salmon fry.

TYING TECHNIQUE: See Figs. 134-135. One configuration is almost identical to that of the Cooper Bug (Fig. 311).

Silver Blue (G)

HOOKS: 10-4, low-water Atlantic-salmon hook.

THREAD: black.

TIP (OPTIONAL): flat silver tinsel.

TAIL: golden-pheasant crest feather.

BODY: flat silver tinsel.

RIBBING: fine oval silver tinsel.

WING : matched sections of barred teal- or brown mallard-breast or -flank feathers, dressed in conventional wet-fly style.

THROAT: small bunch of pale blue hackle fibers. (Joe Bates lists proper dye shade as Cambridge blue.)

NOTES: An old standby English salmon pattern, it's normally dressed low-water style and is useful both on Atlantic salmon and steelheads. A hair-wing version employing gray-squirrel tail for the wing is also useful. TYING TECHNIQUE: See Figs. 250-252.

Shad Flies

Cooney's Shad Fly (E)

HOOK: 8, TDE.

TAIL: small bunch of yellow calf-tail hair.

BODY: white nylon floss.

RIBBING: fine embossed silver tinsel.

HEAD: red thread, wrapped slightly larger than body diameter and lacquered red.

NOTES: This is the fly as dressed by Jesse Harden, and it's excellent for both white and hickory shad in Eastern waters. TYING TECHNIQUE: See Figs. 242-244, though fly is atypical.

Green Dart (E)

HOOK: 8, 2XL Mustad.

THREAD: light green, same shade as body.

BODY: fluorescent green floss, tapered medium-full.

RIBBING: embossed silver tinsel.

WING: green, imitation polar bear.

HEAD: light green, well tapered, with small black dot painted on top.

NOTES: An Eastern pattern, as dressed by Jesse Harden. Another of Harden's ties, called the Shad Queen, is dressed in the same style with a white fluorescent floss body, silver tinsel rib and a fluorescent, dark, pink wing. It's good in the Eastern shad rivers. TYING TECHNIQUE: See Figs. 242-244.

Hayden Shad Fly (W)

HOOK: 6, 2XL, TDE.

THREAD: red.

BODY: medium oval silver tinsel.

WING STUB: short tuft of fluorescent red yarn, tied in on top of hook immediately behind hackle, less than ¼-inch long.

HACKLE: yellow or white, dressed as sparse collar.

EYES: small gold bead-chain beads, tied down with criss-cross thread wraps and well lacquered.

NOTES: Brace Hayden of Seattle, Wash., ties it this way, and it's excellent on the shad rivers of Washington, Oregon and California.

Shad Fly (W)

HOOK: 6, 1XL, 2X-stout, nickel.

THREAD: red.

TAIL: paired sections of red duck pointer-feather, concave sides facing in.

UNDERBODY: lead wire, with white cotton thread or floss wrapped over it.

BODY: silver Mylar tubing. Rear tie-down wrapping is red. Oval silver tinsel is alternative body wrapping.

HACKLE: sparse white collar.

HEAD: large fluorescent-red chenille ball, with fairly large, silver bead-chain eyes, tied in front.

NOTES: This is the shad fly as it's used in southern California shad rivers by the Inglewood Fly Fishermen. It's very productive.

Bass, Pike & Muskie Flies

Calcasieu Pig Boat (G)

HOOK: 1/0, regular weight and length.

THREAD: black.

BODY: large black chenille, dressed fat and heavy.

PALMER HACKLE: black saddle hackle, palmered up body, sometimes trimmed for less bulk.

HACKLE: 6 strands of black rubber hackle tied in at head and extending back over body like a hula skirt, past bend of hook.

NOTES: Pattern supplied by Tom Nixon, author of *Fly Tying and Fly Fishing for Bass and Panfish*, A. S. Barnes, N.Y., 1968. It's great for largemouth bass. Tom says this one is best fished off a #3 off-set or jig spinner. TYING TECHNIQUE: See Figs. 129-132.

Castor Creek (G)

HOOK: 8, 3X fine, regular length.

TAIL (OPTIONAL): black hackle fibers.

BODY: round-clipped deer-body hair, full-length palmered with grizzly saddle hackle.

NOTES: This is an excellent example of a high-floating dry fly as dressed by Tom Nixon, Maplewood, La., for large or smallmouth bass. The Irresistible and the Wulff-type dry flies are also excellent. TYING TECHNIQUE: See Figs. 129-132, 282-284.

Grizzly Feather Duster (G)

HOOK: 1/0, regular length and weight.

TAILS: eight grizzly hackles, four turned out one way, four the other, tied in on edge to form swallowlike tail.

HACKLE/BODY: densely palmered grizzly hackle at least one-third of shank length.

HEAD: black, small.

NOTES: Also known as the Gray Hackle Bass, this type of bass fly is in use throughout most of the U.S. and it's effective on pike and muskies as well as largemouths. Colors can be varied to suit regional preferences of the fish. As dressed by Tom Nixon (Fig. 315).

Irresistible (G)

HOOKS: 8-4, fine-wire, or low-water salmon hooks.

THREAD: black or brown.

TAIL: bunch of natural brown bucktail, same length as hook shank.

Fig. 315. Grizzly Feather Duster.

BODY: tapered, round-clipped natural gray deer-body hair, spun on as in Castor Creek. In trout and salmon versions, body is egg-shaped and flattened in the forward portion, occupying about half the distance from tail tie-in to hook eye.

HACKLE: grizzly gamecock or saddle hackles dressed as dry-fly-type collar. For bass, pike and muskie fishing, colors should be varied to suit local preferences of fish.

NOTES: I've hooked some fine bass in eastern Washington and northern Idaho, using the Irresistible dressed with blue-dun hackle in sizes as small as 14 and 12. TYING TECHNIQUE: See Figs. 259-262, 282-284.

Louisiana Mickey Finn (G)

HOOK: 1/0, 4XL, regular weight.

TAIL: black and white barred wood-duck flank feather fibers.

BUTT: orange chenille.

BODY: silver tinsel chenille, ribbed with gold-tinsel chenille.

WING: yellow, over red, over yellow bucktail.

SHOULDER: black and white barred wood-duck feather sections.

Fig. 316. Louisiana Mickey Finn.

HEAD: large, black.

EYES: yellow, with red pupils.

NOTES: This is an intriguing variation of the Mickey Finn, as dressed by Tom Nixon (Fig. 316). TYING TECHNIQUE: See Figs. 242–244.

McNally Smelt (E, EC)

HOOKS: 1/0 tinned, ring-eye saltwater hook.

THREAD: white.

BODY: white tying thread.

WINGS: four six-inch-long hackles, concave sides in, with two slightly shorter grizzly hackles tied outside.

UNDERWING: bunch of white polar-bear hair dressed on bottom and lower sides of hooks.

CHEEKS: two medium-width strips of Mylar or silver tinsel tied inside speckled mallard-breast feathers, about three-quarters of wing length.

HEAD: lacquered-pearl white.

NOTES: Originated by outdoor writer Tom McNally for pike and lake trout in northern waters, it's fished on a stout shock-tippet for pike. Pictured in color plate.

SALTWATER FLIES

Beer Belly (W)

HOOK: 3/0, TDE streamer hook.

THREAD: black.

TAIL: pink over yellow bucktail, dressed about as long as body.

BODY: large Mylar tubing, flattened and heavily cemented to form deep "paunch" under shank. Rear wrap is painted silver.

WING: medium-sized bunch of deep yellow bucktail, same length as tail, over which is tied small bunch of pink bucktail, topped by small

Fig. 317. Beer Belly.

bunch of medium-light blue bucktail (Fig. 317).

HEAD: black.

EYES: white with red and black pupils.

NOTES: Originated by Larry Green, West
Coast field editor for *Field & Stream*, and
Irwin M. Thompson of Sebastopol, Calif.
It's usually fished on a lead-core line, offshore for king salmon called tyee salmon in
British Columbia and Chinook salmon during the spawning runs. There's also a version made from furlike synthetic yarn fibers. TYING TECHNIQUE: See Figs. 242–244.

Bonefish Fly (E)

HOOK: 2, ring-eye, stainless steel.

TAIL STREAMERS: six strands of 1/16- to
1/32-inch Mylar strips.

WINGS: dark gray-green bucktail over
white bucktail, reverse-tied (see
color plate) to form a head of
same color combination. Tie-
down thread is red.

EYES: yellow with black pupils, small.

NOTES: As dressed by William J. Keane,
Bronxville, N.Y. This color combination
has taken plenty of bonefish, and another
excellent version is pink over yellow.

Bristle Back (W)

HOOK: 2, long-shank, nickel, TDE.

THREAD: white.

TAIL: three large white neck hackles,
tied on edge facing inward, tips
trimmed to minnow-tail shape.

BODY: fully dressed with white chenille.

OVERBODY & BRISTLES: spread fibers of
two matched yel-
low or medium-
blue neck hack-
les. Place con-
cave sides to-
gether, strip
fibers from one
side of paired
hackles, lightly
cement center
stems and hackle
fibers of other
side and trim
ends. Tie in be-
fore wrapping
body with strand
of small orange
chenille on each
side. When body
is wrapped, pull
bristles over top
to form dorsal fin
(Fig. 318). Then
pull chenille
strands close
along each side
to form over-
body.

HEAD: white.

EYES: black.

NOTES: Originated by Irwin M. Thompson, this fly has been very successful for
striped bass on the West Coast. It can be

Fig. 318. Bristleback.

fished near the surface or deep with stripping recoveries. TYING TECHNIQUE: See Figs. 134–136.

Brooks Blonde Bucktails (G)

HOOKS: 3/0 tinned or stainless steel, ring-eye O'Shaughnessy.

THREAD: black.

TAIL: long bunch of bright orange bucktail dressed twice as dense as wing.

BODY: wide gold tinsel.

WING: small bunch of dark red bucktail, cocked upward slightly.

HEAD: black.

NOTES: A series of exceptionally deadly, easy-to-tie bucktail flies that are consistent producers in both fresh- and saltwater situations. My favorites are the Platinum Blonde, which is all white with a silver body, and the Strawberry Blonde described above. TYING TECHNIQUE: See Figs. 242–244 and color plate.

Cockroach Tarpon Fly (E)

HOOK: 1/0, ring-eye, Perfect Bend, stainless.

THREAD: black.

TAIL STREAMERS: six 1/32-inch strands of Mylar, about 1½ inches long.

BODY: flat silver tinsel or Mylar.

WINGS: six grizzly saddle hackles, 3½ inches long, dressed in two bunches, concave sides out.

HACKLE: dense collar of natural-brown bucktail, same length as hook bend.

HEAD: long and black.

EYES: white, with black pupils.

NOTES: This description is a dressing supplied by Lefty Kreh and Robert D. Stearns, noted saltwater flyrodders. TYING TECHNIQUE: See Fig. 315.

Gibbs Striper Bucktail (E)

HOOKS: 1/0–3/0, ring-eye tinned O'Shaughnessy.

THREAD: black.

BODY: narrow flat silver Mylar or tinsel.

THROAT: long scarlet hackle fibers.

WING: medium bunch of white Asian goat or polar-bear hair, over which is tied shorter, very small bunch of blue hairs, topped by medium-large bunch of white hairs.

CHEEKS: short barred Bali-duck feathers, or jungle-cock hackle.

HEAD: black.

EYES: yellow with red pupils.

NOTES: The Gibbs is a standard Eastern striped bass bucktail. TYING TECHNIQUE: See Figs. 242–244.

Gypsy Streamer (W)

HOOK: 4, 4XL, TDE.

BODY: medium thick, wrapped out of yellow thread, over which are wrapped four equally spaced bands of heavy black thread. Entire body is heavily lacquered.

WING: equal bunches of yellow, over orange, over green bucktail, extending well beyond hook bend, about same distance past as length of shank.

HEAD: black.

EYES: white with red pupils.

NOTES: Originated by Irwin M. Thompson, it's good for both coho and king salmon, cast or trolled. A Western pattern. TYING TECHNIQUE: See Figs. 242–244.

Hackle Fly (G)

HOOKS: 1/0–5/0, tinned or stainless-steel, ring-eye.

TAIL STREAMERS: six light blue hackles.

BODY HACKLE: light blue.

HEAD: white.

NOTES: This listing is from a sample fly provided by Lefty Kreh and Bob Stearns. For tying directions, see Gray Hackle Bass, Fig. 315. This is a very basic type of streamer that's effective over a wide range of conditions for numerous saltwater species on the Pacific, Gulf and Atlantic Coasts.

Keys Tarpon Streamer (E)

HOOKS: 1/0–5/0, tinned or stainless steel, ring-eye.

THREAD: scarlet.

TAIL: long thin bunch of orange bucktail, with three orange saddle hackles on each side, concave sides facing outward.

BODY: scarlet hackle, palmered densely as in Hackle Fly or wrapped on as six separate, spaced collars.

HEAD: scarlet.

NOTES: This is a popular type of streamer in Florida, and it should be equally good in other tarpon waters. TYING TECHNIQUE: See Fig. 315.

Paul Kukonen Bluefish Bucktails (E)

HOOKS: 1 & 1/0 Wright & McGill SS-90. (Thinner than most stainless-steel hooks and used for sake of penetration with light trout-action fly rods.)

THREAD: scarlet.

BODY: yellow polypropylene, built up fairly heavy, or silver Mylar built up with heavy thread, yarn or polypropylene.

WING: white or yellow bucktail, combination of green over white or pink over white or all yellow is

Fig. 319. Kukonen Bluefish Bucktail.

used mostly in evening. On some flies, wing butts are left protruding about a half-inch and flared, so that when fished on surface the fly will splash like a popping bug. Butts are flared and cemented to retain flared shape (Fig. 319).

NOTES: These bluefish flies were originated by the noted angler Paul Kukonen of Worcester, Mass.

Lefty's Deceiver (G)

HOOKS: stainless-steel, ring-eye, size to suit species sought.

THREAD: white.

TAIL: six saddle hackles tied in by butts, concave sides out, with six narrow strands of Mylar, slightly shorter than the feathers, tied on top.

BODY: silver Mylar.

COLLAR: calf tail or bucktail, tied on in bunches all around to form collar about same length as hook bend.

NOTES: The listing is from a sample fly supplied by Lefty Kreh himself. Dressed in all white, white tails with red collar, or yellow tails with red collar, this is an all-purpose saltwater pattern useful virtually anywhere. TYING TECHNIQUE: Roughly like Fig. 315.

Little Jak (W)

HOOK: 6 or 4, TDE, regular length and weight.

TAIL: three hot-orange hackle tips trimmed to shape at ends.

BODY: white chenille with three evenly spaced small black dots painted on sides.

OVERBODY & BRISTLES: hot-orange bristles, yellow overbody strips.

NOTES: This is one of Irwin Thompson's innovative striped-bass streamers, dressed in the same fashion as the Bristle Back. It can be fished either near the surface or deep. TYING TECHNIQUE: See Figs. 134–136, 318.

McKim's Anchovy (W)

HOOK: 2, short-shank, nickel, large ring-eye.

THREAD: scarlet.

WING: 4½-inch-long white bucktail under green bucktail, topped with medium-blue bucktail. Over the bucktail are tied several kinky, narrow Mylar strands stripped from tubular piping.

TOPPING: peacock herl.

NOTES: This anchovy is attributed to one John McKim. It's for use on any saltwater fish—including bonito—that feeds on anchovies. A West Coast pattern that has to be fished very fast. TYING TECHNIQUE: See Fig. 263–265 for adaptable techniques.

Mono-Fly (G)

HOOKS: stainless steel, ring-eye, size to suit species.

BODY: silver Mylar, overwrapped with clear 20- or 30-pound-test monofilament. Use 20-pound mono for fly sizes less than 1. Allow 3/16-inch space behind eye for tying in wing.

WING: choice of blue over white, brown over white or green over white calf-tail, polar-bear, or artificial polar-bear hair.

WING STRIPS: 1/64-inch Mylar strips on each side of wing.

HEAD: to match color of overwing.

EYES: white with black pupils.

NOTES: This is from a sample fly provided by Lefty Kreh and Bob Stearns. It suggests a small minnow. TYING TECHNIQUE: See Figs. 242–244 for adaptable techniques.

Phillips Bead Head (E)

HOOKS: tinned or stainless steel, size to suit species sought.

THREAD: scarlet.

BODY: yellow chenille.

HACKLE: long scarlet hackle collar, extending beyond bend.

WINGS: six bright yellow saddle hackles.

BEAD HEAD: large clamp-on brass bead, painted red with white eyes and black pupils.

NOTES: This is one of the many effective saltwater flies dressed by the Phillips Fly & Tackle Company of Alexandria, Pa. TYING TECHNIQUE: See Figs. 269–270 for adaptable techniques.

Phillips Pink Bonefish Fly (E)

HOOKS: 1 & 1/0 stainless steel, ring eye.

THREAD: bright red.

BODY: pale pink chenille.

THROAT: long pink hackle, a shade darker than body.

WING: pale pink bucktail, extending length of body beyond the bend.

HEAD: bright red.

NOTES: Pink is an excellent color for bonefish. Brown, orange, yellow and white also produce but some anglers rank this pink fly as tops. TYING TECHNIQUE: See Figs. 242–244 for adaptable techniques.

Phillips Shrimp, Pink (E)

HOOKS: 6–2, ring-eye, stainless steel.

TAIL: dark-pink bucktail, tied in slightly down on bend.

BODY: oval silver tinsel over padding, palmered with trimmed pink hackle.

OVERBODY: dark-pink bucktail, twisted.

HEAD: white.

EYES: red with black pupils.

NOTES: As dressed by Phillips Fly & Tackle Company. It's a good bonefish fly in both pink and natural-colored versions. The tail and overbody on the natural version are natural-brown bucktail. The hackle is grizzly, the head black with a white eye and black pupil. The Phillips pink shrimp was the favorite bonefish fly of the late Joe Brooks. TYING TECHNIQUE: See Figs. 129–136 for adaptable techniques.

Striped Bass Popper (E)

HOOK: 1/0 low-water salmon with trailer hook, size 2, short-shank, ring-eye tinned or stainless steel, point up, attached by length of mono.

TAIL: four-inch-long bunch of white bucktail.

BODY: clipped, spun-on white (albino) deer-body hair.

HEAD: white.

NOTES: This is one of the William Keane ties. Stripers tend to hit short at times, and a trailer hook is a good way to booby-trap them. Fished on the surface with slow stripping recoveries. Bill Keane says he fishes the popper sometimes fast, sometimes slow, until he gets a strike or the fish stop feeding. In tidal rivers he usually works the run at the head of a deep pool, casting the popper or a streamer fly out and letting the current and line pull them down-and-across-stream, with the speed of the fly depending on what works best. The fish, he says, usually take on the swing when the fly is moving quite rapidly; he cites the chapter on controlled drag in Jock Scott's book *Fine and Far Off* and Balfour-Kinnear's book *Flying Salmon* as good technique references. TYING TECHNIQUE: See Figs. 282–284.

Stu Apte Tarpon Fly (E)

HOOKS: scaled to size of tarpon in water being fished—up to 5/0 for tarpon in excess of 90 pounds.

THREAD: scarlet.

TAIL: two hot-orange saddle hackles, inside two pairs of yellow saddle hackles.

HACKLE: mixed hot-orange and yellow, extending about half the rear portion of hook shank.

HEAD: scarlet.

NOTES: This thoroughly tested tarpon taker is from a dressed sample provided by Lefty Kreh and Bob Stearns. TYING TECHNIQUE: See Fig. 315.

Upperman Streamer, White (E)

HOOKS: scaled to species and size of fish sought.

BODY: white chenille.

THROAT: red hackle.

WINGS: three-inch-long white saddle hackles, back to back.

NOTES: It's given here as described by P. G. "Perk" Angwin of Margate, Fla. Alternative colors include black or yellow body, yellow wings, and either yellow or red throat. TYING TECHNIQUE: See Figs. 269–270 for adaptable techniques.

Appendix I

Regional Fly Patterns

ONE OF fly fishing's many charms is the special flavor inherent in the fishing of diverse regions. It is not just that game fish in different areas exhibit peculiarities of diet and behavior, although such peculiarities are of paramount importance. Each region also imposes its own unique moods and challenges. There are the complexities and elegance of the Beaverkill; the quietly frustrating limestone streams flowing from the Appalachians; the demanding spring creeks of the Gallatin and other Western valleys; the awesome thrust of British Columbia's Thompson River; the relentless Caribbean sun; the incredible blue and purple-bronze of an Arctic grayling materializing from tea-colored depths; the silhouettes of scurrying caddis flies hatching by moonlight; the aromas of cedar smoke, frying bacon, hot buttered Scotch; the sounds of salmon and steelheads relentlessly surging upstream through riffles in midnight counterpoint to the river's steady throbbing. These are some of the other things fly fishing is all about.

There is an unchanging quality of discovery and delight, but other aspects do change. The flies probably undergo the most frequent variations and innovations. Any listing of regional fly dressings can therefore pose a number of hazards. For one thing, patterns vary considerably within the regions where they enjoy their greatest popularity. This is true even in the case of time-tested favorites like the Light Cahill, which is dressed in versions ranging from ginger to almost cream-white, depending on the immediate locale. Similar variations are noted in other varietal and imitative flies of broad general interest, including the Royal Coachman, Mosquito, Black Quill and March Brown, to name just a few.

Often a so-called variation is actually a totally different fly in configuration and coloration.

Another problem is that regional popularity lists of flies sometimes undergo dramatic changes over a two-year period as a result of spectacular but short-lived successes with a few new patterns. (To some degree, fluctuating popularity is more frequently noted in regions where the sport of fly fishing is relatively young—where the innovative surge of local anglers is at a peak.)

Therefore, in compiling regional pattern lists for this appendix, I undertook a study based not so much on the flies' market popularity as on their consistent effectiveness as fish-catchers. To be sure, there is some correlation between market popularity and effectiveness, but a standard fly's popularity in a given region doesn't necessarily mean it's the most killing fly of its type for that region.

So I wrote to over 100 knowledgeable

fly fishermen, amateur and professional fly tiers and technical consultants for tackle manufacturers—persons whose knowledge of the fly fishing in their home regions is unsurpassed.

Each regional contributor was asked to recommend the six most killing patterns for his area in each of four categories: dry flies, nymphs, wet flies and streamer flies. The criteria were that each fly must be consistently effective throughout a given region or regions, that it must have been used for no less than two full seasons by a significant number of anglers and that it must be capable of being dressed by an amateur tier of average skill.

I believe the results of the study—this appendix plus the dressing details found in Chapter 14—represent as true a picture of recent trends in innovative fly design and use across North America as I can possibly paint.

NORTHEAST

Compiled from lists supplied by Art Flick, Abercrombie & Fitch, the Orvis Company, Jesse Harden, S. V. Yaruta, Don Shiner, Harry Darbee, Joseph D. Bates, Jr., A. I. "Pal" Alexander, Percy Tackle Company and William Keane. Sizes are not listed since the dressings for many of the patterns are included in the book.

Dry Flies

Adams
Badger Spider
Black Ant
Black Beetle
Black Gnat
Blue Dun Midge
Brown Drake
Cahill, Dark
Cahill, Light
Cooper Bug
Cream Variant

Dark Blue Quill
Dun Variant
Ginger Quill
Grasshopper
Gray Fox
Gray Wulff
Green Drake
Hendrickson
Hornberg
Jassid
March Brown (Jennings)
Mosquito
Pale Watery Dun
Quill Gordon
Red Quill (Flick)
Royal Wulff
White Wulff

Wet Flies

Beaverkill
Black Gnat
Black Wooly Worm
Blue Winged Olive
Brown Hackle
Cahill, Dark
Cahill, Light
Coachman
Cow Dung
Ginger Quill
Gold-Ribbed Hare's Ear
Gray Hackle
Leadwing Coachman
March Brown
Montana Nymph
Pal's Wire Body
Picket Pin
Quill Gordon
Royal Coachman
Yellow Dun

Nymphs

Bread Crumb
Breadcrust
Caddis Worm
Casual Dress (Rosborough)

Connett Nymph
Early Brown Stone (Flick)
Gold-Ribbed Hare's Ear
Gray Nymph
Light Cahill Nymph
Light Stone
Montana Nymph
Muskrat Nymph
Pumpkin Pupa
Savage Special
Slate/Brown Emerger
Stone Fly Nymph
Tellico Nymph
Zug Bug

Streamer Flies

Allagash Al
Black Ghost
Black Knight
Black Marabou
Black-Nosed Dace
Colonel Bates
Dobson
Edson Dark Tiger
Gray Ghost
Gray Marabou
Green Ghost
Herb Johnson Special
Hornberg
Labrador Special
Little Brown Trout
Marabou Muddler, White
Maynard's Marvel
Mickey Finn
Muddler Minnow
Nine-Three
Parmachene Belle
Pink Ghost
Pink Lady Streamer
Red Ghost
Royal Coachman Streamer
Supervisor
Thunder Creek Series (Fulsher)
Winn. Smelt
Yellow Marabou
York's Kennebago

Midwest

Compiled from lists supplied by Doug Swisher and Ed Haaga.

Dry Flies

Adams
Adams, Hairwing
Blue Dun
Dun/Brown Hen Spinner
Dun/Yellow Hen Spinner
Gray/Olive No Hackle
Gray/Yellow No Hackle
Michigan Hopper
Slate/Tan No Hackle

Nymphs & Wet Flies

Artesan Green
Cahill, Dark
Cahill, Light
Slate/Brown Emerger

Streamer Flies

Black-Nosed Dace
Hornberg
Muddler Minnow
Royal Coachman

Rocky Mountain States

Compiled from lists supplied by Bud Lilly, George F. Grant, Mrs. Merton J. Parks, Dan Bailey, George Bodmer and Bob Terrell.

Dry Flies

Adams
Badger Hackle

Bird's Stone Fly
Blue Dun
Blue Quill
Cahill, Light
Colorado King
Gray Hackle, Yellow
Grizzly Wulff
Hatch Matcher
Joe's Hopper
Muckledun
Quill Gordon
Red Variant
Renegade
Rio Grande King
Royal Coachman
Royal Wulff
Sofa Pillow
Yellow-Bodied Grayback

Wet Flies

Bloody Butcher
Blue Quill
Brown Hackle
Ginger Quill
Gold-Ribbed Hare's Ear
Gray Hackle, Yellow
March Brown
Orange Asher
Rio Grande King
Royal Coachman
Wooly Worm (various colors)

Nymphs

Black Drake Nymph
Colorado Caddis
Ed Burke Nymph
Fledermaus
George Bodmer's Brown Stone Nymph
Gold-Ribbed Hare's Ear
Grant's Black Creeper
Grant's Brass Bug
Gray Nymph
Martinez Black Nymph
Muskrat Nymph

Slate/Brown Emerger
S. Platte Brassie
Trueblood Otter Nymph

Streamer Flies

Black-Nosed Dace
Brown Bear
Gray Ghost
Hornberg
Integration Bucktail
Marabou Muddler, White
Marabou Muddler, Yellow
Muddler Minnow
N. Platte Special
S. Park Special
Spruce Fly, Dark
Spruce Fly, Light
Spuddler
Whitlock's Sculpin
Wooly Worm Streamer

SIERRA-NEVADA

Compiled from lists supplied by Stu Kaplan, Milt Kahl, Ray Johnson and Milt Huber.

Dry Flies

Adams
Adams, Female
Black Gnat
Blue Dun
Brown Sedge
Cahill, Light
Ginger Quill
Gray Sedge
Grizzly Mosquito
Jassid
Little Marryat
Near-n-Nuff
Picket Pin
Quill Gordon
Royal Whisker

Sierra Brite Dot
Sierra Sedge
Yellow Mayfly

Wet Flies

Black Gnat
Brown Hackle, peacock
Gray Hackle, peacock
Leadwing Coachman
Picket Pin
Wooly Worm (various colors)

Nymphs

Blue Dun
Muskrat Nymph
Turkey Quill

PACIFIC NORTHWEST

Compiled from lists supplied by the author, Fenton Roskelley, Jim Kilburn, Stan Engle, Gil Nyerges, and A. A. "Tony" Whitney.

Dry Flies

Adams
Black Midge
Black Quill
Blue Upright
Brown Bivisible
Brown Midge
Edward's Sedge
Flot-n-Fool
Flying Black Ant
Grizzly Wulff
Humpy
Irresistible
Joe's Hopper
Kolzer Caddis, Dark
Kolzer Caddis, Light
Meadow Grasshopper
Mosquito

Renegade
Royal Wulff
Salmon Candy
Tom Thumb

Wet Flies

Black Hackle, Peacock
Brown Hackle, Peacock
Bucktail Coachman
Gold-Ribbed Hare's Ear
Gray Hackle, Peacock
Gray Hackle, Yellow
March Brown

Nymphs

Anderson Stone Nymph
Beaverpelt Nymph
Big Ugly Nymph
Carey Special
Casual Dress (Rosborough)
Damselfly Nymph (Gerlach)
Dark Stone Nymph (Rosborough)
Dragonfly Nymph
Ed Burke Nymph
Heather Nymph
Leech (various ties)
Light Stone Nymph (Rosborough)
Mosquito Larva
Muskrat Nymph (Rosborough)
Nyerges Nymph
O'Gara Shrimp
Pinto Nymph (Engle)
PKCK
Slate/Brown Emerger
TDC
Terry's Stone Fly Nymph
Tied-Down Caddis
Trueblood's Otter Nymph
Werner Shrimp

Streamer Flies

Bandit, Gray
Black Knight (Whitney)

Crane Prairie Special Silver
Deschutes Special
Hussy
Integration
Muddler Minnow
Orbit, White
Orbit, Yellow
Oregon Special, Gold
Oregon Special, Silver
Royal Coachman
Snollygoster
Spruce, Dark
Spruce, Light
Spuddler
Supervisor
Wick-i-up Empress
Wick-i-up Special

Steelhead Flies

Blue Charm (low-water)

Boulton Special
Chappie Streamer
Comet
Fall Favorite
Golden Demon
Golden Squamish
Kalama Special
Lady Caroline (low-water)
McLeod's Ugly
Orange Optic
Pink Frammus
Red Ant
Royal Coachman
Scarlet Woman
Skunk
Skykomish Sunrise
Stillaguamish Sunrise
Thor
Toley's Polar Shrimp
Van Luven, Fluorescent
Western Steelhead Bee (dry)

Appendix II

Selected Fly-Tying Material Suppliers

THIS LIST is included for the convenience of amateur fly tiers in various regions. Most of these firms publish catalogs or material lists that will be of considerable help to the beginning tier.

Dan Bailey's Fly Shop
209 W. Park St.
Livingston, Mont. 59047

Bodmer's Fly Shop
2404 E. Boulder
Colorado Springs, Colo. 80909

Bonner & Johnson Fly Tying Kits
629 Anthony St.
Anaheim, Calif. 92804

Buz's Fly and Tackle Shop
805 W. Tulare Ave.
Visalia, Calif. 93277

E. B. & H. A. Darbee
Livingston Manor, N.Y. 12758

The Feather Vendor
N. 1512 Jefferson
Spokane, Wash. 99201

Fireside Angler, Inc.
P.O. Box 823
Melville, N.Y. 11748

The Fly Fisherman's Bookcase
   Tackle Service
138 Grand St.
Croton-on-Hudson, N.Y. 10520

The Fly Tyer's Supply Shop
P.O. Box 153
Downington, Pa. 19335

Gene's Tackle Shop
P.O. Box 7701
Rochester, N.Y. 14622

Herter's Inc.
R. R. 1
Waseca, Minn. 56097

E. Hille, Inc.
Williamsport, Pa. 17701

Joe's Tackle Shop
P.O. Box 156
Warehouse Point, Conn. 06088

Bud Lilly's Trout Shop
Box 387
West Yellowstone, Mont. 59758

The Orvis Co., Inc.
Manchester, Vt. 05254

Rangeley Region Sports Shop
28 Main St.
Rangeley, Me. 04970

Reed Tackle
Box 390
Caldwell, N.J. 07006

Sawtooth Quality Stores
120 W. 13th Ave.
Spokane, Wash. 99204

Tackle-Craft
P.O. Box 489

Chippewa Falls, Wis. 54729

E. Veniard (Retail) Ltd.
138 Northwood Rd., Paramount
    Warehouse
Thornton Heath
England CR4 8YG

Bud Wilcox
Rangeley, Me. 04970

Appendix III

Selected Dressers & Suppliers of Quality Flies

Abercrombie & Fitch Co.
Madison Ave. at 45th St.
New York, N.Y. 10017

Dan Bailey's Fly Shop
209 W. Park St.
Livingston, Mont. 59047

Bentz Fly & Tackle Co.
5427 Pacific Ave. S.
Tacoma, Wash. 98408

George M. Bodmer
2404 E. Boulder
Colorado Springs, Colo. 80909

E. B. & H. A. Darbee
Livingston Manor, N.Y. 12758

R. K. "Granny" Granstrom
P.O. Box 1162
Klamath Falls, Ore. 97601

Edward Haaga
White Lake, Wis. 54491

Jesse Harden
Walnut Ave.
Owings Mills, Md. 21117

Mrs. Audrey Joy
4720 S. E. 52nd Ave.
Portland, Ore. 97213

William J. Keane
Box 371
Bronxville, N.Y. 10708

Bud Lilly's Trout Shop
Box 387
West Yellowstone, Mont. 59758

The Orvis Co., Inc.
Manchester, Vt. 05254

Parks' Fly Shop
Gardiner, Mont. 59030

Patrick's Fly Shop
2237 Eastlake Ave. E.
Seattle, Wash. 98102

Percy Tackle Co.
22 Monument Sq.
Portland, Me. 04111

Phillips Fly & Tackle Co.
P.O. Box 188
Alexandria, Pa. 16611

Poulsen Quality Flies
73 N. E. 43rd
Portland, Ore. 97213

Bob Roberts
226 East View Ave.
Everett, Wash. 98204

E. H. "Polly" Rosborough
Box 36
Chiloquin, Ore. 97624

Terry Tyed Flies

220 Custer Rd. S.
Spokane, Wash. 99206

A. A. "Tony" Whitney
1928 Mt. Diablo Ave.
Stockton, Calif. 95203

Appendix IV

Bibliography

Bates, Joseph D., Jr. *Atlantic Salmon Flies & Fishing.* Stackpole Books, Harrisburg, Pa., 1970.

———. *Streamer Fly Tying & Fishing,* rev. ed. Stackpole Books, Harrisburg, Pa., 1966.

Bergman, Ray. *Trout.* Alfred A. Knopf, New York, 1945.

Brooks, Joe. *Trout Fishing.* Outdoor Life-Harper & Row, New York, 1972.

Combs, Trey. *The Steelhead Trout.* Northwest Salmon-Trout-Steelheader Co., Portland, Ore., 1971.

Flick, Art. *Master Fly Tying Guide.* Crown Publishers, New York, 1972.

———. *New Streamside Guide to Naturals and Their Imitations.* G. P. Putnam's Sons, New York, 1970.

Gabrielson, Ira N., et al. *The Fisherman's Encyclopedia,* 2d ed. Stackpole Books, Harrisburg, Pa., 1963.

Gerlach, Rex R. *Fly Fishing the Lakes.* Winchester Press, New York, 1972.

———, & Fenton S. Roskelley, *Flies of the Northwest.* Inland Empire Fly Fishing Club, Spokane, Wash., 1965, 1970.

Gordon, Sid W. *How to Fish from Top to Bottom.* Stackpole Books, Harrisburg, Pa., 1955.

Grant, George F. *Montana Trout Flies.* George F. Grant, Butte, Mont., 1972.

———. *The Art of Weaving Hair Hackles for Trout Flies.* George F. Grant, Butte, Mont., 1971.

Green, Jim. *Fly Casting from the Beginning,* Sevenstrand Tackle Mfg. Co., Westminster, Calif., 1971.

Herter, George Leonard. *Professional Fly Tying and Tackle Making Manual and Manufacturer's Guide,* special rev. 10th edition, Herter's, Inc., Waseca, Minn., 1955.

Hidy, V. S., and the editors of *Sports Illustrated. Sports Illustrated Fly Fishing.* J. B. Lippincott Co., Philadelphia and New York, 1972.

Jennings, Preston J. *A Book of Trout Flies.* Crown Publishers, New York, 1970.

Leisenring, James E., & V. S. Hidy, *The Art of Tying the Wet Fly and Fishing the Flymph.* Crown Publishers, New York, 1971.

Leonard, J. Edson. *Flies.* A. S. Barnes & Co., New York, 1950.

Lynde, John G. *34 Ways to Cast a Fly.* A. S. Barnes & Co., Cranbury, N.J., 1969.

McClane, A. J. *The Wise Fishermen's Encyclopedia.* Wm. H. Wise & Co., New York, 1954.

Marinaro, Vincent C. *A Modern Dry Fly Code.* Crown Publishers, New York, 1970.

Migdalski, Edward C. *Angler's Guide to the Salt Water Game Fishes, Atlantic and Pacific.* Ronald Press Co., New York, 1958.

———. *Angler's Guide to the Freshwater Sport Fishes of North America.* Ronald Press Co., New York, 1962.

Nixon, Tom. *Fly Tying and Fly Fishing for Bass and Panfish.* A. S. Barnes & Co., New York, and South Brunswick, N.J., 1968.

Rice, F. Phillip. *America's Favorite Fishing.* Outdoor Life-Harper & Row, New York, 1964.

Schwiebert, Ernest. *Remembrances of Rivers Past.* The Macmillan Co., New York, 1972.

———. *Nymphs.* Winchester Press, New York, 1973.

Swisher, Doug & Carl Richards. *Selective Trout.* Crown Publishers, New York, 1971.

Taverner, et al. *Salmon Fishing.* The Lonsdale Library, Volume X. J. B. Lippincott Co., Philadelphia, Pa.

To Cast a Fly. Scientific Anglers, Inc., Midland, Mich., 1966.

Veniard, John. *A Further Guide To Fly Dressing.* Adam & Charles Black, London, 1964.

———, & Donald Downs. *Fly Tying Problems and Their Answers.* Adam & Charles Black, London, 1970.

Walden, Howard T., 2nd. *Familiar Freshwater Fishes of America.* Harper & Row, New York, 1964.

Index